THE COMPLETE BOOK OF
ENGLISH

By HENRY THOMAS, Ph.D.

(*Author of* THE STORY OF THE HUMAN RACE,
THE WONDER BOOK, THE COLLEGE
COURSE CULTURE BOOK, *etc.*)

GARDEN CITY PUBLISHING COMPANY, INC.

GARDEN CITY   NEW YORK

PART I

THE ESSENTIAL BASES OF GOOD ENGLISH

v

Chapter

PART II
THE PRACTICAL USES OF EFFECTIVE ENGLISH

CONTENTS

Introduction

THE STORY OF WORDS

Their Origin and Their Meaning

ONE of the most fascinating studies in the world is the study of words. For words are the materials out of which thoughts are built, just as bricks and stones are the materials out of which houses are built. But, unlike bricks and stones, words are alive. They keep growing and changing and moving from one meaning to another. The ancient poets said that words were the winged creatures of the air, carrying their precious message from mind to mind.

The study of words, therefore, is the study of things that have life and growth and motion. As nations develop, so do their words develop both in form and in meaning. In tracing the evolution of words, we are able to throw a vivid flashlight upon the evolution of the race that employs them.

Let us, for example, consider the word *sarcasm*. At present it means *a cutting jest*. Originally, however, it signified something much more severe than that. The Greek word from which it comes is *sarkadzein,* which means *to cut off the flesh.* The development in the meaning of this word is parallel to the progress of the human race. It is a long step from actually *cutting the flesh* of those whom you dislike to giving them merely *a severe tongue lashing.*

In the course of their history, a number of words have undergone a very interesting evolution. Take the word *gossip.* This word, which is derived from *God* and *sip,* means literally a *God-relation.* At first the word meant *a godfather* or *a godmother.* Then it came to mean *a friend.* But a friend is a person who comes to visit you often. The word *gossip,* therefore, took on the new meaning of *a frequent visitor.* From that point on, the next steps in the evolution of the word *gossip* were quite logical. A frequent visitor in one house is likely to be a frequent visitor in other houses. And a person who visits many houses is very likely to become a runabout and to carry news from one house to another. Hence the present meaning of *gossip: a person who runs about and tattles.*

Thus we sometimes discover an entire story in the evolution of a single word. When we examine the evolution of a group of words in a sentence or in a paragraph, we behold a colorful panorama not only of one nation, but of several nations. For the English language, like every other language, is the result of the intermarriage of many tongues. The English that we use today is a compound of elements borrowed from the Saxons, the Greeks, the Romans, the French, the Scandinavians, the Russians, the Arabians, the Turks, the Indians, and even the Chinese and the Jews. All the nations that have done business with us, and all the countries whose inhabitants have migrated to our shores, have enriched us not only with goods and with deeds, but with words. The following passage will in a small way point out the great debt which the English-speaking peoples owe to the tongues of other nations:

> "The lady and her companion had just visited the cardinal in the chapel of the church. He was reading a religious pamphlet when they arrived. They told him about their trials and tribulations. The cardinal listened attentively, and then said:
>
> " 'I can easily see why you are in such a quandary. I do not blame you for being so embittered against the scoundrel. When did you say you met him?'
>
> " 'Right after we had witnessed the tragedy of *Hamlet.* We had gone to the theatre for amusement, little dreaming that the Tory would accost us on the way out.'
>
> " 'Never you fear,' said the cardinal. 'Go home and sew that wedding dress you have been working on. I will ask my friend, the admiral, to arrest that scoundrel. You shall be able to marry in April just as you have been planning to do. And then you shall enjoy your honeymoon,—thirty happy days without a cloud.' "

Let us examine the origin and the meaning of some of the words in the above passage:

Lady. This word is of Saxon origin. It is derived from the term *hloefdige,* which means *loaf-keeper.* In the early days of England the lady of the house took care of the bread and handed it out to those who were hungry.

Companion. A companion is a person who, in accordance with the Latin derivation, *cum* (with) + *panis* (bread), shares bread with another person.

Cardinal. This word is derived from the Latin word *cardo, a hinge.* A cardinal, therefore, is the *hinge* by which the door of salvation may be opened.

Chapel. This word has an even more interesting history than *cardinal. Chapel* is derived from *capella, a little hat.* The word comes to us from the Latin, through the French. In the early history of France, the kings and the generals used to carry into their campaigns, as a token of good luck, the hat of their patron saint. This hat was called a *capella.* Later, the term was transferred from the hat to the little tent in which the hat was kept. Still later, *capella* came to mean a sacred little edifice, or *chapel.*

Church. This is derived from the Greek *kyrios* (Lord) + *akos* (the place of, or the house of). A *church,* therefore, is *the house of the Lord.*

Pamphlet. The origin of this word is French. A *pamphlet* is a brochure which consists of a number of sheets stitched together by means of a thread, *par-un-filet.* These three French words, *par-un-filet,* became welded into one and took the form of *pamphlet.*

Tribulations. This word is of Graeco-Latin origin. It means a threshing machine with iron prongs. Hence the term *tribulation* (Latin, *tribulum*) is that which crushes you as with prongs of iron.

Quandary. This word dates back to the Norman conquest of England. When William of Normandy came to England, he introduced this word, among many others, into the English language. Originally, it consisted of the French phrase, *qu'en dirai-je, what shall I say of it?* Gradually, the phrase became contracted into a single word, *quandary.*

Scoundrel. For the origin of this word we must go to Italy. *Scoundrel* is derived from the two Italian words *sconder* +

ruolla, one who hides himself when the muster roll is called; a soldier who is afraid to fight; a coward; hence, *a wicked person.*

Tragedy. For this interesting word we are indebted to the Greeks. A Greek tragedy was called *tragoedia,* from *tragos* (goat) + *ode* (song), because in ancient Greece the dramatist who produced the best tragedy received a goat as a prize.

Tory. This word has come to us as a contribution from the Irish. It is derived from *tor,* which means *a bush.* A *Tory* originally was *a man who hid behind a bush, a robber.*

Sew. This verb comes from the Latin *suo,* which in turn is derived from *sus, a sow.* The reason for this derivation is that the ancients did their sewing with needles made out of a pig's bristles. It is interesting to note, incidentally, that the modern needle was invented by a Negro in 1557.

Admiral. This is an Arabian word, contracted from the phrase *emir-al-bahr, commander of the sea.* It dates from the time when the Arabians were masters of the Mediterranean.

April. This is a rather pretty and poetical word. It comes from the Latin verb *aperio, I open,*—a fitting name for the month which opens the flowers to the sun.

Honeymoon. This is another poetical word. When people married in the olden days, they were given a beverage made of honey, and they were asked to drink it for thirty days, or a whole *moon.* Hence the term *honeymoon.*

Cloud. This, too, is a word that is pregnant with poetry. It is derived from the Latin *claudere, to shut* or *to enclose.* A *cloud* is an object which *shuts* the sun away from us. It is also an object which *encloses* the rain. It is probable that both these ideas were present in the minds of our ancestors when they fashioned the word *cloud.*

Thus we see that a study of words not only shows the inner meaning of our thoughts, but also throws the searchlight of knowledge upon the history of the past. For words develop as thoughts and institutions develop. Just as some institutions that once were radical become conservative with the passing of the years, so do certain words completely change their meaning and come to denote the very opposite of that which they denoted in the first place. This can be vividly, and interestingly, demonstrated in the following passage:

"Mary was a sensible and giddy young lady, wise and silly beyond compare. She was a slight and small creature, yet so large that everybody who knew her loved her. She felt rather lonely, because she lived in a town with no other houses or people for miles around. But when she did go to visit other people, she was so cheerful that everybody called her the saddest young lady in the country, and her intellect was so sharp that everybody regarded her as a veritable dunce. It is a pity that we have so little information about her. Yet it is her own fault. For she wrote her diary, and that is why we are unable to know what was in it. Yet this we know: that much as people admired her intellect and her beauty, they admired even to a greater extent the exquisite stench of her person and her clothes."

This passage, which sounds like so much gibberish, will be found to be clear and simple and logical when we examine some of the words in the light of their former meaning. Let us do so:

Giddy. This word, derived from the same stem as *God*, originally meant *divinely possessed, enthusiastic*. There was no sense of dizziness or foolishness attached to the word in the primitive stages of the English language.

Silly. Derived from the word *soelig* (German *selig*), it meant *blessed* or *happy*. As the language developed, the word began to be used in a satirical sense. According to the wise old philosopher, Solon, no man had a right to call himself happy until he was dead. Accordingly, he who regarded himself as *blessed* was *a fool*. And this is how it came about that the word *silly* acquired its present meaning.

Large. In the early English language the word *large* meant not *big*, but *generous*. We still find the trace of the old meaning in the related noun *largess*, which signifies *a generous present*.

Town. This is the same as the old English word *zaun, a farm*. Originally a *zaun*, or *town*, was an isolated farm in the country. Centuries later, when a number of farms were grouped closely together, they became what we now know as a village or *town*.

Saddest. The word *sad* started on its career with a cheerful meaning. It is derived from *satt*, which means *full, satisfied, contented, happy.* Our wise ancestors began to notice, however, that a *full* person was likely to be *unexcited.* Hence *sad* assumed the meaning of *calm.* But, our ancestors observed as time went on, a *calm* person was inclined to be *reflective.* And so *sad* became *serious.* The next step was the conclusion that a *serious* person is often *gloomy.* This is how the word *sad* finally evolved into its present meaning of *sorrowful.*

Dunce. This word is a misspelling of the middle name of Johannes Duns Scotus. This medieval scholar was so brilliant that everybody who showed a marked aptitude in his studies was called a regular *Duns,* or *Dunce.* Later, when the philosophy of Johannes Duns Scotus became unpopular, his enemies began to apply his name in a sarcastic sense, and a *Dunce* became a *fool.*

Wrote. The verb *write* comes from the German word, *reissen, to tear.* Later on, it meant *to scratch.* Still later, it developed into its present meaning, *to make signs upon a piece of parchment,* or *paper.*

Stench. This ugly word, strange as it may seem, originally had a pleasant meaning. A *stench* was an *odor* or *scent.* It was quite proper, in the early history of our language, to speak of the exquisite *stench* of the rose. Indeed, according to the Old English writers, man was said to possess the following five senses: sight, hearing, taste, touch, and *stench.*

Let us now rewrite the passage with the modern equivalents for the old meanings:

"Mary was a sensible and enthusiastic young lady, wise and blessed beyond compare. She was a slight and small creature, yet so generous that everybody who knew her loved her. She felt rather lonely because she lived on a farm with no other houses or people for miles around. But when she did go to visit other people, she was so cheerful that everybody called her the most contented young lady in the country, and her intellect was so sharp that everybody regarded her as a veritable scholar. It is a pity that we have so little information about her. Yet it is her own fault. For she tore up her diary, and that is why we are unable to know what was in it. Yet this we know: that much as people admired her intellect and her beauty, they admired even to a greater extent the exquisite scent of her person and her clothes."

We have just taken a hasty peep into the treasure-house of English words. We have glanced at the origin and the meaning of some of them. Our next step is to open the door and to enter this house where words are minted and grouped into the glories of the English language. An adventure of rare interest and beauty awaits us.

PART I

The Essential Bases of Good English

CHAPTER I

Simplified Grammar

§ I

THE PARTS OF SPEECH

IN THE EARLY DAYS of our language, when the scholars began to study the behavior of words under certain conditions, they discovered the interesting fact that all words may be divided into eight groups. These groups are known as parts of speech, and they are named as follows: *Noun, Pronoun, Adjective, Verb, Adverb, Preposition, Conjunction,* and *Interjection.* Since English grammar is patterned after Latin grammar, the names of the English parts of speech are derived from the Latin. Let us examine the meanings and the uses of these eight parts of speech:

Nouns. The word *noun* comes from the Latin *nomen,* meaning *name.* A *noun,* therefore, is a word which *names* a person or a thing. In the sentence

Jerry was ordered to *bed.*

the word *Jerry* is a noun because it names a person, and the word *bed* is a noun because it names a thing.

Pronouns. The word *pronoun* comes from the Latin *pro +
nomen,* meaning *for a name.* A *pronoun* is therefore a word which stands *for,* or *in place of* a *noun.* A pronoun is not a *name,* but a *substitute* for a name. In the sentence

John married Jennie because *he* loved *her.*

he is a pronoun because it is a substitute for John, and *her* is a pronoun because it is a substitute for Jennie.

Adjectives. The word *adjective* is derived from the Latin *ad + jectivus,* meaning *thrown to* or *added to.* An *adjective,*

3

therefore, is a word *added to* a noun or a pronoun in order to qualify or to describe its meaning. Thus, in the expression

a *little* boy with a *big* drum

little is an adjective because it describes boy, and *big* is an adjective because it describes drum.

Verbs. The term *verb* comes from the Latin *verbum,* meaning *word.* A verb is *the most important word* in a sentence. Without a verb, either expressed or understood, you cannot have a complete sentence. On the other hand, a verb may all by itself make a complete sentence. For example, the verb

Stop!

is a complete sentence.

A *verb,* therefore, is a word that makes a statement about some noun or pronoun. It denotes action or a state of being. In other words, it tells what a noun or pronoun *does* or *is.* Consider, for example, the following passage from *The Vicar of Wakefield:*

> I *was* ever of opinion, that the honest man who *married,* and *brought up* a large family, *did* more service than he who *continued* single, and only *talked* of population.

The italicized words in the above passage are verbs, because each of them denotes either *action* or *being.*

Adverbs. The word *adverb* comes from the Latin *ad + verbum,* meaning *added to a verb.* Hence an *adverb* qualifies or describes a verb. Observe, for example, the sentence

He greeted her *joyously.*

In this sentence the word *joyously* is an adverb because it describes the *manner* in which he greeted her.

An adverb may also qualify or describe an adjective, another adverb, a preposition, or a conjunction.

Prepositions. The word *preposition* comes from the Latin *prae + positus,* meaning *placed before.* A preposition, therefore, is a word that *precedes* a noun or a pronoun in order to *introduce* it, or to *relate* it, to the rest of the sentence. Thus, in the sentence

The book is *on* the table.

the word *on* is a preposition because it relates the table to the book. In other words, it points out to us the position where the book is lying.

Conjunctions. The word *conjunction* comes from the Latin *coniunctio,* meaning *a joining together.* Therefore a *conjunction* is a word which *joins* or *ties together* two or more words, or two or more groups of words. In the following passage all the italicized words are such connecting links, or *conjunctions:*

> I chose my wife, *as* she did her wedding gown, not for a fine glossy surface, *but* for such qualities as would wear well. To do her justice, she was a good-natured, notable woman; *and* as for breeding, there were few country ladies who could show more. She could read any English book without much spelling; *but* for pickling, preserving *and* cookery none could excel her. She prided herself also upon being an excellent contriver in housekeeping; *though* I could never find *that* we grew richer with all her contrivances.

Interjections. The word *interjection* is derived from the Latin *inter* + *jacere,* meaning *to throw between.* An *interjection* is something that is cast in between other words without having any grammatical relation to them. It has the same effect on a sentence that a stranger would have if he suddenly rushed, uninvited, into a formal gathering. Hence an *interjection* is generally followed by an exclamation point. In the expression

> Oh! He hurt himself.

The word *oh* is an interjection. It adds nothing to the grammatical construction of the rest of the sentence.

In addition to the eight parts of speech, we have the three articles: the indefinite articles *a* and *an,* and the definite article *the.* These three articles are really adjectives. The indefinite articles refer to *any,* but no particular, object, as in the sentences

> I saw *a* boy (any boy).
> I saw *an* animal (any animal).

The definite article refers to *a specific* object, as in the sentences

> I saw *the* boy (a specific boy).
> I saw *the* animal (a specific animal).

Before we proceed with the next step, let us pick out the different parts of speech in the following exercises. Name for yourself each word in the four sentences, and then check your answers with the key as given below:

1. Our doubts are now at an end.
2. He and she played equally well.
3. Alas! Poor Yorick.
4. Her quiet eyelids closed—she had another morn than ours.

KEY TO THE ABOVE EXERCISES

1. *Our* is an adjective, modifying the noun *doubts;* *are* is a verb, and *now* is its qualifying adverb; *at* is a preposition; *an* is the indefinite article; and *end* is a noun which is related to the rest of the sentence by the preposition *at*.
2. *He* is a pronoun, connected to the pronoun *she* by means of the conjunction *and;* *played* is a verb modified by the adverb *well,* which in turn is modified by the adverb *equally.*
3. *Alas* is an interjection; *poor* is an adjective which describes the noun *Yorick*.
4. *Her* and *quiet* are adjectives which modify the noun *eyelids; closed* is a verb; *she* is a pronoun; *had* is a verb; *another* is an adjective which qualifies the noun *morn; than* is a preposition which relates the pronoun *ours* to the rest of the sentence.

§ 2

CLASSES OF NOUNS

There are in the English language two general classes into which all nouns may be divided: **Concrete Nouns** and **Abstract Nouns.**

A *Concrete Noun* is the name of an object which we can perceive with our senses. We can see a house, or hear a tune, or touch a table, or taste an apple, or smell a rose. All these are therefore called *Concrete Nouns*. An *Abstract Noun* is the name of an idea which we can conceive in the mind but which we cannot perceive with the senses. We can think of fear and courage and philosophy and hope and love, but we cannot see or hear or touch or taste or smell these conceptions. Hence they are called *Abstract Nouns*.

Concrete Nouns

Concrete Nouns may be divided into three groups: *Common Nouns, Proper Nouns,* and *Collective Nouns.*

A *Common Noun* is a word which names an object, not as an individual, but as one of a class. For example, such words as *book, city,* and *college* are *Common Nouns*.

A *Proper Noun* is a word which names an object as an individual unit. Thus the *Bible* is the name of an individual book; *Boston* denotes a particular city; and *Harvard* refers to a definite college. These names, therefore, are *Proper Nouns*. *Proper Nouns* are always spelled with a capital letter.

A *Collective Noun* is a word which refers to a collection or group of things as one. Thus we speak of a *flock* of birds, a *class* of pupils, a *regiment* of soldiers, a *herd* of sheep, and a *congregation* of men and women. All these are *Collective Nouns*.

Abstract Nouns

An *Abstract Noun,* as we have observed, is the name of an idea. It cannot be perceived by the senses. It may denote a quality, such as *brightness;* a state or condition, such as *illness;* or an action, such as *growth*. Sometimes the same noun may be used either in an abstract or in a concrete sense. *Beauty* is such a noun. It is used in an abstract sense in the sentence

Beauty is truth, truth beauty,—that is all
Ye know on earth, and all ye need to know.

In the following sentence, however, the same word assumes a concrete meaning:

She is a regular *beauty*.

Inflection of Nouns

In order to serve their purpose in the English language, nouns may change their form in different kinds of sentences. This change of form is called *Inflection*.

Nouns change to designate:

1. *Number.* When a noun refers to only *one* object it is said to be in the *Singular Number.* When it refers to *more than one* object, it is said to be in the *Plural Number.* The plural is formed regularly by the addition of *s* or *es* (*book, books; beach, beaches*); irregularly, by the addition of *en* (*child, children; ox, oxen*), or by changing the vowel within the word (*mouse, mice; foot, feet*), or by changing the vowel or the consonant at the end of the word before adding *s* or *es* (*fly, flies; wife, wives*). Some nouns are the same in the singular and in the plural (*sheep, deer*).

2. *Gender,* or *Sex.* A man who acts is an *actor;* a woman who acts is an *actress.* Similarly, we have *hero, heroine; author, authoress; widower, widow.*

3. *Case.* There are three cases in English: *Nominative, Possessive,* and *Objective.*

The Nominative Case generally designates the *subject* of a verb:

The *man* came home (*man* is the subject of *came*).

The Possessive Case denotes *ownership:*

This is *John's* book (John is the owner of the book).

The Objective Case designates the *object,* or the person or thing *receiving the action* of a verb or a preposition. For example:

He struck the *prisoner* (object of the verb *struck*). She gave the book to her *son* (object of the preposition *to*).

The only case in which a noun changes its form is the Possessive.

EXERCISE

Point out, in the passage below, (1) the *Common Nouns;* (2) the *Proper Nouns;* (3) the *Collective Nouns;* (4) the *Abstract Nouns:*

"The famous Gyges," wrote Plato, "was a shepherd and servant of the king of Lydia. One day, while he was in the field feeding his flock, there was a storm and earthquake, which made an opening in the earth.

After some hesitation, Gyges descended into the opening, where he beheld a bronze horse with a human body upon it wearing a golden ring. This he took from the finger of the dead man, and re-ascended out of the opening. He came into the assembly of the shepherds; and as he was sitting among them, he chanced to rub the ring upon his finger. Immediately, to everybody's amazement, he became invisible."

Having picked out the various types of nouns in the above passage, compare your results now with the following answers:

1. Common Nouns: shepherd, servant, king, day, field, storm, earthquake, opening, earth, horse, body, ring, finger, man.
2. Proper Nouns: Gyges, Plato, Lydia.
3. Collective Nouns: flock, assembly.
4. Abstract Nouns: hesitation, amazement.

§ 3

CLASSES OF PRONOUNS

Pronouns may be divided into five classes: *Personal, Possessive, Demonstrative, Interrogative,* and *Relative.*

Personal Pronouns

A *Personal Pronoun* is a pronoun which denotes either the person who is *speaking,* or the person who is *spoken to,* or the person who is *spoken of.*

A pronoun denoting the person *speaking* is a pronoun of the *First Person.* For example, in the sentences

> *I* love my mother.
> *We* love our mother.
> My mother loves *me.*
> My mother loves *us.*

the words *I, we, me,* and *us* are pronouns of the *First Person,* because they indicate the person who is speaking these sentences.

A pronoun denoting the person *spoken to* is a pronoun of the *Second Person*. In the sentences

> *Thou* art a good man.
> *You* are good men.
> All good men love *thee*.
> All good men love *you*.

the words *thou, you, thee,* and *you* are pronouns of the *Second Person*, because they indicate the person spoken to.

A pronoun denoting the person *spoken of* is a pronoun of the *Third Person*. In the sentences

> *He* believes his friends.
> *She* believes her friends.
> *They* believe their friends.
> His friends believe *him*.
> Her friends believe *her*.
> Their friends believe *them*.

the words *he, she, they, him, her,* and *them* are pronouns of the *Third Person*, because they indicate the person spoken of.

In using the personal pronouns, be careful to avoid the following mistakes:

> (Wrong form) *Him* and I are friends.
> (Correct form) *He* and I are friends.

> (Wrong form) You and *me* are partners.
> (Correct form) You and *I* are partners.

> (Wrong form) Between you and *I*.
> (Correct form) Between you and *me*.

On the other hand, do not make the mistake of using the personal pronoun *them* for the demonstrative adjective *those*.

> (Wrong form) Give me a dozen of *them* crullers.
> (Correct form) Give me a dozen of *those* crullers.

Possessive Pronouns

When a Personal Pronoun denotes ownership, or possession, it is called a *Possessive Pronoun*. The following sentences will illustrate the use of the *Possessive Pronouns:*

> The pleasure is all *mine*.
> Take what is *thine*.

This book is *his*.
The beautiful dress is *hers*.
Ours is the duty to love our country.
If it is *yours*, I shall give it to you.
If they are our friends, we are *theirs*.

A common error is to spell some of these Possessive Pronouns with an apostrophe (your's, their's). Be sure to avoid this error.

Demonstrative Pronouns

A *Demonstrative Pronoun*, from the Latin *de* + *monstrare*, is a pronoun which *points out* a particular noun or phrase or clause to which it refers. In the passage from Keats which we have already quoted

Beauty is truth, truth beauty,—*that* is all
Ye know on earth, and all ye need to know.

the word *that* is a Demonstrative Pronoun because it *points out* the clause "Beauty is truth, truth beauty".

Interrogative Pronouns

An *Interrogative Pronoun* is a pronoun used in asking a question, either directly or indirectly. For example:

Who has just come in?
He wants to know *who* has just come in.
Whom do you take me for?
What is the price of this book?
I can tell you *whose* ideas I like best.

Frequent mistakes are made in the usage of *who* and *whom*. You can avoid these mistakes if you remember that the pronoun *who* must be used only as the *subject* of a verb (that is, the person who *does* something), and that we must use the pronoun *whom* only as the *object* (that is, the person to whom something *is done*). For example:

(Wrong form) *Whom* married that girl?
(Correct form) *Who* married that girl?

(Wrong form) *Who* did you see at the game?
(Correct form) *Whom* did you see at the game?

(Wrong form) *Who* do you want?
(Correct form) *Whom* do you want?

(Wrong form) He asked me *whom* would come to visit me.

(Correct form) He asked me *who* would come to visit me.

Relative Pronouns

A *Relative Pronoun* is a pronoun which *relates,* or *is related to,* a noun or a phrase or a clause. When the words *who, whom, whose,* and *what* ask a question, they are Interrogative Pronouns. When they do not ask a question, they are Relative Pronouns. In the following passage the italicized words are Relative Pronouns:

We honor the man *who* is truthful and *whose* words we can therefore trust. Such a man, *whom* we can all take into our confidence, is indeed fortunate. We love him for *what* he is, and for *what* he does.

PRACTICE DRILL

In the following sentences point out the pronouns and give the name of each:

1. Honesty is the best policy; of this I am certain.
2. What did you say?
3. I believe what you say.
4. Henry would like to know who is here.
5. Henry would like to know the man who is here.
6. Thine is the power and the glory.

In the following sentences point out those pronouns that are correct:

7. Whom, do you believe, came to see me today?
8. I know the man who, I think, will be elected.
9. Whom are you speaking of?
10. Whom do you expect to entertain at the party?
11. Whom do you expect will entertain at the party?

KEY TO THE ABOVE PRACTICE DRILL

1. *This* is a Demonstrative Pronoun. *I* is a Personal Pronoun.
2. *What* is an Interrogative Pronoun. *You* is a Personal Pronoun.

3. *I* and *you* are Personal Pronouns. *What* is a Relative Pronoun.

4. *Who* is an Interrogative Pronoun.

5. *Who* is a Relative Pronoun.

6. *Thine* is a Possessive Pronoun.

Sentences 8, 9, and 10 are correct. Sentences 7 and 11 are incorrect.

§ 4

CLASSES OF ADJECTIVES

Adjectives may be divided into four classes: *Descriptive, Demonstrative, Possessive,* and *Numeral.*

Descriptive Adjectives

A Descriptive Adjective is, obviously, an adjective that *describes* a noun or a pronoun. For example: a *red* robe, a *tall* man, a *warm* summer, an *English* book, a *Homeric* poem. These adjectives enable us to get a more vivid picture of the nouns which they modify.

Demonstrative Adjectives

A *Demonstrative Adjective* is an adjective which *demonstrates,* or *points out* the noun that it modifies. For example: *this* robe, *those* men, *another* summer, *neither* book, *some* poem.

Note the following usage: *this kind* of book; *these kinds* of books; *that kind* of book; *those kinds* of books.

Be careful not to confuse the Demonstrative Adjective with the Demonstrative Pronoun. In the sentence

I enjoyed *that* book; *that* is certain.

the first *that* is an adjective; the second is a pronoun.

Possessive Adjectives

A *Possessive Adjective* is an adjective which denotes *possession.* For example: this is *my* house; this is *your* car; this is *her* coat. These adjectives are equivalent to the pronouns *mine, yours,* and *hers.* If we prefer to use the pronouns, we can express the above sentences as follows:

This house is *mine.*
This car is *yours* (no apostrophe).
This coat is *hers* (no apostrophe).

Note: The word *its,* when spelled without an apostrophe, means *belonging to it.* For example: I like this house, particularly *its* roof. When *it's* is spelled with an apostrophe, it stands for *it is.* For example: *It's* a beautiful day today.

Numeral Adjectives

A *Numeral Adjective* is an adjective which indicates the *number* of the noun that it modifies. There are two kinds of numbers: Cardinal, like *one, two, three;* and Ordinal, like *first, second, third.* Here are a few examples of numeral adjectives:

Cardinal: One class; *ten* children; *fifty-one* dollars.
Ordinal: The *first* class; the *tenth* child; the *fifty-first* dollar.

EXERCISE

In the following sentences point out the adjectives and give the name of each:

1. For the twentieth time I have warned you that you must not take my shirt and pretend that it is yours.
2. The king abdicated when he learned that his personal interests conflicted with the interests of the people over whose country he ruled.
3. Theirs was not to question why, for it was their business to do and die.
4. That is why I enjoy this drama.
5. It's my decision to buy the older animal because its fur is thicker.

KEY TO THE ABOVE EXERCISE

1. *Twentieth* is a Numeral Adjective. *My* is a Possessive Adjective.

2. *His* is a Possessive Adjective. *Personal* is a Descriptive Adjective. *Whose* is a Possessive Adjective.
3. *Their* is a Possessive Adjective. (The first word in the sentence, *theirs*, is not an adjective but a pronoun.)
4. *This* is a Demonstrative Adjective.
5. *My* is a Possessive Adjective. *Older* and *thicker* are Descriptive Adjectives. *Its* is a Possessive Adjective.

§ 5

VERBS

There are two classes of verbs: *Transitive* and *Intransitive*.

Transitive Verbs

A *Transitive Verb* (from the Latin *trans* + *ire*, meaning *to go over*) is a verb that expresses action which *goes over to*, or *influences* or *affects* some object. Thus, in the sentence

The batter *hits* the ball.

the word *hits* is a Transitive Verb because it expresses an action which goes over to the ball and impels it to travel in a certain direction. A transitive verb requires an object, or receiver, for its action. For example: He sold the *house;* he likes *cheese;* the pianist struck the *keys;* the congregation heard the *sermon;* the senate passed the *law.*

Intransitive Verbs

An *Intransitive Verb* (from the Latin *in* [*not*] + *trans* + *ire*) is a verb that does not require an object. In the sentence

The man *rises* from the ground.

the word *rises* is an Intransitive Verb. But in the sentence

The man *raises* himself from the ground.

the word *raises* is a Transitive Verb, because its action affects the pronoun *himself.*

Frequently, the same verb may be used both in a transitive and in an intransitive sense. For example:

TRANSITIVE	INTRANSITIVE
He *smelled* the rose.	The rose *smelled* sweet.
She *looked* her scorn.	She *looked* charming.
The sexton *sounded* the bell.	The bell *sounded* in the belfry.
He *felt* his way.	He *felt* ill.
They did not *choose* him president.	He did not *choose* to run.

Bear in mind the fact that intransitive verbs can *not* take an object. All parts of the verb *to be*—I *am*, you *are*, he *is*, etc. —are intransitive. It is therefore wrong to say *it's me*, since *me* is an object. The correct form is *it is I*.

Many people confuse the transitive verb *to lay* with the intransitive verb *to lie*. The principal parts of the transitive verb are *I lay, I laid, I have laid*. The principal parts of the intransitive verb are *I lie, I lay, I have lain*. The confusion arises from the similarity in form between the present tense of *to lay* (*I lay*) and the past tense of *to lie* (*I lay*). But if you remember the fact that only a transitive verb can take an object, you will be able to use these verbs correctly. The correct usage is as follows:

> I (now) *lay* me down to sleep (transitive).
> The teacher *laid* the book on the table (transitive).
> We have *laid* our plans (transitive).
> The book *lies* on the table (intransitive).
> The snow *lay* on the ground (intransitive).
> I have *lain* in bed all week (intransitive).
> *Lie down!* (Do not say *Lay down!*)

EXERCISE

In the following passage point out the verbs and indicate in each case whether the verb is transitive or intransitive:

> Although they smiled and greeted each other courteously enough, they were ready to fly each at the other's throat. Outwardly they remained friends; they seemed, in the eyes of the casual spectator, to be on the best of terms. They dared not admit their quarrel, even to themselves. Yet all their friends recog-

nized the fact that a great companionship had run its course and was now dead.

KEY TO THE ABOVE EXERCISE

smiled, intransitive
greeted, transitive
were, intransitive
fly, intransitive
remained, intransitive
seemed, intransitive
to be, intransitive
dared, transitive
admit, transitive
recognized, transitive
had run, transitive
was, intransitive

Inflection of Verbs

Verbs, like nouns, may change their form in order to express different shades of meaning. These changes are designed to indicate:

1. *Person.* The first person indicates the one who is *speaking;* the second person, the one who is *spoken to;* the third person, the one who is *spoken of.* For example: I *give;* thou *givest;* he *gives.*

2. *Number.* A verb may be either singular or plural. For example: he *gives;* they *give.*

3. *Tense,* or *Time.* By changing its form, a verb may change the time of its action. There are six *tenses,* or *times,* when an action can take place:

Present: I *go.*
Past: I *went.*
Future: I *shall go.*
Present Perfect: I *have gone* (denoting a past action that has just been completed).
Past Perfect or Pluperfect: I *had gone* (denoting an action that was completed before another past action: *When John came, I had already gone*).
Future Perfect: I *shall have gone.*

Each one of the above tenses may also have a *progressive* form, denoting an action that is, was, or will be going on for some time: *I am going; I was going; I shall be going; I have been going; I had been going; I shall have been going.*

4. *Mood.* A Mood shows the *manner* or *condition* of an action. The English verb has three moods: *Indicative, Subjunctive,* and *Imperative.*

Indicative. The Indicative Mood states a fact, asks a question, or utters an exclamation: *He rides. Does he like it? He certainly does!*

Subjunctive. The Subjunctive Mood is frequently used to express an *if* clause, especially when the idea is doubtful or contrary to fact. Observe the following examples carefully:

If I *were* you, I would act differently.

The word *were* expresses an idea which is contrary to fact, since I am *not* you. Hence *were* is in the Subjunctive Mood.

If he *come,* I shall see him.

The word *come* expresses a doubtful future, since I do not know whether he will come or not.

Some of the other chief uses of the Subjunctive Mood are to express wishes (Long *live* the King!),—obligations (I think that he *ought* to come),—possibility (You *may* like this dinner),—and concessions (Though he *speak* with a voice of thunder, I shall not believe him).

Imperative. The Imperative Mood may be used to express a command or a request. Its form is the same in the singular and in the plural. It has but one tense, the present, and one person, the second. It generally is used without an expressed subject. Examples:

Go on!
Please forgive me!

5. *Voice.* A verb may be expressed either in the *Active* or in the *Passive Voice.* Let us, for example, consider the two following sentences:

Active: The captain shot his enemy.
Passive: The enemy was shot by the captain.

You will note that the *object* of the *active* verb becomes the *subject* of the *passive* verb. It is a good idea to avoid the passive voice wherever possible, especially if you want to acquire a vigorous style. The passive voice, like the passive person, is a weaker form than the active.

6. *Infinitives.* The infinitive is a verb which may be used either as a noun, an adjective, or an adverb. It has two tenses: present (*to read*), and perfect (*to have read*). Examples of its use:

Noun: *To read* is a pleasure (*to read* is the subject of the verb *is*).
I asked him *to read* (in this sentence, *to read* is the object of the verb *asked*).
Adjective: His ability *to read* was amazing (in this sentence, the infinitive modifies the noun *ability*).
Adverb: *To get* information, he read the book (*to get* modifies the verb *read*).

When you use the infinitive, be careful to avoid the following error: *I should have liked to have met him.* There are two correct ways of expressing this thought: *I should like* (now) *to have met him* (in the past); or, *I should have liked* (in the past) *to meet him* (at that time).

§ 6

ADVERBS

An *Adverb* may express one of the following ideas with respect to the verb that it modifies: Place, Time, Manner, Degree, Number, Assertion, Denial.

Adverbs of Place: She met him *here.*
Whence came the army of locusts?
Where are the snows of yesteryear?
Adverbs of Time: Now is the time to act.
I shall see you *soon.*
Yesterday it rained.
Adverbs of Manner: He walked *rapidly.*
He spoke *well.*
She sang *sweetly.*
Adverbs of Degree: He knows *more* than I do.
The game was *very* exciting.
This is *too* good to be true.

Adverbs of Number: He arrived *first.*
    She won the prize *twice.*
    Thrice he attempted to cross the river.
Adverbs of Assertion and Denial: Are you listening?
    Yes.
    Are you fond of pastry? *No.*
    Did you go to the dance? Certainly *not!*

Errors in the Use of Adverbs

A common error in the use of adverbs is to place two negatives together. It is wrong to say

There *ain't* (*isn't*) *nobody* here.

Since two negatives are equal to an affirmative, *there isn't nobody here* really means *there is somebody here.* There are two correct ways of expressing the negative idea in the above sentence:

There is nobody here; or, *there isn't anybody here.*

Some of the other common errors in the use of adverbs may be observed in the following sentences:

(Wrong form) He played very *good.* (*Good* is an adjective and cannot modify a verb.)
(Correct form) He played very *well.*

(Wrong form) He earns money *easier* than I do. (*Easier* is an adjective.)
(Correct form) He earns money *more easily* than I do.

(Wrong form) He speaks very *independent.*
(Correct form) He speaks very *independently.*

(Wrong form) He seemed *some* tired.
(Correct form) He seemed *somewhat* tired.

(Wrong form) You can *only* come by train.
(Correct form) You can come *only* by train; or, you can come by train *only.* (The adverb *only* must, if possible, immediately precede or immediately follow the word or phrase or clause that it modifies.)

(Wrong form) She is *not as* clever as her brother.
(Correct form) She is *not so* clever as her brother.

(Wrong form) He rises *up* from the ground.

(Correct form) He rises from the ground. (Since the word *rises* means *gets up,* the repetition of the adverb *up* is unnecessary.)

(Wrong form) The airship descended *down* to the earth.

(Correct form) The airship descended to the earth.

EXERCISE

In the following sentences name the adverbs and point out the errors if you find any:

1. Whither are you going?
2. Don't do nothing about it.
3. I've taken the medicine, and now I can work excellent.
4. Tomorrow will be her birthday.
5. He was the first to fight courageously.
6. I only see him occasionally.
7. He fell down on his face.

KEY TO THE ABOVE EXERCISE

1. *Whither* is an adverb of place.
2. *Don't* do *nothing* is incorrect,—a double negative.
3. *Excellent* is an adjective and is here used incorrectly as an adverb. The adverbial form is *excellently.*
4. *Tomorrow* is an adverb of time.
5. *Courageously* is an adverb of manner. Note: The word *first* in this sentence is not an adverb. It is an adjective, because it modifies the pronoun *he.*
6. This sentence is wrong. The correct form is *I see him only occasionally.*
7. The word *down* is unnecessary, as the downward idea is contained in the verb *fell.*

§ 7

PREPOSITIONS

A *Preposition,* you will recall, is a word which as a general rule is placed before a noun or pronoun in order to connect it with the rest of the sentence. The noun or pronoun thus connected by means of the preposition is the *object* of the preposition. The prepositions most frequently used are:

at	of
but (meaning *except*)	on
by	over
down	past
for	to
from	under
in	up
into	with

Errors in the Use of Prepositions

Prepositions are troublesome words, and they are often misused. Following is a partial list of the commonest errors in the use of prepositions:

(Wrong form) Between you and *I*.
(Correct form) Between you and *me*.

(Wrong form) Between me and *she*.
(Correct form) Between me and *her*.

(Wrong form) There is no one here except *she* and *I*.
(Correct form) There is no one here except *her* and *me*.

(Wrong form) There is no one here but *he* and *we*.
(Correct form) There is no one here but *him* and *us*.

(Wrong form) I shall bring my sister *for* supper.
(Correct form) I shall bring my sister *to* supper.
(Correct form) I shall bring a steak *for* supper.

(Wrong form) I live *at* Boston.
(Correct form) I live *in* Boston.
(Correct form) I live *at* Cambridge (University).
(Correct form) I live *in* Cambridge (city).

(Wrong form) Come *in* the house.
(Correct form) Come *into* the house.

(Wrong form) Where do you live *at?*
(Correct form) Where do you live?

(Wrong form) He will be home tonight.
(Correct form) He will be *at* home tonight.

(Wrong form) He lives near *to* the boundary.
(Correct form) He lives near the boundary.

Prepositional Idioms

Accompanied by:

> The boy was *accompanied by* his sister.

Accompanied with:

> The angry retort was *accompanied with* a blow.
> Note: the best present usage requires *by* to denote a person, and *with* to denote a thing.

Angry at:

> He is *angry at* his friend's suggestion.

Angry with:

> He is *angry with* his friend.
> Note: We are angry *at* a thing said or done, and *with* a person.

Appropriate for:

> The furniture was *appropriate for* the house.

Appropriate to:

> The speech was *appropriate to* the occasion.
> Note: In this idiom, *for* is used to denote objects or persons; *to* is used to denote occasions.

Blush at:

> He *blushed at* his brother's demand.

Blush for:

> He ought to *blush for* his ignorance.
> Note: We blush *at* another's speech or action, and *for* our own speech or action or condition.

Concur in:

> He *concurs in* the ideas of the committee.

Concur with:

> He *concurs with* the other members of the committee.
> Note: We concur *in* ideas or opinions, and *with* persons.

Contemporary of:

> Molière was a *contemporary of* Louis XIV.

Contemporary with:

>Molière was *contemporary with* Louis XIV.
>When *contemporary* is a noun, use *of;* when it is an adjective, use *with.*

Disappointed in:

>He was *disappointed in* his friend.

Disappointed with:

>He was *disappointed with* the house he bought.
>Note: We are disappointed *in* a person, and *with* a thing.

Distinguish among:

>We must *distinguish among* several types of literature: the novel, the drama, the poem, the biography, the essay, and so forth.

Distinguish between:

>We must *distinguish between* two important types of literature: the novel and the drama.

Divide among:

>The prizes were *divided among* twenty-five winners.

Divide between:

>The prizes were *divided between* the two winners.

Enraged at:

>He is *enraged at* Mr. Smith's accusations.

Enraged with or against:

>He is *enraged with* Mr. Smith.
>He is *enraged against* Mr. Smith.
>Note: We are enraged *at* a thing said or done, and *with* or *against* a person.

Favor of:

>He is in *favor of* the administration (meaning, *he favors* the administration).

Favor with:

>He is in *favor with* the administration (meaning, *he is favored by* the administration).

Impatient at:

He was quite *impatient at* the long delay.

Impatient with:

Don't be *impatient with* the boy.
Note: We are impatient *at* things, and *with* persons.

Indignant at:

He became *indignant at* the carelessness of the students (*at* a thing).

Indignant with:

He became *indignant with* his students (*with* a person or persons).

Liable for:

All men are *liable for* their actions.

Liable to:

The clerks are *liable to* their employer.
Note: We are liable *for* a thing, and *to* a person.

Vexed at:

She was *vexed at* his clumsiness (*at* a thing).

Vexed with:

She was *vexed with* him (*with* a person).

Exercise

In the following passage, point out the prepositions and their objects:

So, with a smile upon thy face, thou passest gently to another measure—to a quicker and more joyful one—and little feet are used to dance about thee at the sound, and bright young eyes to glance up into thine. And there is one slight creature, Tom—her child; not Ruth's—whom thine eyes follow in the romp and dance: who, wondering sometimes to see thee look so thoughtful, runs to climb upon thy knee, and put her cheek to thine; who loves thee, Tom, above all the rest, if that can be; and falling sick once, chose thee for her nurse, and never knew impatience, Tom, when thou wert by her side.

Thou glidest now, into a graver air; an air devoted to old friends and bygone days; and in thy lingering touch upon the keys, and the rich swelling of the mellow harmony, they rise before thee. The spirit of that old man dead, who delighted to anticipate thy wants, and never ceased to honor thee, is there among the rest : repeating, with a face composed and calm, the words he said to thee upon his bed, and blessing thee!

KEY TO THE ABOVE PASSAGE

PREPOSITION	OBJECT
with	smile
upon	face
to	measure
to	one
about	thee
at	sound
into	thine
in	romp—dance
on	knee
to	thine
above	rest
for	nurse
by	side
into	air
to	friends—times
in	touch
upon	keys
of	harmony
before	thee
of	man
among	rest
with	face
to	thee
upon	bed

§ 8

CONJUNCTIONS

There is an important distinction between a *Preposition* and a *Conjunction*. A *Preposition* takes an object; a *Conjunction* does not. In the phrase

John *with* his brother

with is a Preposition and *brother* is its object. But in the phrase

John *and* his brother

and is a Conjunction and *brother* is *not* its object. A Conjunction, therefore, is a word which does not take an object and which connects words, phrases, clauses, sentences, or paragraphs. There are two kinds of Conjunctions: *Coördinate* and *Subordinate*.

Coördinate Conjunctions

A *Coördinate Conjunction* is a word that connects expressions of *equal grammatical rank*. For example:

Mary *and* her sister are twins.

The words *Mary* and *sister* are of equal grammatical rank, because they are both subjects of the verb *are*. Therefore the conjunction *and* is a *Coördinate Conjunction*.

Some of the other Coördinate Conjunctions are: *but, or, yet, neither . . . nor, not only . . . but*. Examples:

John is rich, *but* his brother is poor.
Did you speak to them *or* to us?
He is disappointed, *yet* he is not discouraged.
He is *neither* very tall *nor* very short.
She *not only* admired him, *but* loved him.

Position of Coördinate Conjunctions

When you use Coördinate Conjunctions, especially when you use them in pairs, be sure to put them into the right position. Each member of the pair of conjunctions should immediately precede the same part of speech. Examples:

(Wrong form) They were ready *either* for peace *or* war.
(Correct form) They were ready *either* for peace *or* for war.

The words *either* and *or* should both precede the same part of speech: in this case, the preposition *for*.

(Wrong form) I am pleased *neither* with him *nor* her.
(Correct form) I am pleased *neither* with him *nor* with her.

(Wrong form) The reading of the book *both* helped him mentally *and* financially.

(Correct form) The reading of the book helped him *both* mentally *and* financially.

In the above sentence, each of the two conjunctions should immediately precede the adverb.

(Wrong form) He *not only* saw the parade, *but also* the fireworks.

(Correct form) He saw *not only* the parade, *but also* the fireworks.

Subordinate Conjunctions

A *Subordinate Conjunction* is a word that connects expressions of *unequal grammatical rank*. The clause that is introduced by a Subordinate Conjunction is *dependent upon* the principal clause, just as a lieutenant is dependent upon a captain. A subordinate clause can never stand by itself without the aid of the principal clause. For example, in the sentence

He answered *when his name was called*.

the clause *when his name was called*, introduced by the subordinate conjunction *when*, does not make complete sense without the help of the principal clause *He answered*.

Some of the more common Subordinate Conjunctions are: *though, because, unless, until, as, than*. Examples:

Though he pleaded his innocence, the jury found him guilty.

They liked him *because* he was so willing to help.

I refuse to go *unless* you come along.

They waited *until* the end came.

She is not so tall *as* I.

He is taller *than* I.

Warning: It is incorrect to say: *He is taller than me.* The word *me* is in the objective case. But since the word *than* is a conjunction, it can take no object. The above sentence, fully expressed, would be as follows:

He is taller *than I am tall*.

The same warning applies to the sentence *She is not so tall as I*. Never fall into the common error of saying *She is not so tall as me*.

The Difference between *Like* and *As*

Like is a preposition and takes an object. *As* is a conjunction and does *not* take an object. It is wrong to say: *He looks exactly like I do*. The correct way to express this idea is as follows:

He looks exactly like me. (*Me* is the object of *like*.)

We frequently hear the expression: *He acted like he meant it*. This is wrong. The correct expression is: *He acted as if he meant it*.

(Wrong form) He believes *like* I do.
(Correct form) He believes *as* I do.

Prepositions and Conjunctions

There are a number of English words which may be used either as Prepositions or as Conjunctions. The grammatical construction of the sentence will enable us to distinguish the difference in every case. Examples:

PREPOSITION	CONJUNCTION
He came *before* six o'clock.	He came *before* I left.
He died willingly *for* his country.	He died willingly, *for* he was a patriot.
Work *until* the end.	Work *until* you come to the end.
I have not seen him *since* yesterday.	I have not seen him *since* he arrived.
All came *but* us.	All came, *but* we remained behind.

EXERCISES

Name the conjunctions and point out the errors in the following sentences:

1. He was popular; therefore they elected him.
2. If a man is contented, he may be envied.
3. He is neither wise nor is he handsome.

4. He is both faithful and a friend.
5. We eat that we may live.
6. He is not good like you and I.
7. Since we understand each other, we may now speak plainly.
8. Between you and I, let us keep this a secret.
9. There is nothing meaner than them.
10. There is nothing meaner than them people.

Key to the Above Exercises

1. *Therefore* is a coördinate conjunction.
2. *If* is a subordinate conjunction.
3. *Neither . . . nor:* coördinate.
   This sentence is incorrect. The words *is he* should be omitted.
4. *Both . . . and:* coördinate.
   This sentence is wrong. The two words connected by the conjunctions should belong to the same part of speech. The words *a friend* should be changed to the word *friendly,* an adjective, just as *faithful* is an adjective.
5. *That* is a subordinate conjunction.
6. *And:* coördinate.
   This sentence should read: *He is not good like you and me.*
7. *Since:* subordinate.
8. *And:* coördinate.
   This sentence should read: *Between you and me,* etc.
9. *Than:* subordinate. *Them* should be changed to *they.*
10. *Than:* subordinate. *Them people* should be changed to *those people.*

§9

INTERJECTIONS

The *Interjection* is a very easy part of speech to master. We may therefore dismiss this subject with the warning that if you wish to become a good speaker or writer you will be very sparing in the use of interjections. A dramatic style with too many interjections becomes *melodramatic*.

Some of the more common interjections are: *good! halt! bang! alas! ha! bosh! hurrah!*

College yells consist almost entirely of interjections. For example:

> Har-vard! Har-vard! Har-vard!
> Rah! Rah! Rah!
> Rah! Rah! Rah!
> Rah! Rah! Rah!
> Har-vard! Har-vard! Har-vard!

A style that is full of interjections depicts a highly emotional, and probably very illogical, state of mind.

§ 10

CAPITALIZATION

The word *Capital* has a picturesque meaning. It comes from the Latin word *caput, a head*. A *capitalized* word is a word *crowned with a head*. It is, so to speak, the king of the passage in which it stands. A capital is a grammatical mark of respect.

RULES FOR THE USE OF CAPITALS

1. Use a capital at the beginning of every sentence:
   John came home early. He found the door locked.

2. Every line of poetry should begin with a capital:

   > If we shadows have offended,
   > Think but this, and all is mended,
   > That you have but slumbered here,
   > While these visions did appear.
   > —*Shakespeare.*

3. Use a capital at the beginning of every formal resolution or question:

   > Resolved, That this meeting give a rising vote of thanks.
   > Whereas, The guest of honor is one of the leading scientists of our generation, therefore be it unani-

mously agreed that we invite him to become a member of our learned society.

The question is, Shall we or shall we not surrender?

4. Use a capital for every noun or pronoun referring to God:

Our Father in Heaven, give us this day our daily bread.
Hallowed be Thy name.

5. Use a capital for every proper noun and every proper adjective.

Proper nouns: Henry, Sarah, Monday, December.
Proper adjectives: American, Darwinian, French.

6. When you quote the title of a book, use capital initials for the nouns, pronouns, adjectives, verbs, and adverbs. Do not use any capitals for the prepositions and conjunctions:

The Call of the Wild
How to Talk Entertainingly
The Prince and the Pauper
The Royal Road to Success

7. Use a capital for the pronoun *I*.

8. Use a capital to denote titles of rank and position when followed by a noun.

He was faithful to King George.
Introduce me to Professor Smith.

When such titles are *not* followed by a noun, you may use small letters:

He was faithful to his king.
Introduce me to the professor.

9. Every direct quotation should begin with a capital:

She said, "It is very warm today."

10. Use capitals to abbreviate degrees, eras, and personal titles:

A.B.	A.D.
A.M.	Mr.
Ph.D.	Mrs.
B.C.	Esq.

11. Use capitals to denote important events in history:

> The Civil War
> The French Revolution

12. Use capitals for the nouns (but not for the adjectives) in the salutation of a letter:

> My dear Brother Jack

In the conclusion of a letter, the common nouns are not capitalized:

> Your loving brother Jack

13. When an abstract noun is personified, use a capital:

> The Greeks regarded *Charity* as a goddess, and they worshipped it accordingly.

As the English nations are becoming more democratic, the best English writers are gradually reducing the number of their capitals. It is not an uncommon practice among certain types of modern poets to begin every line in a poem with a small instead of with a capital letter. Some writers even go so far as to begin all their sentences with small letters. The general usage, however, is in accordance with the thirteen rules as outlined above.

EXERCISES

In the following passages, place the capitals where they belong:

1. o hearts that break and give no sign
save whitened lips and fading tresses,
till death pours out his longed-for wine
slow-dropped from misery's crushing presses,—
if singing breath or echoing chord
to every hidden pang were given,
what endless melodies were poured
as sad as earth, as sweet as heaven!
—*Oliver Wendell Holmes.*

2. "listen, hawkeye," said the indian, "we mohicans came and made this land ours. then came the dutch, and gave my people the fire-water. then they parted with their land. now i, a chief and a sagamore, have never seen the sun shine except

through the trees, and have never visited the
graves of my fathers. and my son, uncas, the last
of the tribe, is the last of the mohicans."

—*James Fenimore Cooper.*

3. twilight and evening bell,
    and after that the dark!
   and may there be no sadness of farewell
    when i embark;

   for tho' from out our bourne of time and place
    the flood may bear me far,
   i hope to see my pilot face to face
    when i have crossed the bar.

   —*Alfred Tennyson.*

4. and so he did! it was old roger chillingworth
   that entered. the minister stood white and speech-
   less, with one hand on the hebrew scriptures,
   and the other spread upon his breast.

   —*Nathaniel Hawthorne.*

5. willingly resign yourself to the goddess, destiny. permit her to guide your life whithersoever
   she may. all things are for a day. observe con-
   tinually that all things change, and keep this
   thought ever with you, that nature loves nothing
   more than destroying one thing and giving birth
   to another.

6. "very well," he said, "what is your remedy for
   this evil?"

7. "we must trust to fate," she replied. "the future
   will take care of itself."

THE ABOVE EXERCISES CORRECTED

1. O hearts that break and give no sign
    Save whitened lips and fading tresses,
   Till Death pours out his longed-for wine
    Slow-dropped from Misery's crushing
      presses,—
   If singing breath or echoing chord
    To every hidden pang were given,
   What endless melodies were poured
    As sad as earth, as sweet as heaven!

2. "Listen, Hawkeye," said the Indian, "we Mohicans came and made this land ours. Then came
the Dutch, and gave my people the fire-water.
Then they parted with their land. Now I, a chief
and a Sagamore, have never seen the sun shine
except through the trees, and have never visited
the graves of my fathers. And my son, Uncas, the
last of the tribe, is the last of the Mohicans."

3. Twilight and evening bell,
   And after that the dark!
And may there be no sadness of farewell
   When I embark;

For tho' from out our bourne of Time and Place
   The flood may bear me far,
I hope to see my Pilot face to face
   When I have crossed the bar.

4. And so he did! It was old Roger Chillingworth
that entered. The minister stood white and speech-
less, with one hand on the Hebrew Scriptures,
and the other spread upon his breast.

5. Willingly resign yourself to the goddess, Destiny. Permit her to guide your life whithersoever
she may. All things are for a day. Observe con-
tinually that all things change, and keep this
thought ever with you, that Nature loves nothing
more than destroying one thing and giving birth
to another.

6. "Very well," he said, "what is your remedy for
this evil?"

7. "We must trust to Fate," she replied. "The future will take care of itself."

§ 11

HYPHENATION

The *Hyphen,* from the Greek *hyp'+hen* (*combined into
one*), is a mark which connects two words that are too
closely related to stay apart and yet not closely enough related
to combine into a single word. It is, so to speak, a link that

enables two words to become engaged before they are ready
to be married.

Rules for the Use of Hyphens

1. Use a hyphen to show connection between related dates,
page references, Bible references, and the like:

> Augustus ruled 31 B.C.-14 A.D.
> To get the answers, consult pages 41-58.
> Genesis I: 9-13.

2. Use a hyphen to show temporary connection between
words that are not ordinarily connected:

> He is a *matter-of-fact* young man.

Ordinarily the words *matter of fact* are not hyphenated.

3. Use a hyphen whenever two words are in the *engaged*
stage. Words are living things. Their form and their meaning keep constantly changing. A hyphenated word today may
be either a single word or two separated words tomorrow.
Frequently your own best judgment will tell you whether or
not a word should be hyphenated. When you are in doubt,
consult the most recent dictionary.

In accordance with the best usage of today, such combina-
tions of words as the following are hyphenated:

> He took a *ten-mile* drive (adjective+noun com-
> pound used as an adjective).
> He was *editor-in-chief* (noun+preposition+noun
> compound used as a noun).
> His *well-groomed* figure attracted everybody's atten-
> tion (adverb+participle compound used as an
> adjective).
> I like this *half-dark* room (adjective+adjective com-
> pound used as an adjective).

4. When a word is preceded by *self* and is compounded
with it, use a hyphen:

> This rule is *self-evident.*

5. Use a hyphen when a single word is temporarily separated at the end of a line. In order to do this properly, you

must know how to divide a line into syllables. The principles
that govern syllabication are as follows:

a. In general, words are divided as they are pronounced.

b. Never divide a word in such a manner as to leave
a single letter dangling either at the beginning or at
the end of a line: *a-long, ver-y, I-tal-y*.

c. Separate the *prefix* and the *suffix* from the rest of
the word: *pro-tect, mono-syllable, real-ize, end-ing*.

d. Do not separate such words as *twin-kle, sti-fle,
ti-tle*.

e. Do not separate two vowels that form a diph-
thong: *roy-al, bay-ou, Lou-is*.

f. When two consonants come at the junction of two
syllables, try to separate them so that each syllable
gets a consonant: *in-ven-tion, gram-mar, doc-tor*.

g. The last and most important principle is this:
When in doubt, consult the dictionary.

§ 12

PUNCTUATION

The ancient Greek and Latin manuscripts that have come
down to our own day are not punctuated. It is a physical
and mental torture to read them. To prove this point, let me
quote the following passage from Shakespeare in the Latin
manuscript style:

andinthiswoodwhereoftenyouandiuponfaintprimrose-
bedwerewonttolieemptyingourbosomsoftheircounsel-
sweettheremylysanderandmyselfshallmeet

Punctuation, you see, is of the utmost importance. It serves
no *grammatical* purpose, but it serves a very definite *logical*
purpose. It puts *reason* into your style, and it enables the
reader to follow you simply, accurately, and pleasantly.

Punctuation is a complicated matter. The rules of punctuation are not easy to apply. There is, however, *one* rule that
includes many of the others and that even a child can learn
to apply without much difficulty. It is this: *Punctuation reflects
the inflection of your voice*. Whenever you speak, you punctu-

ate your statements by means of your voice. You raise it; you lower it; you make a brief pause or a longer pause; you whisper; you exclaim. Try to write as you speak. *Imagine* that you are actually speaking what you are writing. You will then have very little difficulty with your punctuation. A comma will mean that your voice is making a brief pause; a semicolon, that the pause is a little longer; a period, that the pause is still longer. If your voice hurries over a group of words without any pause at all, that group of words does not require even a comma.

The above principle, however, does not cover *all* the rules of punctuation. Let us, therefore, examine the more important of these rules. And let us, if possible, try to simplify them.

The Comma

The Comma is used under the following conditions:

1. To separate the members of a series:

He went to see John, Peter, James, and Mary.
It is man's duty to live nobly, to suffer courageously, and to die peacefully.

2. To separate a dependent clause from the principal clause, when the dependent clause *precedes* the principal clause:

When he arrived, she was gone.

When the dependent clause *follows* the principal clause, the comma may sometimes be omitted:

She was gone when he arrived.

3. To separate a dependent clause that gives a *reason* for the principal clause. Such a dependent *causal* clause is generally introduced by some such word as *for, since,* or *because:*

I helped him, for he needed my help.
He bought the book, since he needed it for his examination.
I was happy to see him free, because I believed him innocent.

4. To separate two clauses of parallel construction:

He was born rich, but he died poor.

5. To separate a relative clause that is *distantly* related to the principal clause:

> This city, whose mayor is a Frenchman, is unusually well governed.

When the relative clause is *closely* related to the principal clause, the comma may be omitted:

> This is the only city whose mayor is a Frenchman.

Note: In the first sentence we may omit the clause *whose mayor is a Frenchman* and still make good sense. Hence this clause is said to be *distantly related* to the principal clause and is not necessary to its existence. In the second sentence, if we omit the clause *whose mayor is a Frenchman,* we leave the principal clause dangling in the air. Hence the relative clause in this sentence is *closely related* to the main clause, since without it the main clause loses its meaning. Note the following further examples:

> I honor the man who gives his life for his friend (a *closely related* relative clause).
> This man, who was a neighbor of mine, gave his life for his friend (a *distantly related* relative clause).

To repeat rule 5 in somewhat different words: When a relative clause may be removed (like an appendix) without changing the vitality of the sentence, separate the clause with commas in order to show its unimportance. When its removal (like some vital organ) would kill the sense of the sentence, use no comma but keep it closely connected to the body of the sentence.

6. To separate a parenthetical expression from the rest of the sentence:

> This sentence, *for example,* illustrates the above point.

A parenthetical expression may also be separated by parentheses or by dashes:

> *This* sentence (*for example*) illustrates the *second* point.
> And *this* sentence—*for example*—illustrates the *third* point.

7. To mark the omission of one or more words:

This book is bound in red; that one, in blue.

The complete sentence, without the omissions, would read as follows:

This book is bound in red; that one is bound in blue.

The Semicolon

The *Semicolon* stands between the Comma and the Period. The pause indicated by the semicolon is longer than that indicated by the comma and shorter than that indicated by the period. It is of particular help in dividing long and unwieldy sentences into shorter and more intelligible groups. For example:

> She stood immovable close to the grim old officer, and remained immovable close to him; remained immovable close to him through the streets, as Defarge and the rest bore him along; remained immovable close to him when he was got near his destination and began to be struck at from behind; remained immovable close to him when the long-gathering rain of stabs and blows fell heavy; was so close to him when he dropped dead under it, that, suddenly animated, she put her foot upon his neck and with her cruel knife—long ready—hewed off his head.
>
> —*Charles Dickens.*

The Colon

The *Colon* is a punctuation mark that is designated to arrest the attention. It indicates that the next phrase or clause is about to explain the previous clause:

> He wrote three kinds of books: a novel, a drama, and an epic poem.

The Colon is also used under the following conditions:

1. Before a long quotation. A short quotation is introduced by a comma. Examples:

> He said:
> "If I knew then what I know now, I would have acted differently. I would have realized my limita-

tions, and I would not have undertaken a task so obviously beyond my endurance."

She replied, "I am glad to hear you speak so sensibly at last."

2. To introduce a formal letter:

Dear Sir:
We are happy to announce that we can fill your order.

The Period

The *Period* is used under the following conditions:
1. To mark the end of a declarative sentence:

He closed the office and went home.

2. To mark abbreviations:

Dr. O. W. Holmes   F.R.S.
A.B.   etc.

3. To indicate that something in a quoted passage has been omitted, three periods (. . .) are used:

He that by the plough would thrive,
Himself must . . . drive.
—*Benjamin Franklin.*

The Exclamation Point

The *Exclamation Point* is used to indicate excitement of any kind.

Halt!
Hush!
I wouldn't have believed it!
I'm terribly afraid!

The Question Mark

The *Question Mark* is used at the end of a *direct* question. It is not used in indirect questions. Examples:

Do you think she has told the truth? (direct)
He asked whether she had told the truth. (indirect)

The Parenthesis

The *Parenthesis* indicates a word or a phrase or a clause that adds very little (if anything) to the meaning of the rest of the sentence.

In the following sentences, note carefully the punctuation marks within, and just outside of, the parentheses:

> He told her (as who wouldn't?) that she was very beautiful.
> The article appeared in the *Nation* (November, 1936).

When a parenthesis follows a clause that requires a comma at the end, the comma goes *after* the parenthesis:

> Ever since he came here (to my sorrow), I have been under a terrific burden.

The Dash

The *Dash* is used to mark off an abrupt or informal group of words in the middle of a passage. It is the black sheep of the punctuation family. It adds spice and color to a style. It may be used either singly or in pairs. Examples:

> He feared nobody—except his wife.
> When he asked her to marry him—it was so sudden—she didn't know what to say.
> No—listen to me!—I say emphatically no.

The Apostrophe

The *Apostrophe* is used under the following conditions:
1. To mark the omission of one or more letters:

> *doesn't*   *o'clock* (of the clock)
> *I'm*   *'tis*

2. To denote possession:

> The *boy's* (singular) sister.
> The *boys'* (plural) sister.
> *Burns's* poems. (This is a better form than *Burns'* poems.)

3. To form certain plurals:

Dot your *i's*.
Cross your *t's*.

Quotation Marks

Quotation Marks are used under the following conditions:
1. To enclose matter that is *directly* quoted:

> He said, "This is quite true."

Matter that is *indirectly* quoted is not enclosed in quotation marks:

> He said that this was quite true.

2. To point out a slang expression:

> This man, with his constant "ataboy", is a regular nuisance.

3. To designate words or phrases used for illustration or explanation:

> Be careful to distinguish between "like" and "as."

Note: It is more common to designate such words or phrases by means of italics:

> Be careful to distinguish between *like* and *as*.

4. To indicate the title of a book or of a picture:

> Thackeray's "Vanity Fair"
> Leonardo da Vinci's "The Last Supper"

Note: Here, too, it is more common to use italics:

> Thackeray's *Vanity Fair*
> Leonardo da Vinci's *The Last Supper*

Quotations Within Quotations

A quotation within a quotation is expressed by means of single marks within double marks:

> "I heard him say 'You are quite right,' " she explained. "Those were his exact words."

Long Quotations

When a quotation continues beyond a single paragraph, use quotation marks at the beginning of *each* paragraph and at the end of the *final* paragraph:

He expressed his philosophy in three short paragraphs:

"I believe in justice. Let there be justice between man and man and between nation and nation.

"I believe in mercy. Justice without mercy is a tempest without a shelter. Justice is revenge; mercy is forgiveness.

"I believe in peace. Without peace there can be no justice or mercy. Without justice and mercy there can be no peace."

Exercises

Punctuate the following passages:

1. And so guiltless very likely she was writhing and pushing onward toward what they call a position in society and the servants were pointing at her as lost and ruined so you see Molly the housemaid of a morning watching a spider in the door-post lay his thread and laboriously crawl up it until tired of the sport she raises her broom and sweeps away the thread and the artificer

—*William Makepeace Thackeray.*

2. It was and I said not but

3. How much was the reward offered did you say asked Dupin

Why a very great deal a very liberal reward I don't like to say how much precisely but one thing I will say that I wouldn't mind giving my individual cheque for fifty thousand francs to anyone who could obtain me that letter I can do no more can I

Why yes said Dupin I really think you might do a little more

How

Why puff puff you might puff puff do this you might

at least so it seems to me employ counsel in the matter
do you agree with me

I most emphatically do not

—*Edgar Allan Poe* (paraphrased).

Key to the Above Exercises

1. And so—guiltless very likely—she was writhing
and pushing onward toward what they call "a position in society," and the servants were pointing at her
as lost and ruined. So you see Molly the housemaid of
a morning watching a spider in the door-post lay his
thread and laboriously crawl up it, until, tired of the
sport, she raises her broom and sweeps away the
thread and the artificer.

2. It was "and" I said, not "but."

3. "How much was the reward offered, did you say?"
asked Dupin.

"Why, a very great deal—a *very* liberal reward—
I don't like to say how much, precisely; but one thing
I *will* say, that I wouldn't mind giving my individual
cheque for fifty thousand francs to anyone who could
obtain me that letter. I can do no more, can I?"

"Why, yes," said Dupin. "I really think you might
do a little more."

"How?"

"Why—puff, puff—you might—puff, puff—do
this: you might (at least, so it seems to me) employ
counsel in the matter. Do you agree with me?"

"I most emphatically do not!"

Before we leave this subject, let us remember that punctuation is an art and not a science. No two writers punctuate
exactly alike. Where one uses a comma, another may use a
dash; where one finds a semicolon satisfactory, another may
insist upon a period; where the scholar is content with a period,
the poet may require an exclamation point. To some extent,
punctuation is to a writer what shading is to a painter. In
developing your style, learn the general rules of punctuation,
and then apply them freely in accordance with your own personality. For every writer must cultivate two important characteristics: *accuracy* and *individuality*.

CHAPTER II

Correct Spelling

§ I

CARELESS PRONUNCIATION

THE COMMONEST REASON for poor spelling is poor pronunciation. Let us, for example, look at a few words that are frequently mispronounced and therefore frequently misspelled:

aerial. Many people pronounce this word as if it contained *three* syllables, *ay-ri-al*. If we learn to pronounce it properly, as a word of *four* syllables, *a-e-ri-al*, we can make no mistake about the spelling.

separate. This word is often mispronounced and misspelled as a word of *two* syllables, *sep-rate*. It should be pronounced and spelled as a word of *three* syllables, *sep-a-rate*.

grievous. This is often mispronounced as a word of *three* syllables, *griev-i-ous*. Pronounce and spell it in *two* syllables, *griev-ous*.

Other words that are misspelled because they are mispronounced:

WRONG PRONUNCIATION	CORRECT PRONUNCIATION
ac-ci-dent-ly	ac-ci-dent-al-ly
ath-e-let-ic	ath-let-ic
ge-ne-o-logy	ge-ne-a-logy
gover-ment	govern-ment
i-den-ity	i-den-tity
ir-rev-e-lant	ir-rel-e-vant
lin-a-ment	lin-e-a-ment
min-er-ol-ogy	min-er-al-ogy
min-a-ture	min-i-a-ture
Ni-ag-ra	Ni-ag-a-ra
pro-gi-dy	pro-di-gy
su-prise	sur-prise
twelth	twelfth
val-u-ble	val-u-a-ble

§ 2
SILENT LETTERS

Another common reason for poor spelling is the frequency of silent letters in the English language. Here are just a few examples:

coco*a*	*m*nesic (relating to memory)
extr*a*ordinary	colum*n*
plum*b*er	solem*n*
redou*b*t	*p*neumonia
indi*c*t	recei*p*t
vi*c*tu*a*ls (pronounced vittles)	apo*ph*the*g*m (maxim)
ya*c*ht	cor*p*s
han*d*kerchief	ai*s*le
han*d*some	vi*s*count
lunch*e*on	bouque*t*
campai*g*n	chas*t*en
diaphra*g*m	chris*t*en
poi*g*nant	mis*t*letoe
brou*g*ham	pes*t*le
besou*g*ht	bisc*u*it
catarr*h*	croqu*e*t
da*h*lia	ga*u*ge
r*h*ythm	g*u*erilla
busi*n*ess	g*u*itar
parl*i*ament	gun*w*ale
*k*nack	*w*reak
*k*nuckle	*w*reath
ba*l*k	*w*ren
*p*sa*l*m	*w*roth

To*w*ard is pronounced as *one* syllable (*tord*)

In the matter of silent letters, we Americans are more fortunate than the English. Just consider, for instance, the following names that have so peculiar a pronunciation in England:

Saint John (pronounced *Sinjun*)
Magdalene (pronounced *Maudlin*)
Cholmondeley (pronounced *Chumly*)

These names are but extreme examples of the orthographic (spelling) difficulties of the English language. No other language, perhaps, contains so many words in which the spelling is divorced from the sound. "No wonder," said Mark Twain, "that so many good English writers are such poor *spelers*."

Yet there is no excuse for poor spelling. All in all, there are only a few hundred words that give even the most careless among us any trouble. Learn these few hundred words, at the rate of five a day, and in two or three months you will have conquered most of your spelling difficulties. Examine the list that follows; check off those words that have been bothering you; look at them not only with your *eyes,* but with your *mind;* use your eyes as lenses and photograph the words upon your consciousness; and then see how easy it is to master these difficult words.

§ 3

WORDS OFTEN MISSPELLED

1. abridgment	24. amethyst
2. abscess	25. ammunition
3. abyss	26. analysis
4. accede	27. annotate
5. accept	28. annunciation
6. accessible	29. anoint
7. accommodate	30. appall
8. accredit	31. apparatus
9. acetylene	32. apparel
10. achieve	33. appraise
11. acknowledge	34. architect
12. acquiesce	35. Arctic
13. acquire	36. arraign
14. adamant	37. ascension
15. admissible	38. asparagus
16. adolescent	39. asphyxiate
17. advice (noun)	40. assassin
18. advise (verb)	41. asterisk
19. aeroplane	42. asthma
20. aggravate	43. auspices
21. all right	44. avoirdupois
22. allege	45. bachelor
23. amateur	46. banana

47. battalion
48. bazaar
49. beauteous
50. beguile
51. behoove
52. benefiting
53. benign
54. benzene
55. benzoin(e)
56. bequeathed
57. bereave
58. bicycle
59. biennial
60. bilge-water
61. bilious
62. biscuit
63. bivouac
64. bizarre
65. blackguard
66. bludgeon
67. bluish
68. boudoir
69. bourgeois
70. boycott
71. bracketing
72. braggadocio
73. breath (noun)
74. breathe (verb)
75. breathing
76. brethren
77. bridging
78. brochure
79. brougham
80. buccaneer
81. buffoon
82. bureaucracy
83. business
84. busy
85. by-and-by
86. calendar
87. callous
88. calorie
89. calumny
90. calyx
91. capillary
92. carat
93. carburetor
94. carcass
95. carillon
96. casserole
97. catalepsy
98. catarrh
99. catechism
100. caucus
101. cauterize
102. celluloid
103. cemetery
104. chameleon
105. chamois
106. chancellor
107. chaotic
108. chassis
109. chauffeur
110. chiropodist
111. chromium
112. cigarette
113. cinnamon
114. cipher
115. circuit
116. cistern
117. clientele
118. climatic (pertaining to climate)
119. coalesce
120. coerce
121. collateral
122. collusion
123. colonnade
124. colossal
125. column
126. commemorate
127. committee
128. concupiscent
129. concurrent
130. condescend
131. conduit
132. confectionary
133. connoisseur

134. connubial
135. conscience
136. consummate
137. contrariety
138. contumely
139. convalesce
140. coquette
141. corollary
142. corrugated
143. coterie
144. council (assembly)
145. counsel (advice)
146. counterfeit
147. crochet
148. cryptogram
149. cursory
150. cynosure
151. Czechoslovakia
152. dahlia
153. debris
154. deceased (dead)
155. deceit
156. Deity
157. delete
158. delineate
159. deshabille
160. desiccate
161. desuetude (disuse)
162. develop
163. diary
164. dilapidated
165. dilettante
166. diphtheria
167. disappoint
168. discern
169. discipline
170. dissect
171. dissension
172. dissipate
173. dormouse
174. drought (absence of rain)
175. eccentric
176. eclipse

177. ecstasy
178. eczema
179. edgewise
180. eerie
181. effervesce
182. effete
183. ellipse
184. embarrass
185. emissary
186. emulsion
187. encyclop(a)edia
188. enforcible
189. envelope (noun)
190. envelop (verb)
191. ephemeral
192. epic (heroic poem)
193. epoch (era)
194. equilibrium
195. erotic (dealing with love)
196. erratic (eccentric)
197. espionage
198. Ethiopian
199. etiquette
200. etymology
201. eucalyptus
202. exaggerate
203. exceed, excess
204. excerpt
205. excise
206. execrate
207. exempt
208. exhale
209. exhilarate
210. exigence
211. existence
212. exquisite
213. extant
214. extinct
215. façade
216. fanatic
217. fascism
218. fatiguing
219. faucet

220. feasible
221. February
222. felon
223. feign
224. fencing
225. filigree
226. Filipino
227. finesse
228. firing
229. flabbergasted
230. flaccid
231. flamboyant
232. focus
233. forfeit
234. forging
235. forty-four
236. fossilize
237. fractious
238. fraudulent
239. fricassee
240. fringing
241. fuchsia
242. fulfill
243. furore (enthusiasm)
244. fuselage
245. fusillade
246. gamble (to play for money)
247. gambol (to skip)
248. gangrene
249. gaseous
250. gatling-gun
251. gauge
252. gewgaw
253. geyser
254. ghastly
255. gingham
256. giraffe
257. gist
258. gladiolus
259. glucose
260. gluttonous
261. glycerine
262. gnat

263. grammar
264. granddaughter
265. grasshopper
266. grateful
267. gregarious
268. grievous
269. grimace
270. gruesome
271. guiding
272. guillotine
273. guise
274. gutta-percha
275. guttural
276. gyrate
277. gyroscope
278. h(a)emorrhage
279. halcyon
280. hallucination
281. halyard
282. handkerchief
283. harangue
284. harass
285. harelip
286. Hawaii
287. hegemony
288. heifer
289. height
290. heinous
291. heirloom
292. hiccough
293. hideous
294. hiding
295. hijacker
296. hippodrome
297. holiday
298. homicide
299. hoping
300. Hottentot
301. Huguenot
302. hyacinth
303. hybrid
304. hydraulic
305. hydrogen
306. hydrophobia

307. hyena
308. hygiene
309. hypochondria
310. hypocrisy
311. idiom
312. idiosyncrasy
313. idol (an image of worship)
314. idyl (a short poem)
315. illegible
316. illiterate
317. illusion (deception)
318. imbroglio
319. immaculate
320. immemorial
321. impugn
322. inaccessible
323. inadmissible
324. inaugurate
325. incandescent
326. incendiary
327. incisor (one of the front teeth)
328. incredible
329. indecisive
330. indefatigable
331. indefensible
332. indispensable
333. innocuous (2 *n's*)
334. inoculate (1 *n*)
335. interceding
336. introducing
337. inveigh
338. inveigle
339. iridescence
340. isosceles
341. jagged
342. jaguar
343. jaundice
344. jaunt
345. jealousy
346. jejune (uninteresting)
347. jeopardy
348. jonquil
349. judgment
350. juggernaut
351. kaleidoscope
352. keyed
353. khaki
354. kilogram
355. knack
356. knapsack
357. knickknack
358. knoll
359. kyanize
360. labyrinth
361. lachrymose (tearful)
362. lacing
363. laconic (brief)
364. lacquer
365. laity
366. laryngitis
367. lascivious
368. leisure
369. leopard
370. levee
371. leveling
372. liable
373. libel
374. licence (noun) or license
375. license (verb)
376. licentious
377. lichen
378. licorice
379. lief
380. liege
381. lien (a legal claim)
382. lightning
383. likeable
384. linotype
385. lodging
386. loiter
387. lollipop
388. longevity
389. to loose (to untie)
390. to lose (not to gain)
391. loveliness

392. loving
393. loyalty
394. luscious
395. lying
396. macaroni
397. macaroon
398. madeira
399. mademoiselle
400. maestro
401. mahogany
402. maintenance
403. malign
404. management
405. manikin
406. margarine
407. marriageable
408. martyr
409. massacring
410. massaging
411. maudlin
412. mausoleum
413. medallion
414. Mediterranean
415. mellifluous
416. meningitis
417. messieurs
418. metallurgy
419. meteor
420. mettle (courage)
421. miniature
422. miscellaneous
423. mischievous
424. misshaped
425. misstate
426. moccasin
427. molasses
428. mollify (soften)
429. mortgage
430. mucilage
431. mulatto
432. myopia
433. naphtha
434. nauseous
435. necessary
436. neuralgia (pain in a nerve)
437. neurology (study of nerve diseases)
438. niche
439. nuisance
440. numskull
441. obeisance
442. obese (fat)
443. obsession
444. obsolete
445. obstreperous
446. occurrence
447. odious
448. offal (unfit meat)
449. offense
450. omitted
451. omniscient
452. onerous (heavy)
453. operetta
454. opponent
455. opportune
456. oppressor
457. oscillate (to vibrate)
458. osculate (to kiss)
459. outrageous
460. overrate
461. owing
462. oxidize
463. oxygen
464. pageant
465. panacea
466. panegyric
467. pantomime
468. papacy
469. paraffin
470. parallel
471. paralysis
472. parasite
473. parenthesis
474. pariah (an outcast)
475. parishioner
476. parliament
477. parochial

478. parodied
479. paroxysm
480. pasteurize
481. paucity (scarcity)
482. paving
483. peaceable
484. pebbly
485. pecan
486. peddling
487. pedigree
488. perceive
489. percolator
490. perennial
491. pernicious
492. perseverance
493. personnel
494. phaeton
495. phenomenon
496. Philippines
497. philosophy
498. phlegm
499. phosphorus
500. phthisis (consumption)
501. physic
502. physiography
503. physiology
504. piccolo
505. picnic
506. picnicking
507. pigeon
508. pinnacle
509. pistachio
510. pistil (part of a flower)
511. pitiful
512. plagiarize
513. plaguing
514. plaintiff (noun)
515. plaintive (adjective)
516. plaited (braided)
517. plated (covered with metal)
518. plating
519. plausible
520. playwright

521. pleasurable
522. plebeian
523. pleurisy
524. plugged
525. plumber
526. plunging
527. pneumonia
528. poignant
529. poking
530. policing
531. poll-tax
532. polygon
533. Portuguese
534. preference
535. preferred
536. pricing
537. prism
538. privilege
539. precede (to go before)
540. proceed (to go ahead)
541. procedure
542. process
543. profession
544. proffer
545. proficience
546. promising
547. promissory
548. pronounce
549. pronunciation
550. propaganda
551. prophecy (noun)
552. prophesy (verb)
553. proprietor
554. prove
555. pseudonym
556. psychic
557. ptomaine
558. pugilism
559. purging
560. pursuit
561. pusillanimous (timid)
562. pygmy
563. pyjamas
564. quadrilateral

565. quadrille
566. querulous
567. questionnaire
568. queue
569. quibbling
570. quinsy (sore throat)
571. Quixotic
572. radish
573. raffling
574. raiment (clothing)
575. rancid
576. rarefy
577. raspberry
578. rebellious
579. rebuttal
580. recede
581. receipt
582. receive
583. recension (revision)
584. recipe
585. recollect
586. recommend
587. reconnoiter
588. refugee
589. regatta
590. reimburse
591. relieve
592. reminiscent
593. removable
594. reprieve
595. rescind
596. resurrect
597. resuscitate
598. retrieve
599. reveille
600. reverie
601. rhinoceros
602. rhubarb
603. rhyme
604. rhythm
605. rigmarole
606. roebuck
607. roguishness
608. roulette

609. rueful
610. ruffling
611. Sabbath
612. saccharin
613. sachet
614. sacque
615. sacrilegious
616. saffron
617. salaam
618. salicylic
619. sandwich
620. sang-froid
621. sapphire
622. Saracen
623. sarsaparilla
624. satchel
625. satellite
626. satiate
627. scathing
628. scented
629. scepter
630. schedule
631. scherzo
632. schism
633. sciatica
634. scintilla
635. scion
636. scissors
637. sconce
638. scourge
639. scythe
640. secede
641. secretarial
642. sedentary
643. seething (boiling)
644. seizing
645. seminary
646. separate
647. sepulcher
648. seraglio
649. sewage
650. sheik
651. shellac
652. sheriff

653. shrick
654. Siamese
655. siege
656. sieve
657. silhouette
658. siphon
659. skein
660. sluice
661. snaky
662. sniveling
663. sobriquet
664. solicit
665. soliloquy
666. somersault
667. somnambulist
668. soothing
669. soubrette
670. sovereign
671. spaghetti
672. speech
673. speedometer
674. sphinx
675. spigot
676. spinach
677. staccato
678. statistician
679. stereoscope
680. stiletto
681. stratagem
682. strategic
683. strategy
684. strengthen
685. strychnine
686. stupefy
687. styptic
688. subpoena
689. succinct
690. succulent
691. suffragette
692. supersede
693. supervene
694. supplementary
695. surfeit
696. surgeon

697. surveillance
698. susceptible
699. sycamore
700. symmetrical
701. symposium
702. syncopation
703. synopsis
704. syringe
705. tariff
706. tattoo
707. tee (golf term)
708. teetotaler
709. tenacious
710. tenant
711. terrestrial
712. terrorize
713. thatch
714. thoroughbred
715. thousandth
716. tidily
717. tying
718. tobacconist
719. toboggan
720. toeing
721. tonic
722. tonnage
723. toppling
724. toreador
725. totally
726. trafficking
727. tragedian
728. tragedienne
729. tranquillity
730. transferable
731. trapeze
732. trestle
733. tribal
734. trifling
735. trolley
736. trousseau
737. trudging
738. truly
739. tryst
740. turquoise

741. turreted
742. tyrannous
743. unfeigned
744. unnerving
745. unparalleled
746. unprecedented
747. unsheathing
748. until
749. unwieldy
750. upholstered
751. usable
752. vaccinate
753. vacillate
754. valedictory
755. valorous
756. variegated
757. vaseline
758. vaudeville
759. vermicelli
760. vicissitude
761. victuals
762. villain
763. violoncello
764. voracious
765. waive (to relinquish)
766. weird
767. wherry
768. whistling
769. whooping-cough
770. wizened
771. wondrous
772. woolen
773. woolly
774. worshiping
775. xylophone
776. yeoman
777. yield
778. yoking
779. zephyr
780. zeppelin

All your spelling errors, remember, can be eliminated in a few weeks at the rate of five words a day. And then, in order to make your road to good spelling all the more easy and all the more certain, learn to apply the few simple rules that you will find in the next section.

§ 4

HELPFUL RULES FOR SPELLING

1. A word ending in a consonant and a silent *e*, drops the *e* when *ing* is added. Examples:

give	giving
believe	believing
forge	forging

2. A word ending in a consonant followed by *y*, keeps the *y* when *ing* is added, but changes *y* to *i* when *es* or *ed* is added. Examples:

fly	flying	flies	
deny	denying	denies	denied

3. A word of one syllable containing a single vowel followed by a single consonant, doubles the final consonant when *ing, ed, er, est,* or *y* is added. Examples:

sit	sitting	
grab	grabbing	grabbed
big	bigger	biggest
mud	muddy	

4. A word ending in *x* does not double the final letter. Examples:

fox	foxes	
box	boxing	boxes

5. Use *ei* after *c*. Examples:

receive	receipt
deceive	deceit

6. Use *ie* after *other consonants*. Examples:

believe	belief
grieve	grief
niece	
siege	
field	
pierce	

Warning: You must watch out for exceptions to rules 5 and 6. For example:

financier (*ie* after *c*)
leisure (*ei* after *l*)
seize (*ei* after *s*)

These exceptions, however, are comparatively few in number and can be mastered individually as you run across them in your reading. The above rules will apply to the majority of the cases.

7. Three verbs end in *eed: Exceed, proceed, succeed.* All other verbs in this group end in *ede: concede, precede, recede, secede,* etc.

8. the letters *c* and *g* are hard before *a, o,* and *u.* Examples:

cast	column	cupboard
gash	goitre	gullible

9. The letters *c* and *g* are soft before *e, i,* and *y.* Examples:

| deceased | decipher | cymbal |
| pigeon | gigantic | gyroscope |

The above rule will enable you to spell such words as *traceable, peaceable, changeable,* and *manageable.* Since the *c* and the *g* in these words have a *soft* sound, you can tell at once that they are followed by the letter *e.*

10. Words of *one* syllable with an *l* sound at the end are usually spelled with a double *ll.* Words of two or more syllables are usually spelled with a single *l.* Examples:

WORDS OF ONE SYLLABLE	WORDS OF TWO OR MORE SYLLABLES
till	until
dell	infidei
bell	parallel
roll	expel

Note: This rule, like all other rules, has its exceptions. There are quite a number of words of more than one syllable that end in two *ll's.* For example: *enroll, fulfill, carryall.* You will observe, however, that such words are generally compounds of one-syllable words that end in two *ll's.*

EXERCISES

Correct the misspelled words in the following passages:

1. He made an excellent speach in which he alledged that his opponent's advise was not to be followed. His opponent, he said, had made a greivous mistake on two seperate occasions: first, when he accidently admitted that we would be able to conquer with the addition of but a single batallion; and second, when he dared to hint that we should dismiss so loveable and so indispensible an officer as General Rogers.

2. We had an exhilarating trip to the White Mountains. There was, in our group, a Fillippino who was a consumate story teller. He was somewhat of a braggadocio, but this only made his stories all the more interesting. He was convalessing from a severe attack of diptheria.

3. What an ecstacy to read that novel of Mr. B! It is an

epoch in prose. Its delineation of character is exeedingly fascinating.

4. There is in Mexico an exstinct volcano that still omits a gasseous reminder of its former activity.

5. They had a friccasee of lamb that entirely fullfilled their expectations. One of them, however, paid dearly for it, as he was siezed with a seige of severe cramps right after dinner.

6. The doctor, afraid to vaccinate the child, vaccilated in his decision until it was almost too late. It was a most unfortunate ocurrence, as it almost caused the death of the child. The incompetent doctor was finally superceeded by another physician whose businesslike behavior disippated the anxiety of the parents. They hoped that he would help the child, and they were not dissapointed. He saved the patient and restored the tranquility of the parents. As a result of this, they reccommended him to all their friends.

7. He was a most tenaceous boy. He had a thach of straw-colored hair, a stacato voice, and a most embarrassing way of asking unanswerable questions. Yet there was in his eyes the look of a real thoroughbred, and everybody admitted that it was a priviledge to know him.

8. The plummer came down with neupmonia, and it was neccesary to treat him with oxigen in order to pull him through the crisis. When he recovered, he suffered from neurology for several weeks.

You have observed the misspelled words in the above passages spelled correctly under Section 3. See how many of them you are able to get without the necessity of referring once more to that section. If your percentage of accuracy has not been very high, go back to these exercises a few weeks later and note your improvement. Keep this up until you can spell every word correctly.

In addition to the above drill, you will find the following exercises helpful:

1. Insert either *ei* or *ie* in the blanks below:

rel—f	gr—vous
perc—ve	hyg—ne
conc—t	l—f
ach—ve	financ—r

2. Add *ing* to each of the following words:

try	endorse
gorge	indite
flit	job
dig	compel

3. Correct the spelling of the following words that are spelled incorrectly:

untill	gorgous
parallell	courageous
unmanageable	peaceable
imaginable	asphodell
traceable	forgeable

KEY TO THE ABOVE EXERCISES

1. relief   grievous
    perceive   hygiene
    conceit   lief
    achieve   financier

2. trying   endorsing
    gorging   inditing
    flitting   jobbing
    digging   compelling

3. until   gorgeous
    parallel   asphodel

CHAPTER III

Correct Pronunciation

§ I

PITFALLS IN PRONUNCIATION

ENGLISH is so difficult a language to pronounce because it is so difficult a language to spell. As stated in the previous chapter, there are many English words in which the spelling is completely divorced from the sound. In the pronunciation of some of our commonest words we frequently find neither reason nor rhyme. For example, if *r-o-u-g-h* is pronounced *ruff*, why isn't *d-o-u-g-h* pronounced *duff?* If there were any logic to the pronunciation of many of our words, we should be able to understand the following passage:

> The man who had an irritating cuff walked into the store to buy a pluff. Thuff he was willing to pay enuff, the storekeeper refused to sell him the pluff. For he had learned thruff a mutual acquaintance that this customer was not to be trusted. And so the man with the cuff had a thoruff disappointment.

The difficulty in the above passage arises from the fact that we have several pronunciations for words ending in *ough*. Thus:

enough = *enuff*

but

cough   = *coff*
plough   = *plow*
though   = *thowe*
through = *thru*
thorough = *thorowe*

The same difficulty applies to words ending in *ove*. Thus, if *m-o-v-e* is pronounced *moove*, why isn't *s-h-o-v-e* pronounced *shoove?*

Take the pronunciation of *ea*. If the hunger of the captain is *grate* (great), would he be allowed to devour his *mate* (meat)?

Another difficulty with the pronunciation of English is due to the fact that our words, being alive, may keep changing in sound from place to place and from generation to generation. Thus the same word may have three different pronunciations, depending upon whether it is spoken in London or in San Francisco or in Boston. As regards the change in the pronunciation of a word from one generation to another, a modern wit (was it Bernard Shaw?) has remarked that Chaucer was a great poet, but that he spoke English with a foreign accent. Indeed, the accent of Chaucer would sound very foreign to the educated American or even Englishman of today. Shakespeare, too, spoke very unlike the modern educated man. If we pronounced our words as Shakespeare pronounced them, we should, in the opinion of some scholars, be speaking an Irish brogue.

These, then, are some of the pitfalls we must guard against in our endeavor to master the pronunciation of English. On the positive side, however, we have two distinct aids: the stage and the radio. The more talented actors and the more educated radio announcers have done much to standardize the present-day pronunciation of English.

Pronunciation, like punctuation, is an art rather than a science. Living words keep changing in pronunciation just as living men and women keep changing in habits and in appearance. To cite but a few examples:

yes was formerly pronounced as *yis*
bal'cony was formerly pronounced as balco'ny
golf was formerly pronounced as goff
July was formerly pronounced as Ju'ly

Even today there are many words about the pronunciation of which great authorities differ. "In matters of pronunciation," writes the eminent Professor Lounsbury, "one thoroughly-educated man is as good an authority as another."

In the list that follows in Section 3, the pronunciation adopted is that which has been approved by the greatest number of good authorities. Where authority seems to be equally divided, the *simplest* pronunciation has been adopted for this book.

§ 2

KEY TO PRONUNCIATION

ay as in May	oo (long) as in food
a as in fat	oo (short) as in foot
ah as in father	u as in hut
aw as in all	oi as in oil
ee as in feet	ou as in hound
e as in met	ch as in church
er as in err	g as in go
ai as in aisle or isle	w as in wig
i as in bit	wh as in whip
owe as in gold	zh as in azure
o as in not	

§ 3

WORDS OFTEN MISPRONOUNCED

abash (a-bash'), v. To make ashamed.

abdomen (ab-dowe'men), n. The lower part of the belly.

absent (ab'sent), a. Not present.

absent (ab-sent'), v. To keep away from. Used with reflexive pronoun: *He absented himself.*

abyss (a-bis'), n. A bottomless gulf.

accessory (ak-ses'o-ri), n. An accomplice.

acclimated (a-klai'mat-ed), a. Habituated to a new climate.

acquisitive (ak-kwiz'i-tiv), a. Eager to acquire.

adagio (ah-dah'jo), n. A slow musical movement.

adept (a-dept'), n. One who is skilled.

adjudicate (a-joo'di-kayt), v. To determine judicially.

adjunct (aj'unkt), a. United with.

adventist (ad'ven-tist), n. A believer in the (second) coming of Christ.

adversary (ad'ver-sa-ri), n. An opponent.

advertisement (ad-ver'tiz-ment), n. Published information with a view to selling something.

aeronautic (ay-er-owe-nawt'ik), a. Pertaining to aerial navigation.

aeroplane (ay'er-owe-playn).

aesthetic (es-thet'ik), a. Pertaining to a love for the beautiful.

aggrandise (ag'ran-daiz), v. To make great.

alpaca (al-pak'a), n. Cloth made from the hair of a Peruvian animal.

alternate (al'ter-nayt), v. To act or happen in turn.

alternate (al-ter'nayt), a. Occurring in turn.

alternately (al-ter'nayt-li), adv.

amateur (am'a-ter or am'a-tyure), n. A lover of an art without taking a professional part in it.

amenable (a-mee'na-ble), a. Responsible.

amenity (a-men'i-ti), n. Pleasantness.

anchovy (an-chowe'vi), n. A small fish of the herring class.

ancillary (an'si-lay-ri), a. Pertaining to a maid servant.

antipodes (an-tip'o-deez), n. The opposite side of the world.

aperture (ap'er-choor), n. An opening.

appositeness (ap'po-zit-ness), n. The quality of being appropriate.

armada (ar-may'da), n. A fleet of armed ships.

associate (a-sowe'shi-ayt), v. To keep company with.

association (a-sowe-si-ay'shun), n. A union.

assuage (a-swayj'), v. To calm.

atelier (a-tl-yay'), n. A studio.

atrophy (a'tro-fi), n. A wasting away.

august (aw-gust'), a. Majestic.

automaton (aw-tom'a-tun), n. A self-moving machine.

autonomy (aw-ton'o-mi), n. The right of self-government.

avaunt (a-vawnt'), exclam. Begone!

badinage (bad-i-nahzh'), n. Banter.

ballet (bal'lay), n. A theatrical dance.

banal (ban'al), a. Vulgar, commonplace.

basalt (ba-zawlt'), n. A dark kind of marble.

bas relief (bah ree-leef'), n. Sculpture in which the figures do not stand out prominently.

beatify (be-at'i-fai), v. To make happy.

bedizen (be-dai'zn), v. To adorn gaudily.

Bedouin (bed'oo-in), n. A wandering Arab of the desert.

behemoth (be-hee'moth), n. A Biblical animal believed to be the hippopotamus.

Belial (bee'li-al), n. An evil spirit. Satan.

benign (be-nain'), a. Kindly.

benignant (be-nig'nant), a. Kindly.

benignly (be-nain'ly), adv. In a kindly manner.

bête noire (bayt nwahr'), n. A dreaded object (literally, a black beast).

bicycle (bai'si-kl), n. A two-wheeled vehicle.

bijou (bee-zhoo'), n. A small jewel.

bivouac (biv'wak), n. A night encampment in the open air.

bolero (bowe-lay'rowe), n. A Spanish dance.

Bolognese (bowe-lo-nyeez'), a. Pertaining to Bologna.

bon mot (bong mowe [slur the *g* in pronunciation]), n. A witty saying.

bouillon (bool'yun), n. Soup made from beef.

brasier (bray'sher), n. A pan for holding coals.

brassiere (brahs-yayr'), n. An underwaist for women.

brougham (broom), n. A closed carriage.

Byzantine (bi-zan'tin), a. Relating to ancient Byzantium (Constantinople).

cabal (ka-bal'), n. An intrigue.

caisson (kay'son), n. An ammunition chest.

caldron (kawl'dron), n. A large kettle.

cantabile (kahn-tah'bee-lay), adj. Melodious.

caoutchouc (koo'chook), n. India rubber.

carbureter (kahr'byoo-ret-er), n. Part of a motor.

caricature (kar'i-ka-choor), n. A picture so exaggerated as to arouse ridicule.

carillon (kar'i-lon), n. A musical instrument of bells.

celibacy (sel'i-ba-si), n. Bachelorhood.

centenary (sen'te-ne-ri), a. Pertaining to a hundred years.

chalet (shah-lay'), n. A Swiss cottage.

chameleon (ka-mee'le-on), n. A lizard-like reptile whose color keeps changing.

chamois (sham'i), n. A soft leather.

chef-d'oeuvre (shay-de'vr [pronounce the *e* as in *err*]), n. A masterpiece.

chic (sheek), a. Neat in dress.

chicanery (shee-kayn'e-ri), n. Trickery.

chiropodist (kai-rop'o-dist), n. A foot-healer.

circuit (ser′kit), n. A going around in a circle.

clandestine (klan-des′tin), a. Secret.

clientele (klai′en-tel), n. One's clients.

clique (kleek), n. A small group or set.

clothes (klowethz).

cognizance (kog′ni-zans), n. Notice.

coiffure (koif′yoor), n. A head-dress.

colander (kol′an-der), n. A sieve.

colleague (kol′leeg), n. An associate in a profession.

communal (ko-myoo′nal), a. Pertaining to a community.

concerto (kon-chayr′towe), n. A musical composition.

connoisseur (kon-i-ser′ [pronounce the e as in err]), n. A judge of any art.

contumely (kon′tyoo-me-li), n. Insolent language.

coquetry (kowe′ket-ri), n. Trifling in love.

corporeal (kor-powe′re-al), a. Physical.

corpuscle (kor′pus-l), n. A small particle of matter.

corrigible (kor′ri-ji-bl), a. Capable of being corrected.

cortege (kor-tayzh′), n. A train of attendants.

coryza (ko-rai′za), n. Catarrh.

cosmopolite (koz-mop′o-lait), n. One who is at home throughout the world.

coup d'état (koo-day-tah′), n. An unexpected political move.

courteous (ker′tee-us), a. In an elegant manner.

credence (kree′dens), n. Belief.

cuirass (kwee-ras′), n. A breastplate.

Czech (check), n. A native of Bohemia.

Danish (dayn′ish), a. Pertaining to Denmark.

data (day′ta), n. Given facts.

daunt (dahnt or dawnt), v. To intimidate.

dauphin (daw′fin), n. The eldest son of the king of France.

debacle (de-bahk′), n. A confused rout.

debauchee (deb-o-shee′), n. A dissipated person.

debris (day-bree′), n. Rubbish.

decadent (de-kay′dent), a. Falling away, becoming worse.

defecate (def′e-kayt), v. To expel impurities.

deposition (dep-o-zish′un), n. Written testimony.

deprecatory (dep′re-ka-to-ri), a. Apologetic.

desultory (des'ul-to-ri), a. Without order.

detonate (det'o-nayt), v. To explode with a loud noise.

detour (de-toor'), n. A roundabout way.

dilettante (dil-e-tan'ti), n. An amateur lover of the arts.

dirigible (dir'i-ji-bl), a. That which may be steered.

discern (di-zern'), v. To distinguish.

dishabille (diz-a-beel'), n. The state of being not fully dressed.

disheveled (di-shev'eld), a. Disarranged.

divan (di-van'), n. A cushioned seat.

dolorous (dol'o-rus), a. Sorrowful.

domicile (dom'i-sil), n. A home.

dotage (dowe'tej), n. Feebleness of mind due to old age.

dotard (dowe'terd), n. One who is in his dotage.

dour (dōōr, to rhyme with poor), a. Hard, grim, obstinate.

drought (drout), n. Lack of rain.

eczema (ek'ze-ma), n. A disease of the skin.

efficacy (ef'i-ka-si), n. Power to produce an effect.

ego (ee'gowe), n. The first person, I.

egregious (e-gree'jus), a. Remarkable.

egress (ee'gress), n. An exit.

elite (ay-leet'), n. A select group.

emissary (em'i-sa-ri), n. A secret agent.

entourage (ong-too-rahzh' [slur the *g* in pronouncing this word]), n. A group of followers.

envisage (en-viz'ej), v. To look into the face of.

epistle (e-pis'l), n. A letter.

epitome (e-pit'o-mee), n. A brief summary.

equerry (ek'wer-i), n. An officer in charge of a king's horses.

equivocal (e-kwiv'o-kal), a. Doubtful.

erudite (er'oo-dait), a. Learned.

esoteric (es-o-ter'ik), a. Taught to a select few in the "inner circle," profound.

exacerbate (egs-ass'er-bayt), v. To exasperate.

exigency (eks'i-jen-si), n. A pressing necessity.

explicable (eks'pli-ka-bl), a. Capable of being explained.

façade (fah-sahd'), n. The front view of a building.

facsimile (fak-sim'i-lee), n. An exact copy.

faux pas (fowe-pah'), n. A false step.
febrile (fee'bril), a. Pertaining to fever.
February (Feb'roo-a-ri).
feoff (feff), n. A gift of a fee.
fête (fayt), n. A festival.
fetid (fet'id), a. Having an unpleasant smell.
fetish (fee'tish), n. An object of devotion.
fiat (fai'at), n. A decree.
flaccid (flak'sid), a. Flabby.
flagellate (flaj'el-ayt), v. To flog.
forehead (for'ed).
fraternize (frat'er-naiz), v. To associate as brothers.
fusillade (few'zil-ayd), n. A continuous discharge of
    musketry.
gallows (gal'owes), n. A structure for the hanging of
    condemned prisoners.
garage (ga-rahzh').
generic (je-ner'ik), a. Pertaining to a species.
ghoul (gool), n. An imaginary evil spirit.
giaour (joor), n. An infidel (a Moslem word).
gibberish (gib'er-ish [hard g]), n. Unmeaning talk.
gibbet (jib'et), n. A gallows.
gill (gil [hard g]), n. The organ of breathing in
    fishes.
gill (jil), n. The fourth part of a pint.
gillie (gil'i), n. A Scotch male servant.
gimlet (gim'let), n. A small tool for boring.
gist (jist), n. The main point of a question.
glacier (glay'sher), n. An immense moving field of
    ice.
gladiolus (gla-dai'o-lus), n. The sword-lily.
gneiss (nice), n. A species of rock.
gnome (nome), n. A dwarf.
gondola (gon'do-la), n. A boat used in Venice.
gratis (gray'tis), a. Without pay.
grenade (gre-nayd'), n. An explosive ball of iron.
grimace (gri-mayss'), n. An artificial distortion of
    the face.
guerdon (ger'don [hard g]), n. A reward.
guillotine (gil'o-teen), n. A machine for beheading
    persons.
gyroscope (jai'ro-skope), n. A rotating apparatus.
habitué (ha-bich-you-ay'), n. A frequenter of any
    place.

handkerchief (hang'ker-chif).

handsome (han'sum).

harass (har'as), v. To vex with labor, to wear out.

harem (hay'rem), n. The women of a Mohammedan family.

haricot (har'i-kowe), n. A stew of meat and beans.

hauteur (owe-terr'), n. Haughty manner or spirit.

hearth (hahrth), n. The fireside.

heifer (hef'er), n. A young cow.

heinous (hayn'us), a. Hateful.

hussar (huz-zahr'), n. A light-armed horse trooper.

hussy (huz'zi), n. An impertinent girl.

hysteria (his-tee'ri-a), n. A nervous disease, especially of women.

ignominy (ig'no-mi-ni), n. Public disgrace.

ignoramus (ig-no-ray'mus), n. An ignorant person.

imbroglio (im-browe'lyowe), n. A complicated mis-
understanding or plot.

impolitic (im-pol'i-tik), a. Unwise.

importune (im-por-tyoon'), n. To urge by frequent
entreaty.

impotency (im'po-ten-si), n. The state of being
powerless.

imprecate (im'pre-kayt), v. To invoke a curse upon
someone.

impugn (im-pyoon'), v. To contradict.

inchoate (in'ko-ayt), a. Recently begun.

inclement (in-klem'ent), a. Severe.

incognito (in-kog'ni-towe), a. In disguise.

incomparable (in-kom'pa-ra-bl), a. Not to be compared, matchless.

incorporeal (in-kor-powe're-al), a. Not having a
body.

incorrigible (in-kor'ri-ji-bl), a. Bad beyond the possibility of correction.

indecorous (in-de-kowe'rus), a. Unbecoming.

indefatigable (in-de-fat'i-ga-bl), a. Untiring.

indisputable (in-dis'pyoo-ta-bl), a. Not to be dis-
puted.

indissoluble (in-dis'sol-u-bl), a. That cannot be dis-
solved, firm.

inebriate (in-ee'bri-ayt), n. A drunkard.

inefficacy (in-ef'i-ka-si), n. Lack of power.

inexplicable (in-eks'pli-ka-bl), a. Mysterious.

infamous (in'fa-mus), a. Notoriously wicked.

intermezzo (in-ter-met'zo), n. A musical term, meaning in the middle.

internecine (in-ter-nee'sin), a. Referring to great slaughter between two parties or countries.

invalid (in-val'id), a. Having no power or authority.

invalid (in'val-id), n. An ill person.

irascible (ai-ras'i-bl), a. Readily made angry.

iron (ai'ern).

ironical (ai-ron'ik-al), a. Disguising the meaning, sarcastic.

irony (ai'ro-ni), n. Sarcasm.

irremediable (ir-re-mee'di-a-bl), a. Incurable.

irrevocable (ir-rev'o-ka-bl), a. That which cannot be recalled or reversed.

isthmus (is'mus), n. A neck of land connecting two larger bodies.

itinerary (ai-tin'er-a-ri), n. A travel route.

jardiniere (zhahr-din-yare'), n. An ornamental stand for plants and flowers.

kaleidoscope (ka-lai'do-skope), n. An instrument which exhibits colors moving constantly into different symmetrical patterns.

Kreuzer (kroi'tzer), n. An old German coin.

lamentable (lam'ent-a-bl), a. Wretched.

languor (lang'gur), n. Listlessness.

languorous (lang'gur-us), a. Listless.

laryngeal (la-rin'je-al), a. Pertaining to the larynx.

laver (lay'ver), n. A large wash-basin.

legate (leg'at), n. An ambassador.

lese majesty (leez maj'es-te), n. Treason against the king.

lichen (lai'ken), n. A plant without stem or leaves.

llama (lah'ma), n. A camel-like animal of South America.

locale (lo-kahl'), n. Locality.

loggia (loj'ah), n. A gallery.

longevity (lon-jev'i-ti), n. Long life.

lorgnette (lor-nyet'), n. An opera-glass.

lower (lou'er [to rhyme with flower]), v. To scowl.

lower (lowe'er), a. Less high.

luxurious (lug-zhoo'ri-us), a. Given to luxury, extravagant.

lyceum (lai-see'um), n. A literary institute.

lyonnaise (lee-on-ayz'), a. A style of preparing potatoes.

macadamize (mak-ad'a-maiz), v. To pave a road with small, broken stones.

machinate (mak'i-nayt), v. To plot.

Madeira (ma-dee'ra), n. A wine made in Madeira (a Portuguese island).

maestro (mah-es'tro), n. A master in any art.

Magyar (mod'yor), n. A Hungarian.

malmsey (mahm'zi), n. A wine.

maniacal (ma-nai'a-kal), a. Dangerously insane.

maraschino (mah-ra-skee'no), n. A kind of cordial.

marchioness (mahr'shon-es), n. Wife of a marquis.

margarine (mahr'ga-rin), n. An imitation of butter made from animal fat.

marquis (mahr'kwis), n. A title of honor below a duke, and above an earl.

menage (may-nahzh'), n. A household.

menagerie (me-naj'e-ri), n. A collection of wild animals kept for exhibition.

mercantile (mer'kan-til), a. Commercial.

mezzo soprano (met'zo so-prah'no), n. A voice midway between soprano and alto.

minutiae (mi-nyoo'shi-ee), n. Unimportant details.

mirage (mi-rahzh'), n. An optical illusion.

mischievous (mis'chi-vus).

misconstrue (mis-kon-stroo'), v. To misinterpret.

misogynist (mis-oj'in-ist), n. A woman-hater.

motif (mowe-teef'), n. The leading pattern in a musical composition.

museum (myoo-zee'um), n. A building containing interesting objects of literature, art, or science.

naïveté (nah-eev-tay'), n. Native simplicity.

necromancy (nek'ro-man-si), n. Sorcery.

neophyte (nee'o-fait), n. A novice, a beginner.

nephew (nev'yoo).

nomenclature (nowe'men-cla-choor), n. A system of names.

noncombatant (non-com'bat-ant), n. A non-fighting member of the army.

nonpareil (non-pa-rel'), a. Unequaled.

obesity (owe-bee'si-ti), n. Excessive stoutness.

objurgate (ob-jer'gayt), v. To chide severely.

obligatory (ob'li-ga-to-ri), a. Binding.

oblique (ob-leek'), a. Slanting.

oboe (owe'boy), n. A musical wind-instrument.

oleomargarine (owe-li-o-mahr'ga-rin), n. Artificial butter made of animal fat.

palanquin (pal-an-keen'), n. A Chinese carriage borne on the shoulders of men.

palisade (pal-i-sayd'), n. A wooden fortification.

pariah (pah'ri-a), n. An outcast.

parsimony (pahr'si-mo-ni), n. Miserliness.

parvenu (pahr've-nyoo), n. An upstart.

pastel (pas'tel), n. A colored crayon.

pecan (pe-kan'), n. A kind of nut.

penalize (pee'nal-aiz), v. To punish.

peregrinate (per'e-gri-nayt), v. To travel from place to place.

persiflage (per'see-flahzh), n. Idle bantering talk.

phthisical (tiz'i-kal), a. Consumptive.

phthisis (thai'sis), n. Consumption.

piquant (pee'kant), a. Interesting, pungent.

poignant (poin'ant), a. Keen, severe.

polytheism (pol'i-thee-izm), n. The belief that there are many gods.

pomegranate (pom'gran-at), n. An orange-like fruit.

pompadour (pom'pa-door), n. A style of dressing the hair.

portiere (por-tiayr'), n. A large curtain used in a doorway.

posse (pos'si), n. A small body of men.

posthumous (pos'choo-mus), a. Published after the death of the author.

potpourri (powe-poo-ree'), n. A mixed dish, a medley.

precedent (pre-see'dent), a. Former, going before.

precedent (press'e-dent), n. Something in the past that serves as a guide for the present.

précis (pray-see'), n. A brief summary.

premise (prem'iss), n. A proposition laid down as the base for an argument.

prescient (pree'shi-ent), a. Foreknowing, far-seeing.

prestidigitator (pres-ti-dij'i-tay-tor), n. A juggler.

prestige (pres-teezh'), n. Authority based on high character.

protein (prowe'te-in), n. A chemical compound.

psalter (sawl'ter), n. A book of Psalms.

purlieus (per'lyoos), n. Outskirts.
pyramidal (pi-ram'i-dal), a. Pertaining to a pyramid.
qualm (kwahm), n. A twinge of conscience.
quasi (kway'sai), conj. As if.
quay (kee), n. A wharf.
query (kwee'ri), n. A question.
quixotic (kwiks-ot'ik), a. Chivalrous to an extravagant degree.
rabies (ray'bi-eez), n. Hydrophobia.
ragout (rah-goo'), n. A dish of spiced meat and vegetables.
rapier (ray'pi-er), n. A long narrow sword.
rapine (rap'in), n. Plunder.
rapport (rap-port'), n. Harmony.
raspberry (raz'ber-i).
ratiocination (rash-i-os-inay'shon), n. The act of reasoning.
rebate (re-bayt'), n. Discount.
recitative (res-i-ta-teev'), n. A musical recitation.
recluse (re-kloos'), n. A hermit.
recognizance (re-kog'ni-zans), n. Acknowledgment of an obligation.
recourse (re-kors'), n. Resort in perplexity.
recreant (rek're-ant), a. Unfaithful, cowardly.
recreate (rek'ri-ayt), v. To refresh.
recreate (ree-kri-ayt'), v. To create anew.
recuperate (re-kyoo'per-ayt), v. To recover.
recusant (rek'you-zant), a. Obstinate in refusal.
redolent (red'ol-ent), a. Full of an odor.
refluent (ref'loo-ent), a. Flowing back.
refuse (re-fyooz'), v. To reject.
refuse (ref'yooz), n. Rubbish.
regime (ray-zheem'), n. System of government.
relapse (re-laps'), n. A falling back, in health or in character.
remediable (re-mee'di-a-bl), a. Capable of being remedied.
remise (re-maiz'), v. To surrender.
repartee (rep-ar-tee'), n. A smart and ready reply.
repertoire (rep-er-twahr'), n. A list of plays that an actor is ready to perform.
residue (rez'i-dyoo), n. Remainder.
respite (res'pit), n. Temporary rest.
restaurant (res'towe-rant), n. An eating place.

reveille (rev'el-ee), n. The morning signal for soldiers to rise.

revocable (rev'o-ka-bl), a. Capable of being called back.

roentgenology (rent-gen-ol'o-jee), n. The science of x-ray.

romance (rowe-mans'), n. A tale of interesting adventure.

sacerdotal (sas-er-dowe'tal), a. Priestly.

sachem (say'chem), n. An Indian chief.

sachet (sa-shay'), n. A small perfume-bag.

sacrilege (sak'ri-lej), n. Violation of sacred things.

sacrilegious (sak-ri-lee'jus), n. Impious.

saga (sah'ga), n. A Scandinavian legend.

salicylic (sal-i-sil'ik), a. An acid used as an antiseptic.

saline (say'lain), a. Consisting of salt.

saliva (sa-lai'va), n. Spittle.

salivate (sal'i-vayt), v. To produce saliva.

samovar (sam-o-vahr'), n. A Russian tea-urn.

sapient (say'pi-ent), a. Wise, in an ironic sense.

satiate (say'shi-ayt), v. To gratify fully.

satiety (sa-tai'e-ti), n. Full gratification.

saturnine (sat'er-nain), a. Morose, gloomy.

sauterne (sowe'tern), n. A French wine.

savant (sah-vahng' [the g should be slurred]), n. A wise scholar, a man of learning.

says (sez).

scallop (scal'op), n. A shell-fish.

scenario (se-nah'ri-o), n. The plot of a photoplay.

scherzo (sker'tsowe), n. A sportive passage in a musical composition.

schism (sizm), n. A separation, a breach.

scourge (skerj), v. To lash.

scrupulous (skroo'pyou-lus), a. Conscientious.

secretive (se-kree'tiv), a. Given to secrecy.

seine (sayn), n. A fish-net.

seneschal (sen'e-shal), n. A steward in a royal house.

señor (sen-yor'), n. A gentleman, the Spanish equivalent of Mr.

señora (sen-yor'a), n. Mrs.

señorita (sen-yor-eet'a), n. Miss.

sentient (sen'shent), a. Having the capacity of sensation.

septuagenarian (sep-tyoo-a-je-nay'ri-an), n. A person seventy years old.

septuagint (sep'tyoo-a-jint), n. A Greek version of the Old Testament.

sepulchral (se-pul'kral), a. Pertaining to a sepulchre.

seraglio (say-rah'lyo), n. A harem.

sesame (ses'a-mi), n. An oil-producing plant.

sidereal (sai-dee'ri-al), a. Starry.

signor (see'nyor), n. An Italian lord.

signora (see-nyowe'ra), n. Italian equivalent for a lady.

signorina (see-nyo-ree'na), n. Miss.

slough (sluff), n. Dead tissue that is cut off and cast away.

slough (slou), n. A place of deep mud.

sobriquet (sowe-bri-kay'), n. A nickname.

sociology (sowe-shi-ol'o-ji), n. The study of society.

solder (sod'er), v. To unite metals by a fused alloy.

soufflé (soof-lay'), n. A dish composed of eggs and flour.

sough (sou or suff), n. A rushing sound, a sigh.

stipend (stai'pend), n. Compensation, pay.

stoicism (stowe'i-sizm), n. Indifference to pleasure or pain.

suave (swahv), a. Sweet.

subaltern (sub-awl'tern), a. Holding an inferior rank.

succinct (suk-sinkt'), a. Brief, concise.

suggestion (sug-jes'chun), n. A hint.

supine (syoo-pain'), a. Lying on the back.

supine (syoo'pain), n. A part of the Latin verb.

suzerain (syoo'ze-rayn), n. A feudal lord.

swath (swawth), n. A line of mown grass.

swathe (swayth), v. To bandage.

synod (sin'od), n. A religious council.

tarpaulin (tahr-paw'lin), n. Canvas covered with tar.

tepee (tee'pee), n. An Indian lodge.

tergiversate (ter'ji-ver-sayt), v. To be evasive.

Thais (tah-ees'), n. An opera by Massenet.

thaumaturgy (thaw'ma-ter-ji), n. Magic.

thearchy (thee'ahr-ki), n. Government by God.

theater (thee'a-ter).

thyme (taim), n. A small fragrant shrub.

tiara (tai-ay'ra), n. A crown.

tirade (tai-rayd'), n. A vehement harangue.

tomato (to-mah'to or to-may'to).

toupee (too-pee'), n. A small wig.

transact (tranz-akt'), v. To carry through.

transfer (trans'fer), n.

transfer (trans-fer'), v.

transferable (trans-fer'a-bl), a. Capable of being transferred.

transference (trans-fer'ens), n. The act of transferring.

transport (trans'port), n. A ship employed to carry soldiers, etc.

transport (trans-port'), v. To carry from one place to another.

travail (trav'ayl), n. Severe toil, anguish.

treacle (tree'kl), n. Molasses.

treatise (tree'tiz), n. A written composition.

trepan (tre-pan'), n. An instrument for brain surgery.

trespasser (tres'pas-er), n. A sinner.

triad (trai'ad), n. A group of three.

tribunal (trai-byoo'nal), n. A court of justice.

tribune (trib'yoon), n. A protective officer of a tribe.

trigon (trai'gon), n. A figure of three sides.

truculent (tru'kyoo-lent), a. Cruel.

tryst (traist), n. An appointment to meet, a place of meeting.

tubercle (tyoo'ber-kl), n. A small knob.

tulle (tool), n. A thin silk fabric.

tumult (tyoo'mult), n. A loud commotion.

turquoise (ter'koiz), n. A greenish-blue precious stone.

tympanum (tim'pan-um), n. The middle ear.

tyrannic (tai-ran'ik), a. Cruel.

tyranny (tir'a-ni), n. Cruel exercise of power.

tyro (tai'rowe), n. A beginner.

ubiquitous (yoo-bik'wi-tus), a. Present everywhere.

ukase (yoo-kays'), n. A decree of the former (imperial) Russian government.

unguent (ung'went), n. An ointment.

unprecedented (un-press'e-dent-ed), a. Without previous example.

usage (yooz'aj), n. Custom.

use (yoos), n. Practice.

use (yooz), v. To employ.

usufruct (yoo'zyoo-frukt), n. The use and enjoyment of lands (a legal term).

usurer (yoo'zhoo-rer), n. One who lends money at an exorbitant rate of interest.

vagary (va-gay'ri), n. A wild fancy.

valet (val'et or val'ay), n. A manservant.

Valhalla (val-hal'a), n. The Heaven of Scandinavian mythology.

vaudeville (vowed'veel).

Veda (vay'da), n. The Hindu Bible.

venous (vee'nus), a. Pertaining to a vein.

venue (ven'yoo), n. The place where a trial is held.

viand (vai'and), n. Meat.

vicarage (vik'ar-aj), n. The office of a parish priest.

vicarious (vai-kay'ri-us), a. Suffering for another.

vicegerent (vais-jee'rent), n. One who acts in the place of a superior.

victuals (vit'ls), n. Food.

vignette (vin-yet'), n. A small photographic portrait.

vinous (vai'nus), a. Pertaining to wine.

viola (vee-owe'la), n. A large kind of violin.

violoncello (vee-o-lon-chel'o), n. A bass violin.

virago (vi-ray'go), n. A scolding woman.

visage (viz'aj), n. Face.

vis-à-vis (veez-ah-vee'), adv. Face to face.

viscid (vis'sid), a. Sticky.

viscount (vai'kount), n. A nobleman of rank between an earl and a baron.

vise (vaiss), n. A tool for gripping.

visé (vee-zay'), n. An indorsement upon a passport.

vivace (vee-vah'chay), a. A musical term meaning in a lively manner.

wassail (wos'el), n. A drinking contest.

wound (woond).

yolk (yoke), n. The yellow part of an' egg.

zoology (zo-ol'o-ji), n. The study of animals.

CHAPTER IV

Correct Use of Words

§ 1

WORDS OFTEN MISUSED

A MISUSED WORD is like an ill-fitting coat. It is a sign of bad breeding and poor taste. In polite society a careless speaker is just as unwelcome—and rightly so—as a careless dresser. There is no excuse for anyone to misuse his words. Fifteen minutes a day spent in pleasant study will, in the course of a few weeks, enable anyone to overcome his carelessness in the use of words.

Let us begin with this study *right now.*

Among the words that are most frequently misused are the following:

Affect and *Effect:*
To *affect* means *to move the feelings of, to influence;* to *effect* means *to bring about, to accomplish.*

> (Wrong use) He *affected* a change in the organization.
> (Correct use) He *effected* a change in the organization.

> (Wrong use) He *effected* her with his pathetic story.
> (Correct use) He *affected* her with his pathetic story.

As and *So:*
As is used in the comparison of equals; *so* is used in the comparison of unequals.

> (Wrong use) He is *so* rich as his brother.
> (Correct use) He is *as* rich as his brother.

> (Wrong use) He is not *as* rich as his brother.
> (Correct use) He is not *so* rich as his brother.

Awful and *Awfully:*

Awful is an adjective; *awfully* is an adverb.

(Wrong use) He is *awful* scared.
(Correct use) He is *awfully* scared.
The word *awfully* means *in a manner to inspire terror*. It is therefore wrong to say: I had an *awfully* good time.

Beside and *Besides:*

Beside means *at the side of; besides* means *in addition to*.

(Wrong use) *Beside* me there was nobody else there.
(Correct use) *Besides* me there was nobody else there.

(Wrong use) He sat *besides* me.
(Correct use) He sat *beside* me.

Can and *May:*

Can denotes *ability; may* indicates *permission*.

(Wrong use) *Can* I stay home today?
(Correct use) *May* I stay home today?

Creditable and *Credible:*

Creditable means *deserving of credit; credible* means *deserving to be believed*.

(Wrong use) This is a *credible* painting.
(Correct use) This is a *creditable* painting.

(Wrong use) Your story sounds *creditable*.
(Correct use) Your story sounds *credible*.

Cunning and *Pretty:*

Cunning means *artful* or *crafty; pretty* means *having a pleasing form*.

(Wrong use) Isn't this a *cunning* child?
(Correct use) Isn't this a *pretty* child?
(Correct use) Isn't he a *cunning* thief?

Decided and *Decisive:*

Decided means *clear, definite; decisive* means *conclusive, that which brings something to an end*.

(Correct use) He won a *decided* victory (a real, definite victory).
(Correct use) He won a *decisive* victory (a victory that brought the war to an end).

Delicious and *Delightful:*
Delicious means *pleasing to the senses; delightful* means *pleasing to the mind.*

> (Wrong use) The ice-cream was *delightful.*
> (Correct use) The ice-cream was *delicious.*

> (Wrong use) The poem was *delicious.*
> (Correct use) The poem was *delightful.*

To Discover and *To Invent:*
To discover means *to uncover, to find something already ex-isting, but previously unknown; to invent* means *to make, as a result of forethought, something that has not existed before.*

> (Correct use) Columbus *discovered* America.
> (Correct use) Harvey *discovered* the circulation of the blood.
> (Correct use) Bell *invented* the telephone.

Each other and *One another:*
Each other refers to *two* persons; *one another* refers to *more than two* persons.

> (Wrong use) John and Mary loved *one another.*
> (Correct use) John and Mary loved *each other.*

> (Wrong use) All the members of the team worked for *each other.*
> (Correct use) All the members of the team worked for *one another.*

Emigrant and *Immigrant:*
Emigrant means *a person who goes away from a country; immigrant* means *a person who comes into a country.*

> (Wrong use) The *emigrants* arrived in the steerage.
> (Correct use) The *immigrants* arrived in the steer-age.

> (Wrong use) The *immigrants* left England on a rainy day.
> (Correct use) The *emigrants* left England on a rainy day.

Eminent and *Imminent:*
Eminent means *outstanding; imminent* means *threatening.*

> (Wrong use) He is an *imminent* doctor.
> (Correct use) He is an *eminent* doctor.

(Wrong use) The danger is *eminent*.
(Correct use) The danger is *imminent*.

Eruption and *Irruption:*
   An *eruption* is something that *breaks out;* an *irruption* is something that *breaks into*.

   (Wrong use) There was a red *irruption* on his skin.
   (Correct use) There was a red *eruption* on his skin.

   (Wrong use) The *eruption* of the army into France was ruthless.
   (Correct use) The *irruption* of the army into France was ruthless.

Fix and *Arrange:*
   To *fix* means to *repair; to arrange* means *to classify, to put in order*.

   (Wrong use) *Fix* the pages in the proper order.
   (Correct use) *Arrange* the pages in the proper order.

Funny and *Queer:*
   Funny means *arousing fun, comical; queer* means *strange, peculiar*.

   (Wrong use) This story is *queer* because it is amusing.
   (Correct use) This story is *funny* because it is amusing.

   (Wrong use) He looks very *funny;* I have never seen anyone like him.
   (Correct use) He looks very *queer;* I have never seen anyone like him.

Genial and *Talented:*
   Genial means *cordial, kindly;* it does *not* mean *possessing genius; talented* means *possessing talent*.

   (Wrong use) Beethoven was a *genial* man. (As a matter of fact, Beethoven was not a cordial man.)
   (Correct use) Beethoven was *a man of genius*. Or, Beethoven was a *talented* man (though *talented* is hardly a strong enough word to use about Beethoven).

Guess and *Think:*

To *guess* is *to judge at random, to form a hasty opinion;* to *think* is *to arrive at an opinion after mature deliberation.*

> (Wrong use) At first glance, I *think* there are 50,000 people in the Stadium.
> (Correct use) At first glance, I *guess* there are 50,000 people in the Stadium.

> (Wrong use) The philosopher *guesses* that the soul is immortal.
> (Correct use) The philosopher *thinks* that the soul is immortal.

Handy and *Convenient:*

Handy means *near at hand, capable of being handled* (in a physical sense); *convenient* means *suitable* (in a mental sense).

> (Wrong use) This is a *convenient* tool to use.
> (Correct use) This is a *handy* tool to use.

> (Wrong use) It is *handy* to understand music.
> (Correct use) It is *convenient* to understand music.

Happen and *Transpire:*

To *happen* means *to come about by chance;* to *transpire* means *to become known.*

> (Correct use) It *happened* that the man was murdered, though nobody knew who the murderer was.
> (Correct use) It *transpired* that the man was murdered by his young rival.

Healthful and *Healthy:*

Healthful means *producing health; healthy* means *possessing health.*

> (Wrong use) Vitamins are *healthy.*
> (Correct use) Vitamins are *healthful.*

> (Wrong use) The fullback was a *healthful* young man.
> (Correct use) The fullback was a *healthy* young man.

If and *Whether:*

If means *on condition that only one thing may happen; whether* means *on condition that one of two things may happen.*

> (Correct use) I shall go *if* you go.
> (Correct use) I shall go *whether* you go or not.

(Correct use) I do not know *whether* to trust or to distrust him.

(Correct use) I do not know *whether* he will come. (In this sentence the words *or not* are understood after the word *come.*)

In and *Within* (when used in expressions of time):
In means *at the end of; within* means *at some time during.*

(Correct use) He will be here *in* a week (*at the end of a week*).

(Correct use) He will be here *within* a week (*at some time during the week*).

Indict and *Indite:*
To *indict* means *to charge with a crime; to indite* means *to write.*

(Wrong use) He *indicted* a letter.
(Correct use) He *indited* a letter.

(Wrong use) He was *indited* by the grand jury.
(Correct use) He was *indicted* by the grand jury.

Ingenious and *Ingenuous:*
Ingenious means *witty, able; ingenuous* means *frank, candid.*

(Wrong use) He was an *ingenuous* liar.
(Correct use) He was an *ingenious* liar.

(Wrong use) He may be stupid, but he is *ingenious.*
(Correct use) He may be stupid, but he is *ingenuous.*

Kind and *Sort:*
These two words may be used interchangeably. Note, however, the proper construction with these words:

(Wrong use) I hate this *kind of a* business (or *sort of a* business).
(Correct use) I hate this *kind of* business (or *sort of* business).

Learn and *Teach:*
Avoid the error of using *learn* in the sense of *teach.* You *learn* a lesson, and you *teach* a pupil (or you teach a lesson *to* a pupil).

(Wrong use) He *learned* his children the Bible.
(Correct use) He *taught* his children the Bible.

Less and *Least:*

Less is used in comparing *two* persons or things; *least,* in comparing *more than two* persons or things.

(Wrong use) He is the *least* wealthy of the two.
(Correct use) He is the *less* wealthy of the two.
(Correct use) He is the *least* wealthy of the three.

The same usage applies to *poorer* and *poorest.*

(Wrong use) He is the *poorest* of the two.
(Correct use) He is the *poorer* of the two.
(Correct use) He is the *poorest* of the three.

Let and *Leave:*

Do not confuse the verb *let,* when it means *permit,* with the verb *leave,* which means *abandon.*

(Wrong use) *Leave* me go.
(Correct use) *Let* me go.

Mad and *Angry:*

Mad means *insane; angry* means *irritated, provoked.*

(Wrong use) Don't be *mad* at me.
(Correct use) Don't be *angry* with me.

More and *Most:*

More is used in comparing *two* persons or things; *most* is used in comparing *more than two* persons or things. See *Less* and *Least.*

Most and *Almost:*

Most, when used as an adverb, means *in the greatest degree, chiefly; almost* means *nearly.*

(Wrong use) I am *most* through with this book.
(Correct use) I am *almost* through with this book.

Noted and *Notorious:*

Noted means *well known* in a *favorable* sense; *notorious* means *well known* in an *unfavorable* sense.

(Wrong use) We honor the *notorious* poet, Shakespeare.
(Correct use) We honor the *noted* poet, Shakespeare.
(Wrong use) Dillinger was a *noted* criminal.
(Correct use) Dillinger was a *notorious* criminal.

Party and *Person:*
   Party means a *group* of individuals; *person* means *one* individual.

>   (Wrong use) Do you know that *party* who is talking
>   to Mrs. Jones?
>   (Correct use) Do you know that *person* who is talking to Mrs. Jones?

Pleasure and *Happiness:*
   Pleasure is a *temporary gratification of the senses; happiness* is a more or less *permanent delight of the mind.*

>   (Wrong use) The cocktail gave him real *happiness.*
>   (Correct use) The cocktail gave him real *pleasure.*

>   (Wrong use) The true philosopher is blessed with
>   *pleasure.*
>   (Correct use) The true philosopher is blessed with
>   *happiness.*

To Present and *To Introduce:*
   To present means *to bring an inferior person to a superior person; to introduce* means *to make two equals known to each other.*

>   (Wrong use) He *introduced* Mrs. Jones to the king.
>   (Correct use) He *presented* Mrs. Jones to the king.

>   (Wrong use) He *presented* the president of Harvard to the president of Yale.
>   (Correct use) He *introduced* the president of Harvard to the president of Yale.

Providing and *Provided:*
   Providing is an *active participle,* and it means *caring for; provided* is a *passive participle,* and it means *on condition that.*

>   (Wrong use) I shall come to New York *providing*
>   you will be there.
>   (Correct use) I shall come to New York *provided*
>   you will be there.
>   (Correct use) He is a good man, faithfully *providing* for his family.

Raise and *Raze:*
   To raise means *to lift, to build up; to raze* means *to destroy, to lay level with the ground.*

>   (Correct use) The toilers *raised* the temple, the soldiers *razed* it.

Raise and *Rise:*
   Raise is an *active* verb; *rise* is a *passive* verb.

>   (Wrong use) *Raise* up from the ground, John!
>   (Correct use) *Rise* from the ground, John!

Relation and *Relative:*
   Relation is generally used in an *abstract* sense, meaning *connection; relative,* when used as a noun, is *concrete,* meaning *some one allied by blood.*

>   (Wrong use) Mary is a *relation* of mine.
>   (Correct use) Mary is a *relative* of mine.

Sanatorium and *Sanitarium:*
   A *sanatorium* is a place where *all sorts* of sick people go for their health; a *sanitarium* is a place where *mentally* sick people go for their health.

>   (Wrong use) He was so tired from overwork that he decided to go to a *sanitarium* for a month.
>   (Correct use) He was so tired from overwork that he decided to go to a *sanatorium* for a month.
>   (Wrong use) The insane woman was sent to a *sanatorium.*
>   (Correct use) The insane woman was sent to a *sanitarium.*

Scholar and *Pupil:*
   A *scholar* is an *outstanding* pupil.

>   (Correct use) Every *scholar* is a pupil, but not every *pupil* is a scholar.

Sensual and *Sensuous:*
   Sensual means *indulging the senses in a lustful manner; sensuous* means *appreciating beautiful things.*

>   (Correct use) Mr. Smith, a *sensual* man, was fond of beefsteak and beer.
>   (Correct use) Mr. Jones, a *sensuous* man, was fond of poetry and drama.

Seat and *Sit:*

Seat is a *transitive verb* and takes an object; *sit* is an *intransitive verb* and takes no object.

> (Wrong use) He *sits* them in their place.
> (Correct use) He *seats* them in their place.

Note: *Set* is also a transitive verb, not to be confused with *sit*.
Example:

> (Wrong use) *Set* down in front there!
> (Correct use) *Sit* down in front there!

Shall and *Will:*

One of the most difficult lessons in English grammar is to learn the correct use of the verbs *shall* and *will*. Yet the whole complicated subject can be reduced to the following simple rule:

a. In the first person *shall* denotes *the simple future,* and *nothing else; will* denotes *the future, plus determination or command.* For example:

> *I* (or *we*) *shall go* means *I* (or *we*) *merely expect to go.*
> *I* (or *we*) *will go* means *I am* (or *we are*) *determined to go.*

b. In the second and the third persons, the meaning of these two verbs is turned completely around. *Will* denotes the *simple future,* and *shall* denotes *the future, plus determination.* For example:

> *You will go* means that *I merely expect you to go.*
> *He* (or *they*) *will go* means that *I merely expect him* (or *them*) *to go.*

But:

> *You shall go* means that *I command you to go.*
> *He* (or *they*) *shall go* means that *I command him* (or *them*) *to go.*

So much for the rule in *declarative* sentences. In *interrogative* sentences, the rule is just as simple. Here it is:

Use in the question the same word which you expect in the answer. For example:

> *Shall you go?* means that you expect the answer to be
> *Yes, I shall go.*
> *Will you go?* means that you expect the answer to be
> *Yes, I will go.*

Should and *Would:*

These verbs follow the same simple rules which govern the use of *shall* and *will*. Examples:

> *I thought that I should go* expresses *no* determination.
>
> *I thought that I would go* expresses determination.
>
> *I thought that you* (*or he or they*) *would go* implies *no* command.
>
> *I thought that you* (*or he or they*) *should go* implies an obligation or command.

Sickening and *Sickly:*

Sickening means *causing sickness; sickly* means *feeling sick, in a sick condition.*

> (Wrong use) This dirty place is *sickly.*
>
> (Correct use) This dirty place is *sickening* (or unhealthful).

To Speak and *To Talk:*

To speak is used in a *formal* sense; *to talk,* in an *informal* sense.

> (Correct use) He *spoke* well in the lecture room.
>
> (Correct use) He *talked* cleverly among his intimate friends.

Stationary and *Stationery:*

Stationary is an *adjective* meaning *not moving; stationery* is a *noun* meaning *articles sold by stationers,* such as pencils, pens, paper, etc.

Stimulant and *Stimulus:*

A *stimulant* is that which *physically* produces quicker action or greater energy; a *stimulus* is that which *mentally* inspires greater action or ambition.

> (Wrong use) Whisky is a *stimulus.*
>
> (Correct use) Whisky is a *stimulant.*
>
> (Wrong use) The lecture served as a *stimulant* to the students.
>
> (Correct use) The lecture served as a *stimulus* to the students.

If, however, the lecture is regarded as a *physical tonic,* we may use the word *stimulant* in connection with it.

Stop and *Stay:*

To *stop* means *to remain for a short period;* to *stay* means *to remain for a longer period.*

> (Wrong use) He *stopped* in Boston for six months.
> (Correct use) He *stayed* in Boston for six months.
> (Correct use) He *stopped* overnight at the Plaza Hotel.

Sure and *Surely:*

Sure is an *adjective; surely* is an *adverb.*

> (Wrong use) I *sure* want to see him.
> (Correct use) I *surely* want to see him.

Therefor and *Therefore:*

Therefor means *for it; therefore* means *for this reason.*

> (Wrong use) He bought a book and paid a dollar *therefore.*
> (Correct use) He bought a book and paid a dollar *therefor.* (It is a good idea to avoid the use of this word, as it is a clumsy word at best.)

Unmoral and *Immoral:*

Unmoral means *not concerned one way or another with the question of morality, neither good nor bad; immoral* means *bad, depraved.*

> (Wrong use) From an ethical standpoint, mathematics is an *immoral* study.
> (Correct use) From an ethical standpoint, mathematics is an *unmoral* study.

> (Wrong use) He is an *unmoral* villain.
> (Correct use) He is an *immoral* villain.

Vocation and *Avocation:*

Vocation means *profession or business; avocation* means *hobby, something apart from one's profession or business.*

> (Wrong use) He was a doctor; his *avocation,* therefore, was the practice of medicine.
> (Correct use) He was a doctor; his *vocation,* therefore, was the practice of medicine.

> (Wrong use) Every man should have a *vocation* in addition to his business.
> (Correct use) Every man should have an *avocation* in addition to his business.

Without and *Unless:*

Without is a *preposition* and takes an object; *unless* is a *conjunction* and takes *no* object.

> (Wrong use) I shall not be there *without* you come also.
>
> (Correct use) I shall not be there *without* you.
>
> (Correct use) I shall not be there *unless* you come also.

§ 2

USING THE RIGHT WORD IN THE RIGHT PLACE

Every word we use in our speech or in our writing must be:

1. A *living* word. Such words as *anon, fain, quoth, spake,* and *withal* are no longer alive. A style that contains such words is dragged down to destruction by the corpses of obsolete or dead words.

2. A *reputable* word. Such words as *burgle, disremember, gent, enthuse,* and *worthwhileness* are disreputable. They have no place in a good style.

3. A *universal* word. Such words as *pan out, I swan,* and *diggings* are used only in a single place or in a single trade. Such words are, if possible, to be avoided.

4. A word that means exactly what we want it to mean. There are many pairs of words that mean *almost,* but not *exactly* the same thing. We must be careful to distinguish between such words. For example:

> *Action* means *a process of doing* or *a series of deeds.*
> *Act* means *a single deed.*
>
> *Amateur* means *a (new or old) lover of any art or science or game.*
> *Novice* means *a newcomer* or *beginner.*
>
> We *begin* a small thing.
> We *commence* a large thing.
>
> *Between* is used of *two* objects.
> *Among* is used of *more than two* objects.
>
> A man *confesses* his guilt.
> A man *admits* the correctness of somebody else's argument.

A *contemptible man* is *a despised man*.
A *contemptuous man* is *a man who despises*.

Criticism may be either favorable or unfavorable.
Fault-finding is always unfavorable.

Cure is used of a disease.
Heal is used of a wound.

A man may have a *deathly* (*death-like*) appearance.
A tiger has a *deadly* (*likely to cause death*) look.

Distinct means *separated by some mark*.
Distinctive means *having distinction*.

Elder is used of people.
Older is used of animals or of things.

Enormousness means *hugeness*.
Enormity means *atrocity, cruelty*.

Feminine means *female*.
Effeminate means *like a female,* used in a sense of ridicule.

Hanged is used of *persons*. The man was *hanged*.
Hung is used of *things*. The flag was *hung*.

House is used in a physical sense.
Home is used in a spiritual sense.

Human means *belonging to mankind*.
Humane means *merciful*.

Imaginary means *existing in the imagination only*.
Imaginative means *having imagination*.

Interior is used of *large* objects.
Inside (as a noun) is used of *small* objects.

Judicial means *in accordance with the law*.
Judicious means *in accordance with justice, wise*.

Manly means *like a man* (in a *good* sense).
Mannish means *like a man* (in a *bad* sense, as: *a mannish woman*).

Official means *acting like an officer* (in a *good* sense).
Officious means *acting like an officer* (in a *bad* sense).

Practicable is used of *things*.
Practical is used of *persons*.

Prescribe means *to direct to be used as a remedy*.
Proscribe means *to outlaw*.

Prosecute means *to pursue lawfully.*
Persecute means *to injure unlawfully.*

Sentiment means *true tenderness of feeling* (in a *good* sense).
Sentimentalism means *false tenderness of feeling* (in a *bad* sense).

Significance means *importance.*
Signification means *sense* or *meaning.*

Solicitation means *request.*
Solicitude means *anxiety.*

Verse means *a single line of poetry.*
Stanza means *a group of lines of poetry.*

Womanly means *like a woman* (in a *good* sense).
Womanish means *like a woman* (in a *bad* sense).

EXERCISES

Correct the errors in the following sentences:

1. He effected a reconciliation between them.
2. A rich man is not as happy as a contented man.
3. A philosopher is as happy as any man.
4. This humorous story is awfully interesting.
5. Beside his other good qualities, he is a persuasive speaker.
6. A credible story is generally a creditable story.
7. Isn't he a cunning little dog?
8. The last election was a decisive triumph for the Democratic Party.
9. What a delicious argument!
10. The countries of Europe are suspicious of one another.
11. When they excavated the tomb of Pharaoh, they discovered in the king's coffin a tool that had been previously unknown to modern scholars.
12. To discover the North Pole, it was necessary to invent the airship.
13. The Pilgrim Fathers were among the first of the American emigrants.
14. A new European war is obviously eminent.
15. The volcanic irruption was appalling.
16. I shall fix up the whole program.

17. The plays of Ibsen are the works of a genial man.
18. The genial Will Rogers is greatly missed at this time.
19. After careful deliberation, I guess I shall come.
20. French is a handy language to know.
21. The climate of California is said to be very healthful.
22. Grapefruit is a healthy fruit for breakfast.
23. When my business is in a healthy condition, I find that almost everything I eat is healthful.
24. He never lived to know if his book was a success.
25. He indicted a long charge against the indited criminal.
26. He is an honest fellow,—not very ingenious, to be sure, but always ingenuous.
27. I have met both Mary and Constance, and I find Mary the least interesting.
28. Let me alone.
29. He was real mad at the way they treated him.
30. I had most forgotten that I was to meet you.
31. I have read a story about the noted soldier, Napoleon.
32. Benedict Arnold was notorious rather than noted.
33. When pleasure is intense and lasting, it becomes happiness.
34. He presented Greta Garbo to Marlene Dietrich.
35. Everything will be all right providing you keep your wits about you.
36. They raised up from their seats and gave a cheer.
37. He married Jeannette, but he did not marry her relations.
38. The inmates of the sanitarium were treated with great cruelty.
39. The sensuous pleasures of life are more refined than the sensual.
40. I insist that you will go.
41. I think we will like her.
42. I'm afraid I will be ill.
43. I hope we shall not miss the train.
44. "The enemy shall not pass!" said the general.
45. I decided that I would never consent.
46. Shall the letter reach me today?

47. This is a sickening sight.
48. He always spoke about trivial matters.
49. He bought a dollar's worth of stationary.
50. When you pass through the town, stop with us for a week or two.
51. He surely is a grand man!
52. He burgled the house of all its jewelry.
53. The saving of the child from the mad dog was a courageous action.
54. An amateur is not necessarily a novice.
55. He commenced his short story at ten o'clock.
56. Who between us all is without sin?
57. The wounded man looked deathly pale.
58. Do you confess your error?
59. Jonathan Swift was a satirical and contemptuous writer.
60. He wrote a very flattering criticism of the book.
61. He cured the gun-shot in two weeks.
62. The excellence of this poem makes it distinct.
63. "All men," wrote a certain wit, "may be divided into two sexes: the masculine and the effeminate."
64. They hung him by the neck until he was dead.
65. The imaginary poet concocts many an imaginative scene.
66. The interior of the palace was even more splendid than the outside.
67. The modern trend in the courts is to be judicious rather than judicial.
68. The policeman was censured because he acted in too officious a manner.
69. This is a practical machine.
70. He proscribed a cough medicine for the patient.
71. Tyrants always persecute minorities.
72. The signification of the accusation consisted in its bitterness.
73. He was all finished with his work, so that he fell into a faint.

KEY TO THE ABOVE EXERCISES

The incorrect sentences should be corrected as follows:

2. A rich man is not *so* happy as a contented man.
4. This humorous story is *very* interesting.

5. *Besides* his other good qualities, he is a persuasive speaker. (The sentence will be still further improved if you change *besides* to *in addition to*.)

7. Isn't he a *pretty* little dog?

8. The last election was a *decided* triumph for the Democratic Party.

9. What a *delightful* argument!

13. The Pilgrim Fathers were among the first of the American *immigrants*.

14. A new European war is obviously *imminent*.

15. The volcanic *eruption* was appalling.

16. I shall *arrange* the whole program.

17. The plays of Ibsen are the work of *a man of genius*.

19. After careful deliberation, I *think* I shall come.

20. French is a *convenient* language to know.

22. Grapefruit is a *healthful* fruit for breakfast.

24. He never lived to know *whether* (or not) his book was a success.

25. He *indited* a long charge against the *indicted* criminal.

27. I have met both Mary and Constance, and I find Mary the *less* interesting.

28. *Leave* me alone.

29. He was *really angry* at the way they treated him.

30. I had *almost* forgotten that I was to meet you.

34. He *introduced* Greta Garbo to Marlene Dietrich.

35. Everything will be all right *provided* you keep your wits about you.

36. They *rose* from their seats and gave a cheer.

37. He married Jeannette, but he did not marry her *relatives*.

40. I insist that you *shall* go.

41. I think we *shall* like her.

42. I'm afraid I *shall* be ill.

46. *Will* the letter reach me today?

48. He always *talked* about trivial matters.

49. He bought a dollar's worth of *stationery*.

50. When you pass through the town, *stay* with us for a week or two.

52. He *robbed* the house of all its jewelry.

53. The saving of the child from the mad dog was a courageous *act*.

55. He *began* his short story at ten o'clock.
56. Who *among* us all is without sin?
58. Do you *admit* your error?
61. He *healed* the gun-shot in two weeks.
62. The excellence of this poem makes it *distinctive*.
64. They *hanged* him by the neck until he was dead.
65. The *imaginative* poet concocts many an *imaginary* scene.
66. The interior of the palace was even more splendid than the *exterior*.
69. This is a *practicable* machine.
70. He *prescribed* a cough medicine for the patient.
72. The *significance* of the accusation consisted in its bitterness.

In order to verify the above corrections, look once more at the definitions of the words under discussion. And, above all, get into the habit of consulting the dictionary whenever you have the slightest doubt as to the exact meaning of a word.

Remember: He who consults, gets results.

CHAPTER V

Synonyms and Antonyms

§ I

DEFINITIONS

A *Synonym* is a word which has the *same meaning* as another. An *Antonym* is a term which is the *opposite* of another.

Synonyms are like twins. Though found to be somewhat different upon close analysis, they are yet sufficiently alike to pass in a crowd. Take, for example, the three words *obstinate, inflexible,* and *unyielding. Obstinate* comes from the Latin word *obstare, to stand against; inflexible* comes from the Latin *in, not + flectere, to bend; unyielding* is derived from *un, not +* the Old English word *gieldan, to pay.* The exact meaning of the three words, therefore, is as follows:

> *obstinate—standing firmly against*
> *inflexible—unbending*
> *unyielding—not willing to pay*

Yet the three words are closely enough related to be called synonyms.

The purpose of synonyms is to give flexibility and variety to a style. The great speakers and writers are lavish in their use of synonyms. That most irresistible of French humorists, Rabelais, once adorned a single noun with no less than 104 synonymous adjectives.

Very few of us are blessed with the imagination of a Rabelais. Yet all of us can acquire a richer and more persuasive style by the habitual use of synonyms.

A good style is distinguished not only by its synonyms, but also by its antonyms. It is important to know when to use a word with the *same* meaning. It is equally important to know when to use a word with the *opposite* meaning. A style con-

taining good synonyms is a *rich* style. A style containing good
antonyms is a *brilliant* style. Two words of opposite meaning,
when cleverly placed in a sentence, are like two skillful swords-
men engaged in a duel. Their ideas clash and glitter before
our eyes, and the victory of the stronger word gives us a keen
mental satisfaction. Note, for instance, the famous line

> To err is human; to forgive, divine.

In this sentence *human* and *divine* are antonyms. They are
brilliantly selected and placed in such a manner as to produce
one of the truly sublime sentences in the English language.

Try to familiarize yourself with the proper use of synonyms
and antonyms. You will become a better speaker and writer as
a result. Study carefully the list that follows in the next section.

§ 2

COMMON SYNONYMS AND ANTONYMS

	SYNONYMS	ANTONYMS
abandon:	quit	keep
	renounce	continue
	forsake	
active:	vigorous	sluggish
	industrious	idle
	hustling	lazy
add:	join	subtract
	unite	deduct
	attach	
advance:	proceed	recede
	press	retreat
	push	
ancestor:	forefather	descendant
	predecessor	offspring
	forebear	
annoy:	distress	please
	vex	calm
	torment	pacify
	harass	
	pester	

	SYNONYMS	ANTONYMS
applaud:	acclaim clap cheer	condemn censure
apprehensive:	fearful anxious	hopeful sanguine
approve:	indorse favor support	disapprove reprove condemn
arrogant:	presumptuous haughty overweening impudent	humble submissive condescending obsequious
artificial:	unnatural false counterfeit	natural genuine
assurance:	confidence self-reliance aplomb	timidity doubt bashfulness
attack (v.):	assault assail charge engage rush	defend protect shelter
avoid:	shun elude evade dodge	face meet approach court
base:	vile mean low	noble lofty
bashful:	shy retiring timid reserved	assured bold impudent conceited
beginning:	commencement start opening inception	end finish closing completion

	SYNONYMS	ANTONYMS
blame:	censure	approve
	criticize	praise
	reprove	excuse
blunt:	dull	sharp
	pointless	pointed
boastful:	bragging	modest
	vaunting	quiet
	vainglorious	unpretentious
boisterous:	noisy	calm
	riotous	motionless
	clamorous	composed
	turbulent	tranquil
	vociferous	silent
	blatant	
brave:	bold	cowardly
	resolute	faint-hearted
	courageous	timid
	daring	pusillanimous
	valiant	craven
business:	occupation	diversion
	employment	relaxation
	vocation	avocation
	pursuit	
	calling	
caprice:	whim	opinion
	freak	conviction
	notion	thought
	fantasy	
	vagary	
careless:	unconcerned	anxious
	blithesome	watchful
	inconsiderate	careful
	nonchalant	conscientious
	heedless	vigilant
	thoughtless	prudent
	negligent	
	remiss	

	SYNONYMS	ANTONYMS
chaste:	pure	unchaste
	clean	lewd
	innocent	immoral
	virtuous	lascivious
		licentious
cheerful:	light-hearted	heavy-hearted
	merry	depressed
	jolly	sullen
	blithe	gloomy
	bright	
clean:	unsoiled	soiled
	pure	filthy
	unblemished	stained
	immaculate	dirty
	stainless	smeary
clumsy:	awkward	skillful
	unhandy	handy
	ungraceful	graceful
	lumbering	
	elephantine	
	ungainly	
compassion:	sympathy	cruelty
	kindness	malevolence
	pity	hate
	tenderness	
conceit:	egotism	modesty
	vanity	humility
	self-admiration	
confuse:	perplex	order
	confound	classify
	bewilder	arrange
	befuddle	elucidate
corrupt (v.):	demoralize	purify
	vitiate	reform
	deprave	purge
	debauch	

	SYNONYMS	ANTONYMS
cruel:	cold-blooded	gentle
	heartless	compassionate
	savage	kindly
	brutal	merciful
	ruthless	
	ferocious	
	truculent	
deceitful:	deceptive	truthful
	insincere	sincere
	fraudulent	frank
	insidious	
defiant:	despiteful	submissive
	rebellious	obedient
	insolent	resigned
destroy:	demolish	build
	devastate	establish
	subvert	construct
	raze	protect
	efface	
disclose:	reveal	conceal
	divulge	hide
	unfold	
	manifest	
discord:	dissension	harmony
	dissonance	euphony
	cacophony	melodiousness
	disagreement	amity
		concord
dishonest:	crooked	honest
	faithless	conscientious
	fraudulent	virtuous
	perfidious	
economical:	thrifty	extravagant
	parsimonious	wasteful
	frugal	
elated:	exalted	depressed
	joyful	downcast
	exhilarated	

	SYNONYMS	ANTONYMS
enemy:	opponent	friend
	antagonist	ally
	adversary	
energy:	activity	weakness
	force	inertia
	power	
exhaust:	weaken	strengthen
	deplete	refresh
	prostrate	restore
extravagance:	excess	economy
	prodigality	moderation
	lavishness	
face (v.):	confront	avoid
	oppose	evade
	dare	shun
fail:	lack	succeed
	miss	prosper
	miscarry	
fault:	failing	excellence
	blemish	worth
	flaw	
	defect	
	demerit	
ferocity:	savagery	gentleness
	brutality	kindness
	truculence	
fiction:	invention	actuality
	fantasy	reality
	fabrication	history
	concoction	truth
firm:	fixed	shaky
	constant	tottering
	solid	unsteady
	secure	loose
	inflexible	unstable
forbid:	prohibit	bid
	enjoin	ask
	taboo	appoint
	proscribe	permit
	veto	

	SYNONYMS	ANTONYMS
foster:	promote	quench
	cherish	subdue
	patronize	extinguish
	encourage	stifle
frank:	free	hypocritical
	outspoken	artful
	candid	affected
	sincere	deceitful
	genuine	dissembling
fruitful:	productive	unproductive
	fertile	barren
gather:	assemble	scatter
	collect	separate
	congregate	disperse
generosity:	liberality	meanness
	magnanimity	stinginess
	bounty	selfishness
gentle:	mild	rough
	benign	harsh
	docile	severe
	kind	cruel
	lenient	blunt
	amiable	
grand:	noble	small
	majestic	mean
	magnificent	insignificant
	superb	
gross:	crass	nice
	coarse	delicate
	stupid	fastidious
	vulgar	refined
	obscene	
	sensual	
hallowed:	consecrated	unholy
	blessed	
harmony:	agreement	discord
	consistency	cacophony
	concord	
	unison	

	SYNONYMS	ANTONYMS
haste:	hurry impetuosity rashness	leisure deliberation
hateful:	disagreeable spiteful malevolent odious	kindly affectionate compassionate
haughty:	arrogant proud lordly supercilious	humble servile
height:	elevation eminence altitude	abyss depth
hidden:	concealed secret obscure latent covert surreptitious	apparent clear unconcealed exposed
hopeful:	expectant sanguine optimistic buoyant	apprehensive desperate despondent hopeless
idle:	indolent dawdling lazy	busy bustling industrious
immoral:	wicked licentious indecent	righteous virtuous upright
impudent:	impertinent saucy insolent contumelious	polite respectful obsequious abject
increase:	grow multiply intensify develop	abate diminish relax

	SYNONYMS	ANTONYMS
innocent:	sinless	wicked
	blameless	sinful
	guiltless	corrupt
	harmless	guilty
irascible:	cranky	calm
	hot-blooded	peaceful
	testy	patient
	peevish	
irritate:	excite	calm
	annoy	pacify
	anger	
	exacerbate	
jerky:	abrupt	smooth
	spasmodic	gliding
join:	connect	separate
	assemble	break
	combine	detach
	consolidate	disconnect
lag:	delay	hurry
	flag	rush
	linger	dash
	loiter	
lasting:	continuing	ephemeral
	durable	temporary
	perennial	passing
	permanent	
laugh (v.):	giggle	cry
	grin	sob
	sneer	wail
	guffaw	weep
	titter	
	chuckle	
	chortle	
lazy:	inert	active
	idle	ambitious
	indolent	enterprising
	slothful	

	SYNONYMS	ANTONYMS
limited:	bounded	boundless
	confined	limitless
	finite	infinite
logical:	sound	absurd
	valid	illogical
	reasonable	inconsistent
love:	attachment	hatred
	adoration	abhorrence
	affection	aversion
	passion	
luxury:	elegance	simplicity
	voluptuousness	
	sumptuousness	
malevolence:	rancor	benevolence
	hatred	compassion
	venom	
manageable:	gentle	unmanageable
	docile	unruly
	flexible	obstinate
	pliant	perverse
	teachable	unteachable
mention:	recount	disregard
	designate	ignore
	cite	omit
	recommend	
merciful:	kind	implacable
	clement	cruel
	gracious	unfeeling
	humane	relentless
mournful:	regretful	glad
	lugubrious	joyful
	sad	festive
	plaintive	
	lamentable	
	doleful	
narcotic:	anaesthetic	stimulant
novice:	beginner	expert
	tyro	
	neophyte	

	SYNONYMS	ANTONYMS
obedient:	submissive	disobedient
	compliant	obstinate
	subservient	defiant
	complaisant	
occupy:	fill	vacate
	inhabit	evacuate
	keep	
odd:	unusual	usual
	peculiar	customary
	strange	commonplace
	bizarre	
	singular	
offensive:	unpleasant	pleasant
	obnoxious	agreeable
	repugnant	inoffensive
opaque:	dull	translucent
	dark	transparent
	non-transparent	
outrageous:	excessive	moderate
	monstrous	gentle
	atrocious	
	heinous	
pacify:	mollify	annoy
	soothe	agitate
	placate	disturb
	appease	irritate
	propitiate	vex
peace:	concord	dissension
	amity	war
	friendliness	
	harmony	
playful:	sportive	earnest
	frolicsome	serious
	mischievous	
pleasant:	agreeable	unpleasant
	enjoyable	unpalatable
	delightful	offensive
	attractive	disgusting
	fascinating	unbearable
	delicious	painful

	SYNONYMS	ANTONYMS
poisonous:	venomous	innocuous
	virose	healthful
	toxic	
	infectious	
poverty:	penury	wealth
	indigence	riches
	destitution	prosperity
progress (n.):	advance	recession
	development	decline
prosperity:	fortune	adversity
	success	calamity
	well-being	
pugnacious:	combative	peaceable
	quarrelsome	quiet
	militant	gentle
	bellicose	
	contentious	
quarrel:	disagreement	agreement
	contention	harmony
	controversy	concord
	imbroglio	
	discord	
rapid:	fast	slow
	swift	sluggish
	quick	
	speedy	
reasonable:	rational	irrational
	logical	absurd
	valid	
receive:	accept	decline
	get	reject
	acquire	
refresh:	invigorate	tire
	recreate	exhaust
	revive	enervate
	regale	
regretful:	repentant	unrepentant
	penitent	impenitent
	compunctious	

	SYNONYMS	ANTONYMS
relentless:	pitiless unyielding obdurate remorseless	merciful compassionate
repel:	repulse rebuff reject frighten	attract fascinate entice
rich:	prosperous wealthy affluent	poor indigent needy
scholar:	student savant bookman pundit	ignoramus blockhead
shelter (v.):	protect screen shield lodge	assail attack expose
slender:	thin lithe tenuous	coarse stout
strengthen:	reënforce brace invigorate vitalize	weaken enervate exhaust
stupid:	unintelligent witless stolid dull inept obtuse crass	intelligent clever sharp shrewd precocious witty
surly:	ill-tempered churlish snarling ungracious	affable agreeable gracious

	SYNONYMS	ANTONYMS
timid:	fearful	assured
	timorous	bold
	shy	confident
	diffident	
	bashful	
transient:	temporary	permanent
	fleeting	constant
	ephemeral	imperishable
	brief	
truth:	constancy	error
	authenticity	untruth
	accuracy	fallacy
	sincerity	lie
vacate:	quit	occupy
	abandon	
virtue:	rectitude	vice
	honor	dishonor
	goodness	wickedness
	uprightness	
waste:	dissipate	economize
	squander	preserve
	devastate	
weak:	feeble	strong
	infirm	able
	impotent	powerful
	enervated	firm
	decrepit	vigorous
wicked:	evil	good
	perverse	virtuous
	iniquitous	upright
	ungodly	godly
	villainous	sinless
	sinful	
wild:	untamed	tame
	savage	domesticated
	uncultivated	cultivated
wise:	sage	unwise
	prudent	foolish
	learned	ignorant

Exercises

I

In each of the following pairs of words indicate whether the two words mean the *same* or the *opposite:*

1.	ordinary	undistinguished
2.	amity	dissension
3.	dark	translucent
4.	bizarre	commonplace
5.	negligent	remiss
6.	novice	tyro
7.	compliant	obstinate
8.	clement	humane
9.	docile	flexible
10.	elegance	simplicity
11.	rancor	malevolence
12.	inert	enterprising
13.	spasmodic	smooth
14.	plaintive	doleful
15.	peevish	testy
16.	impertinent	contumelious
17.	surreptitious	apparent
18.	sanguine	despondent
19.	concord	unison
20.	impetuosity	deliberation
21.	disagreeable	odious
22.	appease	propitiate
23.	monstrous	heinous
24.	toxic	innocuous
25.	indigence	penury
26.	bellicose	contentious
27.	rebuff	entice
28.	repentant	compunctious
29.	invigorate	enervate
30.	stolid	shrewd

II

In each of the following groups of words select the word asked for:

1. The opposite of *valid* is *certain—active—confined—absurd.*

2. A word having the same meaning as *hopeful* is *desperate —sanguine—conscientious—brilliant*.

3. The opposite of *heretic* is *infidel—traitor—convalescent —believer*.

4. The opposite of *immoral* is *righteous—unseemly—insolent—licentious*.

5. A word having the same meaning as *irascible* is *peaceful —obsequious—hot-blooded—respectful*.

6. A word having the same meaning as *docile* is *relentless —dreary—gentle—passionate*.

7. The opposite of *remiss* is *careful—loose—artificial— submissive*.

8. The opposite of *outrageous* is *heinous—gentle—quarrelsome—uneasy*.

9. A word having the same meaning as *contention* is *imbroglio—reception—meeting—harmony*.

10. A word having the same meaning as *obdurate* is *merciful —swift—penitent—relentless*.

KEY TO THE ABOVE EXERCISES

I

1. same	11. same	21. same
2. opposite	12. opposite	22. same
3. opposite	13. opposite	23. same
4. opposite	14. same	24. opposite
5. same	15. same	25. same
6. same	16. same	26. same
7. opposite	17. opposite	27. opposite
8. same	18. opposite	28. same
9. same	19. same	29. opposite
10. opposite	20. opposite	30. opposite

II

1. absurd	5. hot-blooded	8. gentle
2. sanguine	6. gentle	9. imbroglio
3. believer	7. careful	10. relentless
4. righteous		

CHAPTER VI
Similes and Metaphors

§ 1
DEFINITIONS

A *Simile* is a figure of speech consisting in *comparing* one thing to another. The comparison is introduced by *like* or *as*. For example:

My love is *like* a red, red rose.
He is happy *as* a lark.

A *Metaphor* is a figure of speech consisting in *identifying* one thing with another. In a metaphor, a person or a thing is not *like* another person or another thing; it *is* another person or another thing. For example:

John Smith *is* a regular fox.
My heart *is* a heavy stone.

Similes and *Metaphors* are called *Figures of Speech*. A style that is full of similes and metaphors is called a *figurative style*. A good writer uses figures of speech for three reasons:

1. To produce clearness. In the sentence

The bird sits atilt *like a blossom among the leaves.*

the simile makes the picture of the bird clear and unique and beautiful. You can actually *see* the bird tilted like a blossom.

2. To give force. In the phrase

a *gush* of violets

the word *gush,* identifying the violets with a flood of rain-drops, makes the picture not only *clear,* but *forceful.*

3. To suggest *unity.* This is very important. An apt figure of speech stirs us to the depths of our being. Why? Because, as some philosophers maintain, it subtly suggests that *all* things

are essentially *one*. It helps to *unify* the world. The rose in the garden, unfolding its petals to the sun, and the rose of the morning, spreading out its cloud-petals over the earth, are both alike manifestations of the self-same source of beauty. And the great poet, in his moments of real insight—that is, in the moments when he creates a perfect simile or metaphor—realizes that the world is a unit. The figurative language of the poet is therefore a fragmentary sample of the language of Heaven, revealing to us in that moment of inspiration that all men are brothers and all things are one. This is the reason why a beautiful simile strikes us so forcibly as to take away our breath. For it is a revelation of truth.

The above paragraph may strike some readers as a little too mystical. If so, let us not worry about it. Even those of us who are not mystically-minded may find enough clearness and force and beauty in an apt figure of speech to produce the effect of a glass of champagne. A figurative style, if well handled, has an exhilarating effect upon every cultivated reader. And all of us who are aiming to please the cultivated reader should learn to use the appropriate simile and metaphor in the right place.

What is an appropriate simile or metaphor?

1. It must be *brief*. For example:

His shout was a peal of thunder.
He sank like a stone.

2. It must be *vivid*. For example:

His words smashed into the conversation like a brick through a glass window.
The darkness came on like a giant with seven-league boots.

3. It must be *harmonious*. A figure of speech must mix well. The following figure is harmonious:

Born with the spark of genius, he fanned it into a flame through hard work.

The following figure, however, is *not* harmonious:

Born with a spark of genius, he watered it with hard work until it came to full bloom.

In the first place, a *spark* cannot bloom into a *plant*. In the second place, if you *water* a spark, you *extinguish* it. Hence the figure does not mix well.

4. It must arouse in the mind a *familiar* picture. The following simile is good:

His commands were like the blows of a whip.

But note the next simile:

His commands were like a flagellation.

This simile is bad because it arouses an *unfamiliar* and therefore *vague* picture. Unless you know that a *flagellation* is a *whipping,* you miss the entire effect of the figure.

§ 2

A LIST OF STRIKING SIMILES

In choosing the similes for your own speech and writing, be careful to avoid the similes of other people. Borrowed figures of speech are as ill-fitting as borrowed finery. The list printed here is *not* to be copied. It is rather to serve as an inspiration for your own creative work:

The light cut like a dagger through the darkness.
They chattered like a flock of magpies.
Her song was like a slender, silver rivulet of sound.
The clouds were like a bouquet of flowers illumined by the sun.
The autumn leaves lay on the ground like a Persian rug of many colors.
Life is like a falling star. It flashes for a moment, and then all is darkness.
Love descended upon her like the song of an angel.
The waves followed the ship like a pack of howling wolves.
The new moon fluttered like a feather through the clouds.
She is as modest as a nun.
Tyranny is like a desolating pestilence.
Your name is like a bell in my heart.

His one hope still clung to him like the last leaf in the November wind.

The horse's mane was like a flowing river.

From a distance the stones in the field looked like a flock of sheep.

His face was as shriveled as a walnut.

Her mind was as desolate as a tomb.

She was as beautiful as a statue, and as heartless.

The sun came up like thunder.

His sorrows, like worms, gnawed away at his peace of mind.

Her mind was like a weather-vane.

The rising river clutched at the earth as with greedy fingers.

She stepped as noiselessly as a cat.

Her eyes were like pools of fire.

When she wept, her eyes were like dew-covered violets.

Terror like a wild beast gripped his throat.

His senseless words were like pebbles rattling in a hollow cask.

The red flowers were stained as with the blood of the martyrs.

The bonfire rose like a beard of flame into the darkness.

Autumn, like a rich dowager, reclined at her ease in her kimono of colored leaves.

His life was as beautiful as a Persian tapestry.

The day was as gloomy as the thoughts of a dying man.

Her voice was soft, like the whirring of wings in the twilight.

The little boy's life ebbed away, like water dripping from a broken vase.

His arrival was like a golden thread that bound them together.

His heart was like a field of ice on a moonless night.

In the early morning mist, the city rose like a field of gigantic flowers.

The rain came down soft and caressing, like the benediction of a gentle priest.

The wind-lashed waves came rushing to the beach like a cavalcade of white horses.

The cold was as sharp as a razor.

Like a star she came out only at night; and like a star,
she was cold and glittering and distant.

His words were like pebbles dropped into a lake.
They gave rise to thoughts that spread in ever-
widening circles.

Their gaiety sparkled and sputtered like a bunch of
fire-crackers and then melted into the darkness of
their impending doom.

His ugly green eyes were like pools covered with
slime.

The motif ran like a scarlet thread throughout the
symphony.

All dressed in her gauze, she looked like a wisp of
autumn smoke.

The obsession stuck to him like a leech.

> Death lies on her, like an untimely frost
> Upon the sweetest flower of all the field.
> —*Shakespeare*

> . . . my age is as a lusty winter,
> Frosty, but kindly.
> —*Shakespeare*

> She faded, like a cloud which had outwept the rain.
> —*Shelley*

> Her feet beneath the petticoat
> Like little mice stole in and out,
> As if they feared the light.
> —*Suckling*

> . . . our lips would mingle
> With kisses glad as birds are
> That get sweet rain at noon.
> —*Swinburne*

> . . . like the wings of sea-birds
> Flash the white caps of the sea.
> —*Longfellow*

> . . . a small drop of ink
> Falling like dew upon a thought, produces
> That which makes thousands, perhaps millions, think.
> —*Byron*

§ 3
A LIST OF METAPHORS

As compared with a simile, a metaphor is more difficult to create, but more beautiful to behold. Take the two following pictures, for example:

1. The moonlight *looked like* a bridge of silver across the water.
2. The moonlight *built* a bridge of silver across the water.

The first figure, a simile, is pretty, but not pretty enough. The words *looked like* blur the picture and spoil it. The second figure, a metaphor, is much more satisfactory. Here you get not only a *clear* picture, but a picture *in action*. You actually *see* the poetic building of the bridge. The moonlight is here personified. It becomes a magic builder of silver bridges.

A metaphor, therefore, is more vivid and more forceful than a simile. You will see this point clearly illustrated in the following list of metaphors:

The sunlight fell upon the slender cataract and turned it into a glittering golden sword.

She was a very sphinx of mystery.

A wave of hope ebbed and flowed in his heart.

The wind whipped the waves into a pack of howling wolves.

The new moon, a mere feather of light, fluttered through the clouds.

Your name rings a responsive bell in my heart.

His face was a shrivelled walnut.

Her mind was a weather-vane.

The rising river clutched at the earth with greedy fingers.

Her step was the noiseless step of a cat.

Her eyes were pools of fire.

The wild beast of terror gripped his throat.

The bonfire was a ragged beard of flame in the darkness.

That rich dowager, Autumn, reclined at her ease in her kimono of colored leaves.

His arrival was the golden thread that bound them
   together.
His heart was a field of ice on a moonless night.

> Short swallow-flights of song, that dip
> Their wings in tears, and skim away.
> —*Tennyson*

Language is a very good housewife to her husband,
   the human mind.

> Lo! here the gentle lark, weary of rest,
> From his moist cabinet mounts up on high,
> And wakes the morning, from whose silver breast
> The sun ariseth in his majesty.
> —*Shakespeare*

Note the following gorgeous metaphor in *Ode to the West
Wind,* in which Shelley addresses the Wind:

> Make me thy lyre, even as the forest is:
>   What if my leaves are falling like its own?
> The tumult of thy mighty harmonies
>   Will take from both a deep autumnal tone,
> Sweet though in sadness. Be thou, Spirit fierce,
>   My spirit! Be thou me, impetuous one!

> Riches have wings, and grandeur is a dream.
> —*Cowper*

The following passage, from Shakespeare's *Romeo and
Juliet,* combines a metaphor (in the first line) and a simile (in
the second line) into a perfect figure of speech:

> It seems she hangs upon the cheek of night,
> Like a rich jewel in an Ethiope's ear.

With this last example fresh in your mind, take a note-book
and see how cleverly you, yourself, can string together a succession of similes and metaphors into a necklace of linguistic
pearls. And, in order to sharpen your wits for your own
creative attempts, examine the following exercises and separate the good figures from the bad.

EXERCISES

In these exercises select the similes and the metaphors that fail to ring true, and point out in each case the reason for the failure:

1. The surface was as smooth as alabaster.
2. He brought the worm to his knees.
3. The man was dumb with sorrow.
4. He spoke at great length.
5. The darkness strode down like a black-winged bird.
6. His words, like a keen sword, hit the nail on the head.
7. He stood upon the brow of the hill and looked down upon its crowning glory of pines.
8. Her sorrow burned her and made her feel as if she were suffocating at the bottom of a river.
9. Her words were sugared over with the spice of her wit.
10. The time glided on, like a lovely dream.
11. Her dry eyes were inflamed by a sorrow too deep for tears.
12. The train wound over the hills like a serpent with glittering scales.
13. His style flowed on as brilliantly as burnished metal.
14. This fills all the necessary points.
15. His evil fate whipped him with every scourge of poverty and disease.
16. He covered the skeleton of his outline with the flesh of a glittering style.
17. He spoke with the finality of indecision.
18. His decision was as hard as steel, as final as death.
19. Some words are as refreshing as a summer shower, others as sharp as cannon-balls.
20. His announcement fell into their midst like a sudden spurt of flame.
21. His words came thick and fast as hail.
22. He touched a responsive chord upon the flute of his emotions.
23. He molded the soft clay of his character into a thing of gentleness and beauty.

24. The fire of his genius never diminished till the day of his death.
25. The Goddess of Justice spies out every one of our iniquities, hide them as we try.

KEY TO THE ABOVE EXERCISES

2. This figure is wrong. A worm has no knees.
5. Wrong. A bird does not *stride* down through the air. It *flies* down, or *swoops* down.
6. Wrong. You hit a nail with a *hammer*, not with a sword.
7. Wrong. The crown is *above* the brow.
8. Wrong. You cannot *burn* and *drown* at the same time.
9. Wrong. *Sugared* is not a term to be used in connection with *spice*.
13. Wrong. Metal does not flow (except when melted in a foundry).
14. Wrong. You fill a *hollow*, but not a *point*.
17. Wrong. There is no *finality* to *indecision*.
19. Wrong. Cannon-balls are not *sharp*.
20. Wrong. A spurt of flame does not *fall;* it *rises*.
22. Wrong. *Chord* is used of *stringed-instruments,* but a flute is a *wind-instrument*.
25. The Goddess of Justice, generally represented as being *blind,* cannot properly be said to *spy out* anything.

CHAPTER VII

How to Increase Your Vocabulary

§ 1

GENERAL INTRODUCTION

IN THE FOREGOING CHAPTERS we have already touched upon several effective ways of increasing your vocabulary. These ways, to summarize them briefly, are as follows:

1. Study the meaning of every word the spelling of which you are trying to learn. It is useless to know how to spell a word if you do not know how to define it. It is like trying to understand the clothes of a man without trying to understand his character. In the chapter on Correct Spelling (Chapter III) look up every word about whose meaning you have the slightest doubt. This will give you a good starting list for a foundation.

2. Study the meaning of every word the pronunciation of which you are trying to learn. The pronunciation of a word is like the sound of a person's voice. Learn to know the thoughts of your friends as well as the sound of their voices. In the chapter on Correct Pronunciation (Chapter IV) be sure to familiarize yourself with the meaning of every word. This will add to the basic vocabulary which you will have built up in Chapter III.

3. Learn to distinguish between the different shades of meaning in groups of apparently similar words. This will take you a step beyond your knowledge of *individual* words. It is very interesting, and very important, to get the subtle distinctions in the characters of your friends whose clothes and mannerisms and daily routine may be more or less alike. In the chapter on the Correct Use of Words (Chapter V) you have an opportunity to become somewhat of an expert in the fine art of using words. When you have mastered this chapter,

124

you may well claim to be regarded as a legitimate member of that circle of linguistic artists known as Weavers of Words.

4. Learn to classify your words into those groups that have the same meanings and those that have opposite meanings. In the chapter on Synonyms and Antonyms (Chapter VI) you have had an opportunity not only to make this classification, but also to widen materially the circle of your word-acquaintances. For you must remember that words are to be regarded as friends. The more words you know, and the better you know them, the more able you are to call them to your aid when necessary.

§ 2

HEARING GOOD SPEAKERS

In addition to the above methods for increasing your vocabulary, it is very important that you listen to good speakers. In this respect our own generation is more fortunate than any previous generation in the history of the world. The radio, in spite of all its shortcomings, has brought the best speakers within the reach of everybody. Every day you can hear good speeches on almost every subject under the sun. Listen to these speeches with a note-book in your hand. Take down not only what is new to you in the way of substance, but also what is unfamiliar to you in the way of words. Every good speaker has his own vocabulary. In the course of his practice, he has acquired certain special words, and certain special arrangements of these words, which single him out as a speaker worth listening to. Learn these words; make them your own; fit them into your vocabulary so that they will feel at home in the family of your own words. You will be pleasantly surprised at the speed with which your working vocabulary will grow if you get into the habit of using a note-book when you listen to a speech on the radio.

Listening to good speakers on the radio will increase not only your *general* vocabulary, but also your word-knowledge in that *particular* field which a speaker may be covering at a given time. If you hear a speech by a physician, for example, you may come across such unfamiliar words as *tonsilectomy, cardiograph, subcutaneous, iritis, suture.* If you listen to a speech by a publisher, you may hear such words as *brochure, delete, caption, pi, octavo.* If the speaker happens to be a professor of literature, he may introduce you to such outlandish terms as *sestet, pastoral, tribrach, dactyl.* The careful speaker will in each case explain the unfamiliar terms to you, so that, after you have heard the three speeches mentioned above, your note-book and your mind will be enriched with the following knowledge:

> *Tonsilectomy* means *an operation on the tonsils.*
> *Cardiograph* means *an instrument that measures the movements of the heart.*
> *Subcutaneous,* derived from the Latin words *sub* (under) + *cutis* (skin), means *situated under the skin.*
> *Iritis* means *an inflammation of the iris,* which is the curtain that hangs in front of the lens of the eye.
> *Suture* means the *sewing together of a wound.*
> *A brochure* is *a printed and stitched book containing only a few leaves, a pamphlet.*
> *Delete* is a term used in printing, and it means *to erase, to destroy.*
> *Caption* means *the heading of a chapter, section, page,* or *article.*
> *Pi* is a term used in printing, and it means *type that is confusedly mixed or disarranged.*
> *Octavo* refers to a book which is *composed of sheets folded into eight leaves.* Such a book is more or less definite in size. The average size of an octavo book is 5 by 7½ inches. The word *octavo* is generally written *8vo.*
> *A sestet* is a stanza in poetry consisting of six lines.
> *A pastoral,* from the Latin *pastor* (shepherd), is a *poem which describes the life of shepherds.*
> *A dactyl* is a *poetic measure consisting of three syllables with the accent on the first.* The word *syllable* is a dactyl.

The above examples will help to show you how you can enrich your vocabulary by listening to speeches dealing with as wide a variety of subjects as possible. A great Latin poet once said: "I am a human being, and therefore everything that deals with human beings is of interest to me." This is a good motto to apply in our study of English. As students of words, let us interest ourselves in everything that will increase our knowledge of words. One of the ways to increase this knowledge is to listen to all kinds of good speeches on every possible subject. Another way is to read widely and to learn the meanings of all the unfamiliar words that you come across. And this brings us to the next section.

§ 3
READING GOOD BOOKS

You cannot read a good book without becoming enriched, both in thought and in vocabulary. Every good author spreads out before you a treasure house of precious stones. They are there for you to take. But you must *take* them. So many of us leave a book without having taken anything away from it. We shall here consider not the thought of a great book, but its language. Carry away from a book all the new good words that you can find in it. Read Shakespeare or Milton or Dickens, or any of the other masters, with a note-book always at your side.

Let us suppose, for instance, that you are reading *The Tempest*. You come to Prospero's speech in which he explains his exile to his daughter, Miranda:

> This King of Naples, being an enemy
> To me inveterate, hearkens my brother's suit;
> Which was, that he, in lieu o' the premises,
> Of homage and I know not how much tribute,
> Should presently extirpate me and mine
> Out of the dukedom.

You take your note-book and jot down all the words about whose meaning you are not certain:

inveterate
suit
extirpate

Look these words up in the dictionary. You find that *inveterate* means *of long standing;* that *suit* may sometimes mean *petition;* and that *extirpate,* from the Latin *ex* (out) + *stirps* (root), means *to root out, to expel*. Thus, in the short space of five and a half lines, Shakespeare has enabled you to add three words to your vocabulary.

Or take that exquisite sonnet of Keats, *The Terror of Death:*

> When I have fears that I may cease to be
> Before my pen has gleaned my teeming brain,
> Before high-piléd books, in charact'ry
> Hold like rich garners the full-ripened grain;
>
> When I behold, upon the night's starr'd face,
> Huge cloudy symbols of a high romance,
> And think that I may never live to trace
> Their shadows, with the magic hand of chance;
>
> And when I feel, fair Creature of an hour!
> That I shall never look upon thee more,
> Never have relish in the fairy power
> Of unreflecting love—then on the shore
>
> Of the wide world I stand alone, and think
> Till love and fame to nothingness do sink.

Now, just as you did before, jot down in your note-book the words in the above sonnet which are unfamiliar to you:

gleaned
teeming
charactery
garners

On looking these words up in the dictionary, you learn that *to glean* means *to collect patiently,* as one collects the grain that has been left by the reapers; that *teeming* means *abundant, full, overflowing;* that *charactery* means *a system of symbols,* or a collection of letters and syllables that are combined into words and thoughts; and that *a garner* means *a granary,* a place for storing food. This sonnet, therefore, has added four new words to your vocabulary. Incidentally, it has enriched your imagination with a beautiful metaphor, in which the poet identifies his poetry with a harvest of grain. Note how carefully John Keats has carried out this metaphor. Every word he uses in it has been borrowed directly from the language of the field and the farm.

The poets, you will find, are great vocabulary-builders. Your note-book, if used intelligently in your reading of poetry, is an Aladdin's Lamp that will enable you, as if by magic, to build rapidly and permanently a palace of words that will serve and delight you. But the poets, after all, are the friends of our holidays. They are not, in most cases, our everyday companions. What you are after, very likely, is to acquire a good, work-able, *everyday* style. For this purpose you will want to go not so much to the poet who dwells in the clouds, but to the prose writer who feels at home in *your* environment and in whose environment *you* feel at home. Let us, therefore, select at random any prose passage:

> "Dimmesdale's nerve seemed absolutely destroyed. His moral force was abased into more than child-ish weakness. It grovelled helpless on the ground, even while his intellectual faculties retained their pristine strength. . . . Hester Prynne was shocked at the condition to which she found him reduced . . . Years had come and gone since the day of her ig-nominy."
>
> —From Hawthorne's *The Scarlet Letter*

This passage, with the aid of our note-book and dictionary, enriches our vocabulary with *four* hitherto misunderstood or only partially understood words. We find that *abased* means *debased, lowered, reduced;* that *grovel* is a picturesque old English word which literally means *to crawl with the face upon the ground;* that *pristine* means *original, former;* and that *ignominy* means *the loss of one's good name,* hence *dis-grace.*

To come nearer to our own day—since words keep changing all the time—let us see what new words we can add to our vocabulary in a random passage taken from Galsworthy's *Forsyte Saga:*

> "A little private hotel over a well-known restaurant was Jolyon's haunt in Paris. He hated his fellow-Forsyte's abroad—vapid as fish out of water in their well-trodden runs the Opera, Rue de Rivoli, and Moulin Rouge . . . Paris was always to him more at-tractive in winter. The acrid savour from woodsmoke . . . the sharpness of the winter sunshine . . . the

open cafés defying keen-eyed winter . . . all informed
him that in winter Paris possessed a soul which, like
a migrant bird, in high summer flew away . . . Jolyon
soon found that for those who desired a static condition of the affections, Paris was at once the first and
the last place in which to be friendly with a pretty
woman . . . Irene's philosophy of life seemed to march
in admirable step with his own—ironically mistrust-
ful, susceptible to beauty, almost passionately humane
and tolerant, yet subject to instinctive rigidities of
which as a mere man he was less capable."

This passage yields four interesting words with which to
enrich our vocabulary:

Vapid means *spiritless, dead, insipid.*
Acrid means *sharp, harsh, irritating.*
Static in this passage is an adjective, not to be con-
    fused with the radio term which is used as a noun.
    The meaning of *static* here is *standing still, at rest.*
Rigidity means *stiffness.*

To come still nearer to our own time and interests, let us
look at the following passage selected from a recent issue of
the *Saturday Evening Post:*

"The fanatic is a man of transcendental good intentions. He is called of God, as he sees it, to do good to
others, whether the others like it or not. . . .
"Anyone who supposes that the modern dictators
think of themselves . . . in an opprobrious sense, as
oppressors, misreads human nature."

From these few lines we get two words to add to our
vocabulary:

transcendental means *superior, supreme, excelling.*
opprobrious means *disgraceful.*

§ 4

USING THE DICTIONARY

The importance of using the dictionary has been emphasized
so frequently in this book that it is hardly necessary to insist
any longer upon it at this point. If you use the dictionary intel-

ligently, you will find it not only an aid to education, but a source of pleasure. The reading of the dictionary, as Christopher Morley once pointed out, can be turned into one of the most interesting indoor sports. The study of words, their derivations and their meanings and their relations, can be made as exhilarating as the reading of an adventure story. Indeed, the dictionary *is* an adventure story—the story of the adventures of human minds to express themselves and to understand one another.

Read the dictionary. Study it. Help yourself to its treasures. Supply yourself with ample material for building your ideas into the simplest and most beautiful forms. And then you will be ready to practice with your materials by arranging them tentatively into various groups. This will be the next and the most important step in your mastery of English words.

§ 5

LEARNING THROUGH PRACTICE

After you have acquired a sufficiently large vocabulary, learn to use it. Discover for yourself, through the method of trial and error, how the very same words produce different effects in different settings. When words are put into the best arrangement, or setting, they *cohere*—that is, they stick together into an attractive jewel of thought. Every word has not only a *meaning of its own,* but a *music of its own.* It is of the utmost importance to grasp this law and to apply it in your speech and your writing. A number of words put into *one sort of group* will grate upon the ear and antagonize your audience. The very same words, put into *another sort of group,* will delight the ear and *entice* your audience. Let us illustrate the importance of this point by means of a few excerpts. The first of these excerpts is paraphrased from a passage in Oliver Goldsmith's *The Vicar of Wakefield:*

> I therefore now was left upon the world once more at large; but it was then a thing I was used to. However, my skill could avail me nothing in music in a country where every peasant was a better than I musician; but I by this time had acquired another

> talent which answered as well my purpose, and this
> was in disputation a skill.

The above passage is not only meaningless but cacophonous
(harsh-sounding). See how much more pleasantly the self-
same words glide into the ear if we rearrange them as the
author originally wrote them:

> I now, therefore, was left once more upon the
> world at large; but then it was a thing I was used to.
> However, my skill in music could avail me nothing
> in a country where every peasant was a better musi-
> cian than I; but by this time I had acquired another
> talent which answered my purpose as well, and this
> was a skill in disputation.

The next excerpt is even more striking. It is a prose render-
ing of Tennyson's *In Memoriam,* Section LIII:

> O we yet trust that the final goal of ill will be
> somehow good,—that there will be a good end to
> pangs of nature, to sins of will, to defects of doubt
> and to taints of blood: that nothing walks without a
> goal; that not a single life shall be destroyed, or cast
> to the void as rubbish, when God has completed the
> pile; that not a single worm is cut in vain; that not
> a single moth foolishly aiming at the useless fire is
> shrivelled up, in order to serve the gain of another.
> Lo, we know nothing. I can only trust that at last,
> far off, to all, at last, good shall come, and every
> winter shall change to spring.
> This is how my dream runs: but what am I? An
> infant crying in the darkness for the light: and whose
> only vocabulary is a cry.

The words in the above passage have been but slightly
changed from the original. Their *order,* however, has been
changed, and their music almost entirely destroyed. Observe
now how a poet can turn ordinary words into sublime music,
and how *you* can profit by the example:

> O yet we trust that somehow good
>   Will be the final goal of ill,
>   To pangs of nature, sins of will,
> Defects of doubt and taints of blood:

That nothing walks with aimless feet;
  That not one life shall be destroyed,
  Or cast as rubbish to the void,
When God hath made the pile complete;

That not a worm is cloven in vain;
  That not a moth with vain desire
  Is shrivelled in a fruitless fire,
Or but subserves another's gain.

Behold we know not anything;
  I can but trust that good shall fall
  At last—far off—at last, to all,
And every winter change to spring.

So runs my dream: but what am I?
  An infant crying in the night:
  An infant crying for the light:
And with no language but a cry.

To repeat, then,—there are seven good ways to increase your vocabulary:

1. *Study the meaning of every word whose spelling you are trying to learn.*

2. *Study the meaning of every word whose pronunciation you are trying to learn.*

3. *Learn to distinguish between the different shades of meaning in groups of apparently similar words.*

4. *Listen to good speakers.*

5. *Read good books.*

6. *Use the dictionary.*

7. *Learn through practice.*

Then, when you have acquired your stock of words, practice to group them most effectively into phrases and clauses and sentences. This will be discussed in the next two chapters.

CHAPTER VIII

Effective Phrases

§ 1

KINDS OF PHRASES

A *Phrase* is a group of words which has no subject and verb, and therefore does not make a statement. For example:

a group of words	in many ways
over the hills	before Christmas

There are several kinds of phrases:

1. A *Noun Phrase* is a phrase used as a noun. In the sentence

Joan of Arc was called the Maid of Orleans.

Joan of Arc is a *noun phrase*.

2. An *Adjective Phrase* is a phrase used as an adjective. In the sentence

She has a heart *of gold.*

of gold is an *adjective phrase* meaning *golden.*

3. A *Verb Phrase* is a phrase used as a verb. In the sentence

I *have been reading* this book.

have been reading is a *verb phrase.*

4. An *Adverbial Phrase* is a phrase used as an adverb. In the sentence

I saw him *in the evening.*

in the evening is an *adverbial phrase* denoting the time of the action of the verb *saw.*

5. A *Prepositional Phrase* is a phrase used as a preposition. In the sentence

> He did it *for the sake of* his sister.

for the sake of is a *prepositional phrase* modifying the noun *sister*.

6. A *Conjunctional Phrase* is a phrase used as a conjunction. In the sentence

> I am telling you this *in order that* you may know the truth.

in order that is a *conjunctional phrase*.

§ 2

AVOIDING HACKNEYED PHRASES

You will always recognize the uneducated man by the phrases he uses. The less ideas he has of his own, the more hackneyed will be his phraseology. A *hackneyed phrase* is *a phrase which is used too much*. The term *hackneyed* was originally applied to a horse that was let out for hire to anybody— an overworked plug. Avoid such overworked *plugs*. They will not carry your thoughts very far. Following are a few of the phrases—you will easily recognize them and others like them —that have been worked to death through too much use. Avoid them:

a grand and glorious feeling
a charming person
a small world after all
last but not least
nipped in the bud
well done
the blushing bride
fair maiden
plays divinely
along these lines
old as the hills
so long
a brilliant performance
congratulations and good luck

better late than never
parting of the ways
the good old way
hungry as a bear
gales of laughter
ray of hope
tried and true
sly as a fox
filthy lucre
depths of despair
spick and span
smashed to smithereens
with bated breath
as good as gold

§ 3
IS SLANG PERMISSIBLE?

Some of the best authorities would give a negative answer to this question. Yet slang persists; and many a slang word, like an impertinent but brilliant urchin, lives to grow into a respectable citizen in the community of words. Most slang words are, of course, taboo in polite conversation. Yet a judicious and sparing use of slang may sometimes add spice to a conversation or a piece of writing that otherwise would be extremely dull.

But bear this in mind. If you *must* resort to slang, be *very* judicious and *very* sparing in its use. We speak and we write in order to please others. Try to avoid offending those whom you are anxious to please; for some educated people are really offended by the use of slang. Call them prejudiced, if you like; but if you want them to listen to you and to read you, try not to irritate them unduly.

Yet most people are not averse to the use of slang. Even the college professor and the poet will occasionally resort to a bit of *"slanguage"* in order to give more life to their *language*. Here are a number of slang expressions that are almost respectable enough to be admitted to full citizenship in the Republic of English Letters, and yet at the same time spicy enough to supply a relish which the older and more respectable words are unable to give:

lounge lizard	to get a kick out of
to call it a day	sugar-daddy
to fill the bill	gold-digger
to keep tabs on	to soft-soap
to give him the air	a hold-up
to fly off the handle	wise-cracker
to stick to it	to be all in
sob sister	to be all tuckered out
to squeal	to laugh *that* off
to tip off	to give him the cold shoulder
to pussyfoot	to get one's goat
to pull the wool over	to go places and see things
to poke fun at	deep stuff

to get away with	to go over with a bang
happy landings	to take a crack at
to high hat	to go on a joy ride
to flop	to give him the once-over
to go over the top	

§ 4
SELECTING THE RIGHT PHRASE

The best way to select your own phrases is to watch the phrases of the most competent speakers and writers. Let us glance at a few examples:

> Perhaps there is no more impressive scene on earth than the solitary extent of the Campagna of Rome under evening light. Let the reader imagine himself for a moment withdrawn from the sounds and motion of the living world, and sent forth alone into this wild and wasted plain. The earth yields and crumbles beneath his foot, tread he never so lightly, for its substance is white, hollow, and carious (decaying), like the dusty wreck of the bones of men.

Note, in the above passage from John Ruskin's *Modern Painters,* how every phrase has been carefully selected, and how the parts of every phrase have been skillfully put together, in order to produce the effect of wide and lonely stretches of land. Observe especially such striking phrases as: *the solitary extent; withdrawn from the sounds; sent forth alone; wild and wasted plain; the dusty wreck.*

The following selection from Robert Louis Stevenson's *Virginibus Puerisque* (For Girls and Boys) illustrates the same point:

> Happily we all shoot at the moon with ineffectual arrows; our hopes are set on inaccessible El Dorado (an imaginary city full of gold); we come to an end of nothing here below.

What makes this passage so effective is the succession of such phrases as: *with ineffectual arrows; an inaccessible El Dorado; to an end of nothing.*

Or look at the following jewel-box of glittering phrases taken from the Bible:

> clothed with glory and majesty
> wrapped in light as with a garment
> Thy heavens, the work of Thy fingers
> the Lord is my fortress
> the arrows of the lightning
> the shield of Thy salvation
> the molten mirror of the skies
> when the morning stars sang together
> the clouds are His chariot
> the chains of the Pleiades
> a well of living waters
> answer a fool according to his folly
> the vials of the wrath of God

Next to the Bible, the works of the great poets are the repositories of the most beautiful phrases. The word *poet* means *maker*. The poet is a maker of images and of phrases. To take but a single example, let us look at Byron's *She Walks in Beauty:*

> She walks in beauty, like the night
> Of cloudless climes and starry skies,
> And all that's best of dark and bright
> Meet in her aspect and her eyes;
> Thus mellowed to that tender light
> Which heaven to gaudy day denies.
>
> One shade the more, one ray the less,
> Had half impair'd the nameless grace
> Which waves in every raven tress
> Or softly lightens o'er her face,
> Where thoughts serenely sweet express
> How pure, how dear their dwelling place.
>
> And on that cheek and o'er that brow
> So soft, so calm, yet eloquent,
> The smiles that win, the tints that glow
> But tell of days in goodness spent,—
> A mind at peace with all below,
> A heart whose love is innocent.

This poem is like a necklace of phrases. Note how, one after the other, they are strung upon the thread of the poet's thought to produce the effect of dark beauty: *like the night; starry skies; that tender light* which is denied *to gaudy day; every raven tress.* Then note the spiritual tone that the poet weaves into the harmony of her physical beauty by means of the phrases: *thoughts serenely sweet; how pure, how dear; days in goodness spent; a mind at peace.*

Take your great prose writers and poets as models. See how accurately they fit the right phrase into the right place. Then, using whatever powers nature has bestowed upon you, try to do in your modest way what the great writers have done in their sublime way. *You can perfect your phrases, and put beauty and fire into your style, provided you practice and practice constantly and whole-heartedly.* In addition to the above examples, the following section contains a list of good phrases,—not to copy but to serve as models for your own phrase-making.

§ 5

EXAMPLES OF GOOD PHRASES

The following phrases are all selected from the works of the best writers:

    a thing of beauty
    a joy forever
    a vision of delight
    to pay the piper
    a touching face, painted as on vacancy
    a step as light as summer air
    the golden window of the sunrise
    well-apparel'd April
    on the heel of limping winter
    night's cloak
    a fly in your ointment
    the ounce of sour in a pound of sweet
    a pagan suckled in a creed outworn
    like sleeping flowers
    the cruel, crawling foam
    the crocus, with his cup of gold
    the innumerable murmur of the bees
    the velvet hum of bees
    imperious Caesar

books in running brooks
sermons in stones
deluged with sunlight
blue Italian skies: In this phrase, every word is important; *blue skies* or *Italian skies* would not have nearly the same effect as *blue Italian skies*.
the right word for the right idea
the vigorous march of his elocution
noble parenthood
to cleanse and exalt
the saving grace
the brightness of the firmament
Death, the King of Terrors and the Terror of Kings
Death, the Grand Destroyer
Death, the Prince of Phantoms
the dark domain of Death
Death, the Deliverer
the pathetic fallacy
the bright, troubled period of boyhood
an imperious heart
smiling little house
the bridge of chaos
like dying fire on defiled altars
a solemn space of quiet sky
watch-towers of dark clouds
the click of a cane
the sawing of the violins
the deep wail of the bass viols
the liquid trilling of a flute
jerky black eyes
black, raisin-like eyes
wiry moustache
a dumpling of a woman
a sight to beggar description
the clouds—angels of rain and lightning
the locks of the approaching storm
tameless and swift and proud as the wind
the trumpet of a prophecy
perpetual benediction
a silver fleet of fairy sailboats
a tale told by an idiot
full of sound and fury
to outfly the wind
convulsions of laughter

the inward man
leafy seclusion
robed in a marble toga
a healthy mind in a healthy body
a divine despair
the lone couch of his everlasting sleep
a city of shadowy palaces
to justify the ways of God to men
to be or not to be
the bush with frizzled hair
the friendly silence of the quiet moon
a sleep full of sweet dreams
a solemn stillness
the beetle's droning flight
the light that never was on sea or land
the perished leaves of Hope
the white throne of God

You will note that the titles of many successful novels or poems or plays are clever phrases. Here are just a few, for example:

A Midsummer-Night's Dream
A Winter's Tale
Now in November
With Fire and Sword
Gone with the Wind
Journey's End
A Tale of Two Cities
The House of Seven Gables
The Mysterious Stranger
The Good Earth
Beauty and the Beast
The Magnificent Obsession
The Lion and the Mouse
Much Ado About Nothing
The Devil's Disciple
The Garden of Allah
The Vagabond King
The Comedy of Life
The Comedy of Errors
The Divine Comedy
War and Peace
The Old Curiosity Shop

The Three Musketeers
Far from the Madding Crowd
Strange Interlude
Desire under the Elms
Arms and the Man
An Enemy of the People
The Revolt of the Angels

These and similar successful phrases can be multiplied indefinitely. Take any literary masterpiece, and you will find it studded with good phrases as the sky is studded with stars. Every great writer is a master of words and a master of phrases. But words and phrases alone are not sufficient to produce a work of art. The words and phrases must be skillfully combined into clauses and sentences.

This we shall discuss in the next chapter.

CHAPTER IX

Clauses and Sentences

§ 1

BUILDING A CLAUSE

A *Clause* is more than a phrase and less than a sentence. It is more than a phrase because it contains both subject and verb, and therefore makes a statement. It is less than a sentence because it is only *part* of a sentence. In the sentences that follow the *"italicized"* sections are clauses:

> The book *which he is reading* is a masterpiece.
> He stopped *when he saw the traffic light.*
> This is the house *where my brother lives.*

Just as words are combined into phrases, so phrases are combined into clauses. Add a subject and a verb to a phrase, and you have a clause.

There are two kinds of clauses: *independent,* or *co-ordinate* clauses; and *dependent,* or *subordinate* clauses.

An *independent* clause is one which can exist by itself. It is connected to the rest of the sentence by a *co-ordinating* conjunction (*and, or, nor, but*). If you remove the conjunction, the clause can still be written as a complete sentence. Example:

> I opened the door, *and John Smith came in.*

This sentence consists of two parts, and each part is an independent clause. Remove the conjunction, and the two clauses can be written as two separate independent sentences:

> I opened the door. John Smith came in.

A *dependent* clause is one which can *not* exist by itself. It is introduced by a *subordinating* conjunction (*if, that, though, where, when, unless,* etc.). If you remove the conjunction, the clause can *not* be written as a complete sentence. Example:

He was not in *when I arrived.*

In this sentence, if you remove the conjunction and then try to write the two clauses as two separate sentences, you will have destroyed the meaning. The two sentences

He was not in. I arrived.

make no sense.

Dependent clauses, like phrases, may serve as parts of speech:

1. A *Noun Clause* is a clause used as a noun. For example:

That Shakespeare is a great poet is known to all.

The dependent clause introduced by the word *that* is a noun clause and serves as the *subject* of the verb *is.*

I know *who you are.*

The dependent noun clause in the above sentence serves as the object of the verb *know.*

2. An *Adjective Clause* is a clause used as an adjective. For example:

He likes the house *in which he lives.*

The clause *in which he lives* is an adjective clause and modifies the noun *house.*

3. An *Adverbial Clause* is a clause used as an adverb. It may modify a verb, an adjective, or another adverb. Examples:

They arrived *after the play had started* (modifies the verb *arrived*).

He is richer *than I thought* (modifies the adjective *richer*).

He acted more nervously *than he felt* (modifies the adverb *more nervously*).

The clause is a rich and handy tool for the writer. It enables him to express at least nine different ideas. A dependent clause may denote:

1. Time (answering the question *when*).
   Speak to me *before you leave.*
2. Place (answering the question *where*).
   Where thou goest, there go I.
3. Cause (answering the question *why*).
   The judge freed him *because he was convinced of his honesty.*
4. Concession (making an *admission*).
   Although we are defeated, we are not downhearted.
5. Purpose (answering the question *why*).
   Study, *in order that you may learn.*
6. Result (stating the *effect*).
   He was a timid child, *so that everybody bullied him.*
7. Condition (stating the *circumstance*).
   If you come, I shall be pleased.
8. Manner (answering the question *how*).
   He acted *as if he were guilty.*
9. Degree (answering the question *how much*).
   He earns *as much as he deserves.*

§ 2

BUILDING A SENTENCE

A sentence is a group of words which contains a subject and a predicate, and which expresses a complete thought. As words are combined into phrases and phrases into clauses, clauses are combined into sentences. The sentence is the largest grammatical unit in the English language. Yet it may sometimes consist of only a few words, or even a single word. For example:

He speaks well.
Hurry!

In form, there are three kinds of sentences: *simple*, *compound*, and *complex*.

1. A *Simple Sentence* is a sentence which contains but *one subject* and *one predicate*. Examples:

The boy walks.
The entire book was written in the short space of six months.

2. A *Compound Sentence* is a sentence which contains two or more independent clauses. Examples:

> For men may come and men may go, but I go on for ever.
> The whistle blew; the weavers stopped their work; and the doors of the factory opened like the sluices of a mill stream.

3. A *Complex Sentence* is a sentence which contains one principal clause and one or more dependent clauses. Examples:

> Though he studied hard, he found plenty of time for play.
> The stylistic virtues of that book grow out of the fact that there runs through it with almost desperate earnestness a sense of the pain and loveliness that lie at the very heart of life.

§ 3
LOOSE AND PERIODIC SENTENCES

A man's sentences, like his clothes, may fit either loosely or snugly. A loose sentence is a sentence which can be stopped before the end and still make sense. It is, in other words, a *compound* sentence. Examples:

> He fought with his fear again; he overcame it; he hitched the pack over his shoulder; then he lurched on down the slope.
> This is simple; this is clear; this is sublime; this is what I call inspired literature.

Each of the above sentences can be stopped in more than one place and still express a complete thought. They are therefore *loose* sentences.

A periodic sentence is a sentence which can *not* be stopped before the end. It is, in other words, a *complex* sentence. Examples:

> This illustrious general, who was commander-in-chief of the Grecian forces in the Persian War, and who by his services upon that occasion delivered his country from the tyranny with which it was threat-

ened, having been driven into exile by the jealousy which his great talents had raised, did not acquiesce under the ingratitude of his fellow-citizens.

To a mind rightly composed it is not so much the benefits received as the affectionate zeal from which they flow, that gives them their best and most valuable recommendation.

Neither of the above sentences can be stopped before the end without destroying the meaning. They are therefore periodic sntences.

Which type of sentence are you to use—the loose, or the periodic? The answer is: both. On certain occasions your thoughts will be in a relaxed mood. You will want to wrap them in a comfortable, loose robe. On other occasions, your thoughts will be involved. The tight, periodic style, one clause telescoping into another, and all the clauses contributing their complex meaning to the whole, will on such occasions be the best style to follow.

In general, a simple style is preferable to a complex style. The tendency among modern writers is to use short and loose rather than long and involved sentences. Too much simplicity, however, makes for monotony. Avoid monotony. A long succession of short simple sentences, or of sentences strung loosely together, is likely to become jerky. Construct your sentences in such a manner as to produce a *smooth* and *fluent* style. A good writer will vary the form of his sentences in every paragraph. He will never allow any lengthy passage in his work to consist entirely of loose or entirely of periodic sentences. Note, for example, the following passage taken from Arnold Bennett's *Literary Taste:*

Style cannot be distinguished from matter. When a writer conceives an idea he conceives it in a form of words. That form of words constitutes his style, and it is absolutely governed by the idea. The idea can exist only in words, and it can exist in only one form of words. You cannot say exactly the same thing in two different ways. Slightly alter the expression, and you slightly alter the idea. Surely it is obvious that the expression cannot be altered without altering the thing expressed! A writer, having conceived and expressed an idea, may, and probably will, "polish it

up." But what does he polish up? To say that he pol-
ishes up his style is merely to say that he is polishing
up his idea, that he has discovered faults or imper-
fections in his idea, and is perfecting it.

Observe how skillfully Bennett has molded his sentences
into a paragraph of flexible thought. The first sentence is
simple; the second is complex; the third, loose; the fourth,
loose; the fifth, simple; the sixth, loose; the seventh, complex; the eighth, complex and periodic; the ninth, simple; the
tenth, a combination of the complex and the compound; and
the entire paragraph an excellent example of a simple style
with just enough complexity to save it from monotony.

§ 4

ACHIEVING VARIETY IN SENTENCE STRUCTURE

The secret of a good style, like the spice of life, is variety.
One of the best ways to achieve variety is to begin your sentences with different parts of speech. For example:

1. Begin with an adverb:
   Slowly the clock ticked away the seconds.
2. Begin with an adjective:
   Great is the power of the king.
3. Begin with a verb:
   Go to the ant, thou sluggard.
4. Begin with a preposition:
   In the entire assembly there was not a dissent-
   ing voice.
5. Begin with a pronoun:
   Who among you is without sin?
6. Begin with a conjunction:
   While this is true, nevertheless we must be
   cautious.
7. Begin with a noun in the objective case:
   Wisdom he possessed to a large degree.

The successful writer avoids monotony by varying the beginnings of his sentences. Observe the following passage from
Kipling's *Watches of the Night*:

   Mark how Kismet works! *This* would not arrive
   once in a hundred years. *Toward* the end of his din-

ner . . . the Colonel let out his waistcoat and leaned over the table to look at some Mission Reports. The *bar* of the watch-guard worked through the button-hole, and the watch . . . slid quietly on to the carpet. *Where* the bearer found it next morning and kept it.

Then the Colonel went home to the wife of his bosom . . .

In the above passage there are six sentences, and no two of them begin alike. The first begins with a verb; the second, with a pronoun; the third, with a preposition; the fourth, with a noun (preceded by the article *the*); the fifth, with an adverb; and the sixth, with a conjunction. This sort of variety gives flexibility and color to a style.

§ 5

PITFALLS IN STYLE

If you want to become a good stylist, you must try to avoid the following common errors:

Tautology

The word *tautology,* derived from the Greek *tautologia,* means *the repetition of the same thing.* If you can possibly help it, don't use the identical word or phrase twice in the same sentence. A repetitious style sounds slipshod, and at times even ridiculous. A young politician was recently invited to address a group of insurance men at a banquet. Here is how he began his speech:

> "Gentlemen, I am glad to see you have such an enjoyable time enjoying yourselves on this glad occasion."

The chairman, who was more facetious than polite, acknowledged the speech in these words:

> "We are indeed happy and honored to have heard the Honorable Mr. R——'s address on this happy occasion."

Sometimes, in order to produce a certain effect, an author deliberately repeats the same word again and again. For example:

> "Men are born into the State, are members of the State, must obey the laws enacted by the State, in time of danger must come to the defence of the State, must, if necessary, hazard their lives for the State."   —*Lyman Abbott*

If you have a special reason for repeating yourself, do so carefully and, until you have become an expert stylist, somewhat sparingly. Otherwise you must avoid tautological expressions.

Redundancy

Redundancy is closely allied to tautology. Derived from the Latin *redundare,* to overflow, it means *overabundance,* or *superfluity.* Avoid such superfluous expressions as *audible to the ear, visible to the eye, palatable to the taste.* The words *to the ear, to the eye,* and *to the taste* are unnecessary, and therefore redundant.

Following is a list of errors of redundancy into which inexperienced speakers and writers frequently fall:

> *descend down* for *descend*
> *fall down* for *fall*
> *join together* for *join*
> *the real truth* for *the truth*
> *most perfect* for *perfect*
> *panacea for all ills* for *panacea*
>   (The word *panacea* means *remedy for all ills.*)
> *seems evident* for *seems*
> *win out* for *win*
> *lose out* for *lose*
> *start out* for *start*
> *final end* for *end*
> *bibliography of books* for *bibliography*
> *one and the same* for *the same*
> *dead rather than alive* for *dead*

Ambiguity

Avoid ambiguous expressions,—that is, expressions that have a double meaning. For example:

"The *revolting* army of the South fought at Gettysburg."

The word *revolting* may mean either *rebellious* or *disgusting*.

"I will sit on the grass and *rock*."

This may mean either

"I will sit on the grass and I will rock,"

or

"I will sit on the grass and on the rock."

"The colored woman needs washing."

Does she need to take in washing, or does she need to be washed?

Avoid ambiguity in the use of pronouns. Note, for example, the following sentences:

"He said that if he would come to see him, he would go with him to the theatre."

"Jane told Sally that they would probably go to Europe together. She was happy to learn that she would see those famous historical monuments. She herself had already visited them, but she wanted her to enjoy them also. She was therefore very anxious to go."

The above sentences are purposely exaggerated. Yet to a lesser degree even the best of writers are sometimes ensnared in the use of their pronouns. Observe how carelessly the following sentence is constructed:

"The father of Mithridates was murdered when he was a child, and for some time he led a wandering life."   —*Froude*

The above sentence should be rewritten somewhat as follows:

"When Mithridates was a child, his father was murdered, and for some time the young boy led a wandering life."

Dangling Constructions

A dangling construction is a construction in which a participle (a part of the verb used as an adjective) modifies a word to which it does not belong and is therefore left "dangling in the air." For example:

> *Having taken* a bath, the *train* left for Chicago.

The participle *having taken* modifies the word *train* grammatically, but does not belong to it logically. The sentence, therefore, is absurd. There are two ways of correcting it:

1. Having taken a bath, we left on the train for Chicago.
2. After we had taken a bath, the train left for Chicago.

(Wrong form) Approaching the mountain, snow could be seen on the top.
(Correct form) Approaching the mountain, we could see snow on the top.

(Wrong form) Trying to change places, the canoe tipped over.
(Correct form) As we tried to change places, the canoe tipped over.

(Wrong form) Running into the house, a dead man was found in the parlor. (How can a dead man run?)
(Correct form) As they ran into the house, they found a dead man in the parlor.

(Wrong form) Having fallen asleep, the speaker kept on in his monotonous voice.
(Correct form) The audience having fallen asleep, the speaker kept on in his monotonous voice.

Awkwardness

The young writer is frequently guilty of two kinds of awkward expressions:

1. Forgetting that he must write for the ear as well as for the eye, he produces a disagreeable similarity of sounds. For example:

> The continuation of inflation is a danger to the nation.
> He talks equally fluently.
> Napoleon suffered a complete defeat on his retreat from Moscow.
> This is a mystery of history.

2. Neglecting to arrange his thoughts clearly in his own mind, he sets down a jumble of confusing phrases in an incoherent sequence. For example:

> The two brothers, as has been observed, went, in the opinion of their father, too far in their attempt to repay a perhaps unnecessary and, it seemed, at any rate not a very urgent, obligation.
>
> He urged some jam which he had in a jar upon his sister.
>
> The Marathon runner saw a legless man racing by the cheering throng, and a wave of pity came over him.

Avoid all such sentences. Read your sentences aloud, in order to test their sound, and read them critically, in order to verify their clearness. In other words, look upon your writing *objectively* as well as *subjectively*. Try to be the impartial audience, as well as the partial author, of your work.

§ 6

IMPORTANT TERMS IN GRAMMAR AND IN RHETORIC

It is wise to familiarize yourself with the meaning and the usage of some of the more important terms that you will find in the standard books on style.

1. *Rhetoric.* Rhetoric may be defined as Advanced Grammar—the art of clear, forcible, and elegant use of language, either in speech or in writing.

2. *Onomatopoeia.* This term is used to denote the formation of words in imitation of natural sounds. For example: *ding-dong, buzz, hum, bow-wow, hiss, quack-quack.* Note the following line from Tennyson's *Idyls of the King: Oilily bubbled up the mere.* As you pronounce these words aloud, you actually make a bubbling sound with your lips to represent the bubbling sound of the pool.

3. *Personification.* This term denotes the endowment of an inanimate object with the figure or the sentiments of a human being. For example: *April smiled through her tears. Death swooped down on sable wings. The floods clap their hands. The ocean roared with lusty throat.*

4. *Metonymy.* This is a figure of speech in which one word is put for another word that it suggests. For example: He employs fifty *hands* (for fifty *workmen*). He keeps a good *table* (for good *food*). He likes *Thackeray* (meaning *his novels*). The ship went down with all *souls* on board (meaning with all *passengers* on board).

5. *Antithesis.* This term denotes a contrast of words, phrases, or ideas. For example: We are not *machines,* but *men.* The *prodigal* robs his *heir;* the *miser* robs *himself. Excess* of *ceremony* shows *want* of *breeding.*

6. *Cognate Objects.* A cognate object is one that is *related to* the verb. In other words, it repeats the same idea that is already implied in the verb. For example: He prayed a fervent *prayer.* He ran a good *race.* She breathed a deep *breath.* He died an easy *death.* In the above sentences observe that the intransitive verbs become transitive when they are followed by cognate objects.

7. *Elliptical Constructions.* Ellipsis in grammar denotes the omission of a word or words that can be readily supplied. For example: He is not so old as I (for *as I am old*). If so, you are a lucky man (for *if this is so*). While going to New York, they met with an accident (for *while they were going to New York*). Though tired, he won an easy victory (for *though he was tired*).

8. *Expletives.* An expletive (from the Latin *explere, to fill out*) is a *filling-out* word which is not necessary for the meaning or construction, but is added for rhetorical or metrical reasons. For example: *It* is said that you are about to leave for Europe. *It* is pleasant to be here. He found *it* very easy to get the job. He thought *it* proper to tell the truth. In the foregoing sentences, the word *it* has no grammatical construction, and is therefore an expletive.

9. *Parallelism in Sentence Structure.* This term denotes similarity of construction in parts of a sentence that are closely connected. Note the following constructions:

> (Wrong form) He was a lawyer and honest.
> (Correct parallel form) He was a lawyer and an
> honest man.

The first sentence is wrong because the conjunction *and* connects two *dissimilar* elements: the noun *lawyer* and the adjective *honest*. The second sentence is correct because the conjunction *and* connects two *similar* elements: the noun *lawyer* and the noun *man*.

> (Wrong form) What I told you and the thing that he learned from me are absolutely true.
>
> (Correct parallel form) What I told you and what I told him are absolutely true.
>
> (Wrong form) He was hit with the ball and they carried him off the field.
>
> (Correct parallel form) He was hit with the ball and he was carried off the field.
>
> (Wrong form) We came from an eternity and we are driven into an eternal unknown.
>
> (Correct form) We came from an eternity and we go into an eternity.

§ 7

EXAMPLES OF EFFECTIVE CLAUSES AND SENTENCES

> A thing of beauty is a joy forever.
> Beauty is its own excuse for being.
> The beginning of happiness is wisdom.
> Eat not to dullness; drink not to elevation.
> Self-worship means stagnation.
> Love is loveliest when embalmed in tears.
> Literature is the lasting expression in words of the meaning of life.
> The good book is an immortality rather than a life.
> Ye shall know the truth, and the truth shall make you free.
> True wisdom thanks death for what he takes, and still more for what he brings.
> Death is the physician of him whom medicine cannot cure.
> Live today and every day like a man of honor.
> Lord, I am not worthy.
> Let there be light.
> God gave him a great vision. The devil gave him an imperious heart.

Every glade of grass burned like the golden floor of heaven.

The light was all withdrawn; the shining church turned cold and dark; the stream forgot to smile; the birds were silent; and the gloom of winter dwelt on everything.

Truth, crushed to earth, shall rise again.

Forgive them, Father, for they know not what they do.

Syllables govern the world.

He that hath knowledge spareth his words.

Human speech is like a cracked tin kettle, on which we hammer out tunes to make bears dance when we long to move the stars.

In folly's cup still laughs the bubble joy.

True ease in writing comes from art, not chance, as those move easiest who have learned to dance.

He who dances must pay the piper.

The greatest of these is charity.

Laugh, and the world laughs with you; weep, and you weep alone.

Content is better than riches.

Discontent is man's worst evil.

Fortune favors the brave.

Bravery never goes out of fashion.

Fame is a magnifying glass.

Men hate those they have hurt.

We cannot hate those we know.

Hope springs eternal in the human breast.

Life is a long lesson in humility.

Too much humility is pride.

'Tis better to have loved and lost than never to have loved at all.

False love turns to hate.

All mankind loves a lover.

Revenge never repairs an injury.

Half the world laughs at the other half.

Thou stretchest out the heavens like a curtain.

There is nothing new under the sun.

He that increaseth knowledge increaseth sorrow.

The fear of the lord is the beginning of wisdom.

He prayeth best who loveth best.

A merry heart doeth good like medicine.

The desert shall blossom as a rose.

His heart died within him and he became as a stone.

As a jewel of gold in the snout of a swine, so is a fair woman without discretion.

As a dog returneth to his vomit, so a fool returneth to his folly.

He poured out his fury like fire.

The tongue of the just is as choice silver.

Man is born unto trouble, even as the sparks fly upward.

We spend our days as a tale that is told.

Wisdom excelleth folly as far as light excelleth darkness.

He mouths a sentence as a dog mouths a bone.

My age is like a lusty winter, frosty but kindly.

Art is long and time is fleeting.

Death lies on her, like an untimely frost upon the sweetest flower of the field.

Gloomy as night he stands.

Woman's grief is like a summer storm, short as it is violent.

Hope, like a gleaming taper's light, adorns and cheers us on our way.

The childhood shows the man, as morning shows the day.

Words are like leaves; some wither every year, and every year a younger race succeeds.

And now let us close this list of effective sentences with what Robert Louis Stevenson considered as being "the noblest and most useful sentence in modern literature":

It takes two to speak truth—one to speak and another to hear.

§ 8

CONCLUSION

The last sentence of section 7 is quoted from Thoreau's *A Week on the Concord and Merrimack Rivers*. Let us, for the purposes of this book, paraphrase the sentence:

It takes two to teach—one to teach and another to practice.

In other words, the only way for you to become skillful in the use of effective sentences is to practice, practice, and then practice some more. This is the note upon which I want to close the first part of the book. It is a trite, yet none the less true, statement that *practice makes perfect.* The greatest masters of literature have sharpened their talents upon the grindstone of constant toil. Observe what Gautier has to say about this in his essay on Balzac:

> "Sometimes a single phrase would occupy him for an entire sitting; it was appraised and re-appraised, twisted, kneaded, hammered, lengthened, abbreviated—written in a hundred different fashions; and, —strangest thing of all!—the correct, absolute form presented itself only after the exhaustion of all the *nearly*-correct forms. . . . Six, seven, and sometimes ten proofs were sent back, with erasures and retouches, without satisfying this author's desire for perfection."

If you want to become a good speaker or writer, follow the method of Balzac. Or else, follow the equally effective method of Stevenson, one of the truly great masters of English prose. Here, in his own words, is the manner in which he learned to become a writer:

> "I always kept two books in my pocket, one to read, one to write in. As I walked, my mind was busy fitting what I saw with appropriate words; when I sat by the roadside, I would either read, or a pencil and a notebook would be in my hand . . .
>
> "Whenever I read a book or a passage that particularly pleased me . . . in which there was either some conspicuous force or some happy distinction in the style, I must sit down at once and set myself to ape that quality . . . I remember one of these monkey tricks, which was called *The Vanity of Morals.* The first part was written no less than three times: first in the manner of Hazlitt, second in the manner of Ruskin, and third in the manner of Sir Thomas Browne . . .
>
> "That, like it or not, is the way to learn to write."

With this advice fresh in our minds, we can now turn to the second part of our book.

PART II
The Practical Uses of Effective English

CHAPTER X

The Art of Conversation

§ 1

SELECTING THE RIGHT SUBJECT

CONVERSATION is a fine art. It is the art of exchanging thoughts. It is an art which even the least gifted of us can cultivate. Not everybody can paint or play music, but almost everybody can talk. Conversation, therefore, is that art which affords the greatest pleasure to the greatest number. "To talk," writes Robert Louis Stevenson, "is our chief business in this world; and talk is by far the most accessible of pleasures. It costs nothing in money; it is all profit; it completes our education, founds and fosters our friendships, and can be enjoyed at any age and in almost every state of health."

Conversation is the most easily accessible and the most easily teachable of all the arts. All you need to do in order to become a good conversationalist is to find a subject that interests you tremendously. Speak about it in such a way as to show your interest, and you will find ready listeners.

What are the subjects that are most likely to interest you and other listeners? In general, there are three such subjects: myself, yourself, and the rest of the world. Everything you talk about can be reduced to one of these three subjects. Suppose you have selected politics as the theme of your conversation. Very well, ask yourself these three questions about it:

> How does it affect *me?*
> How does it affect *you?*
> How does it affect *the rest of the world?*

A political action may be very good for me, fairly good for you, and decidedly bad for others. Suppose a law has just been passed to regulate the wages of workers in textile mills. Suppose, further, that I am a worker in such a mill, that you are the owner of such a mill, and that a third person present at a certain gathering represents the general public which neither works in textile mills nor owns them. We start the ball of conversation on this subject, and before we know it we find ourselves tossing it about from mouth to mouth and from mind to mind in a dazzling succession of skillful throws and catches. It will be to my interest to prove that high wages are good for everybody. You will try to prove that high wages may compel you to shut down the factory. The third person, who is neither a worker nor a capitalist, will probably maintain that when the employer and the employee get into a fight, the innocent public is caught between them and receives most of the blows. And when our talk is over, each of us will go his way richer and wiser because of the conversation. For we have all had an opportunity to look into the other's mind and to see the complex and subtle motives that regulate our thoughts. "It is only by understanding others," said a great thinker, "that we can get our own hearts understood."

Any subject can be turned into an exhilarating conversation if attacked from this three-fold point of view: its relation to *me,* its relation to *you,* and its relation to *the rest of the world.* There are a large group of topics which may be handled in this way. To mention only a few of them:

1. The *weather.* Is the weather a trite subject for conversation? Yes and no. It is true that about ninety per-cent of our conversations deal with this subject, and that most of these conversations are extremely dull. But they are dull because we touch upon the subject superficially. The other day I overheard the following conversation in the elevator of a Boston office-building:

Elevator Boy: It's nice and bright this morning.
Stenographer: Yes.
Elevator Boy: D'you think it'll stay nice all day?
Stenographer: May be.
Elevator Boy: I think there's a cloud in the east.
Stenographer: I guess you're right.
Elevator Boy: Looks like rain this afternoon.
Stenographer: It sure does.

Most of the conversations about the weather are just as dull and just as pointless. And yet the weather is an interesting subject for conversation. Why? Because it is dramatic. Those who have lived in New England are well aware of the dramatic possibilities of the weather. Mark Twain once said that if you want to experience all the different kinds of weather, you needn't travel over the entire world. Just stay in New England for one day. There is always an unexpectedness in the weather which makes it one of the most dramatic subjects in the world. A flash of lightning may destroy a house or kill a man. A tornado may devastate a whole town. A downpour of rain may cause a Mississippi to overflow its banks and bring ruin to thousands of helpless creatures. The suddenness in the change of the weather is symbolical of the suddenness in the change of human affairs. We are still creatures of our climate. Our business, our health, our very life depends upon the caprices of the weather. Only a few days ago I heard in a friend's house a discussion about the weather which started with a few meaningless and conventional phrases such as those that were exchanged between the elevator boy and the stenographer, and which finally developed into a most fascinating discussion about the mystery of life and human destiny. And it all came about because one of the guests was wise enough to discuss the subject of the weather from the important three-fold point of view: its effect upon *me,* its effect upon *you,* and its effect upon *the rest of the world.*

The weather is the dramatic language in which heaven speaks to earth and discloses to the mind of man some of the mysterious workings of the mind of God. The weather, therefore, though superficially regarded as one of the most inane of subjects, can be made, and often *is* made, into one of the most interesting of conversational topics. From a talk on the weather it is easy for the mind to leap to the next topic of universal interest:

2. *Religion.* We who live in a democratic country are to be congratulated on our possession of free speech. We can discuss religion frankly and honestly and tolerantly without being spied upon. Conversation about religion is most fascinating, because we are all, either positively or negatively, interested in

it. Who are we? What are we doing in this world? Where do
we come from? Whither are we going? What do our Jewish
and Mohammedan friends think of us Christians? What do
we Christians think of the Jews and Mohammedans? Why are
some people atheists? Have they a right to their point of
view? What is the difference between religion and bigotry?
These are just a few of the many questions that can offer
rich fuel for the fire of a glowing conversation. But in a subject of this kind it is necessary to guard against blind passion.
A warm interest in your own point of view—yes; but a flaming hatred against the other fellow's point of view—certainly
not. For then your conversation will degenerate into vitupera-
tion.

Let your conversation, especially on matters of religion, be
always constructive rather than destructive. Even when you
argue with an atheist, try to understand him and try to make
him understand you. Remember the advice of James Whitcomb
Riley:

> And so I charge ye: by the thorny crown
>   And by the cross on which the Savior bled,
> And by your own soul's hope of fair renown,
>   Let something *good* be said.

"The words of the pure," we read in the sacred proverbs,
"are words of pleasantness."

Every conversation should be a duel of tongues. But it should
be a *bloodless* duel. Let the wit flash back and forth, but let it
not be a *cutting* wit. The most *brilliant* speakers are the most
tolerant speakers. It is bad manners, and bad conversation, to
hurt your opponent. A conversation is most witty when those
who take part in it are ready to laugh *with*, rather than *at*, one
another. A religious conversation that I heard a few weeks
ago threatened to become a battlefield of contradictory dogmas. Angry words and veiled insults were thrown about from
one speaker to another. Then there came a slight lull. Both
sides of the controversy were getting ready for the savage
final storm of abuse. But a wise old man saved the situation.
"Gentlemen," he said, "I have heard you discuss Protestantism
and Catholicism, Mohammedanism and Judaism. I have heard
the pros and cons about every 'ism under the sun. Yet I have

found that of all the 'isms there is only one that we ought to try to abolish."

"And what is that?" I asked.

"Rheumatism," he replied.

Needless to say, these words put an end to the tenseness of the situation. The religious opponents had a good laugh and parted as friends.

Religion, then, if discussed honestly and tolerantly, is one of the most interesting subjects for conversation. For in such a conversation we try to understand the purpose of God. The next subject we shall consider as offering good material for conversation is the conduct of men:

3. *Morals.* One of the most fascinating things to talk about is human character. What sort of man is our next door neighbor, our business partner, the fellow I met at the theater, the young doctor who wants to marry my daughter? What standards of right and wrong does he follow? Are these standards good, or bad, or indifferent? How do they apply to me, to you, and to the rest of the world? Start a conversation on any one of the above questions and you have started on a thrilling mental adventure. To discuss the moral values of life is not to indulge in gossip about your friends. Harmless gossip is in itself a good subject for conversation, and we shall consider it later in this chapter. For the present, however, we are interested in the ideals rather than in the doings of our friends.

The question of morals is almost as wide as the question of life itself. Open the morning newspaper. Almost every news-item that you see can be approached from the moral, or ethical, point of view. Every intelligent person should interest himself in the news behind the news, or rather in the *thought* behind the news. We may see the following headlines, among others:

President Plans New Wage Laws
Mussolini Defies the World
Spanish Rebels Mutiny
Movie Star Divorced
Murderer Executed

Each one of these headlines gives us food for thought, and material for conversation. For example:

President Plans New Wage Laws. What are the old wage laws? Are they just? Are they necessary? Is the President right in his effort to change them? Is he using the right methods? Is it possible to have an economic system without wages? Is it *desirable* to have such a system? Has anything of the sort ever been tried? What is the experience of Russia on this question? How does the Russian plan of compensating the workers compare with our own? Get all the information you can on these questions. First, read the editorials of your papers, consult the magazines, and ask your friends about these matters. Then you are ready to converse about them. Give your own opinions, listen to the opinions of those who disagree with you, learn what you don't know about the subject, and teach what you do know. For every intelligent conversation is a learning and a teaching.

Mussolini Defies the World. Why? Has the world offended Mussolini? Is Mussolini's action justified? Are the ideals of Mussolini in harmony with the ideals of the rest of the world? If not, which side is right? What attitude should the world assume in face of Mussolini's defiance? What would be the probable consequences of a defiant attitude? Of a conciliatory attitude? These and similar questions will start you off on a pleasant course of thought and talk. But, first of all, you must learn something about Mussolini and his ideas. Otherwise, your contribution to the talk will be negligible.

Spanish Rebels Mutiny. Why do they mutiny? Have they a right to do so? Just who are the mutineers? What are they fighting for? Is their cause just? Is this mutiny likely to affect the rest of Europe? The United States? If so, what is our *personal* attitude toward the mutiny? Should the United States take an interest in the Spanish Revolution? Is there any similarity between the Spanish Revolution and the Russian Revolution? The French Revolution? Our own Revolutionary War?

Movie Star Divorced. What were the causes of this divorce? What are the causes of divorce in general? Is an artistic career compatible with a happy family life? Can you cite instances to support either side of the question? What, if any, have been your own experiences on this subject? The experiences of your friends? Is there a good substitute for divorce? What can married people do to avoid divorce? To insure marital happiness?

Murderer Executed. What was the murder? What were the motives for it? Was the sentence just? Could it have been avoided? Is capital punishment ever justifiable? What substitutes would you suggest? What should be done to reduce the frequency of murder? Are the G-men more successful than the state police in curbing crime? If so, why? Was John Wesley right in his attitude toward criminals? John Wesley, you will recall, once saw a criminal being led to the place of execution, whereupon he remarked, "There, but for the grace of God, goes John Wesley." What he meant, of course, was this,—that each man is the product of his environment, and that had he, John Wesley, been subjected to an unfavorable environment, he would have turned out to be a criminal rather than a great religious teacher.

From the above examples we have seen how morals can supply us with many a fruitful subject for conversation, and how the daily newspaper can give us the necessary impetus to get such conversations going. From the subject of morals we come to what the philosophers call the subject of aesthetics, but what you and I will call the subject of art.

4. *Art.* Art is long, and life is short. There are enough interesting conversations in the field of art to keep anyone absorbed for a life-time. Whenever you find yourself in a circle of artists, you are lifted above the ordinary world. For artists are creatures of daring imagination. Their talk is generally unbridled. They make you dizzy with the flights of their fancies, but they exhilarate you in spite of your dizziness. The artist "mixes his conversational salad like a drunken god." A well-conducted conversation on art produces a divine intoxication. And, in order to share in such a conversation, it is not necessary to be an artist. A little judicious information, picked up here and there, will enable you to talk sensibly, if not expertly, on the subject. Read the latest articles on the current movements in art. Attend the exhibitions. Learn what the cubists, the dadaists and the surrealists are trying to do. Are their works sincere? Is a fur-lined cup, or a bundle of straw representing a man in love, or a rock with a human eye

in the center, an expression of true art or the reflection of an insane mind? Try to understand what the artist sees in his own work of art, and then decide, intelligently and sincerely, what *you* see in it. Don't be like the woman who attends the Saturday evening concerts of the Boston Symphony Orchestra. After every piece she looks to see what a certain Mr. W——, a well-known critic, is doing. If Mr. W—— applauds, she applauds. If Mr. W—— snickers, she snickers. If Mr. W—— stamps with his feet, she stamps with her feet. In her anxiety to ape the great man's point of view, she has deliberately refrained from cultivating a point of view of her own. As a result, this woman's soul is barren and her conversation, especially in the field of music, is about as stimulating as the cackling of a hen. In all your conversations about art, or about any other subject, be yourself. Try to develop your own taste. Let your thoughts and your words be your own. Don't allow yourself to become the mouthpiece of another person. For then you are nothing more than a ventriloquist's dummy.

In order to acquire a taste for art, learn all you can about it at first hand. To *talk* intelligently, you must *read* intelligently. "There is no charm in conversation without intelligence," writes Robert Collyer. I know a young lady who cannot paint a single stroke on the canvas, yet who is a most charming authority on art. She has read so widely and so carefully on the subject that even the professional artists among her acquaintances sit spellbound at her feet when she talks about art.

Her case is not unusual.

5. *Music.* This is a subject of universal interest. Everybody wants an answer to the following questions: Is jazz good music? Is it the sign of a low-brow to be fond of jazz? What do you think of the modern composers? Of Stravinsky? Of Prokofieff? Of our American composers? Was George Gershwin a great musician? Will his *Porgy and Bess* become a classic? Is he as popular as Jerome Kern? Has the radio advanced, or retarded our appreciation of music? Are there too many musical programs on the air? Too few? Do you know anything about the lives of the great musicians? Beethoven? Verdi? Mozart? Brahms? Wagner? Read the biographies of these men. You will

get out of them many appetizing tid-bits of conversational spice,—little human anecdotes about their lives, their friendships, their sufferings, their triumphs and their works. Take Romain Rolland's biography of Beethoven, for example. It will give you enough ammunition to keep a company spellbound for an entire evening.

6. *Literature.* Everybody nowadays reads. Get into the habit of discussing with your friends your most interesting adventures among books. Read the latest books and see the latest plays that have met with the approval of the critics. Make the characters in these books your intimate friends. Then, when you find yourself in the company of others who have read the same books, you can be talking intimately and interestingly about your mutual friends. A mutual sympathy for the same characters in a great book will turn an evening into a banquet of beauty; and a friendly disagreement about such characters will turn it into a breath-taking game. When you bring a great character in fiction into your conversation, you have enriched your party with an invited guest who will take an aggressive part in the festivities. Through you, *he* will talk; and in return, through him, *you* will glitter.

7. *Hobbies.* We all like to ride our own hobbies. In conversation, however, we get the greatest fun, and win the greatest enthusiasm, by riding *each other's* hobbies. It is a dull and dangerous thing to talk to people about what interests *you.* Talk about what interests *them,* and they will set you down as a good fellow and brilliant wit. Theodore Roosevelt traced his popularity to this fact. Whenever he had an appointment to meet anybody whom he was anxious to please, he spent the evening before the appointment in studying the man's hobby. The next day, when he met him, he spoke with such knowledge and such conviction and such *interest* about the thing that lay nearest to his visitor's heart that the visitor at once set him down as one of the most sympathetic and therefore one of the most *charming* men he had ever met.

The good teacher, the good doctor, the good lawyer, and the good salesman have all learned this lesson. They try to sell *you* to yourself. And in so doing, they sell *themselves* to you.

8. *Gossip.* This is the last, the most universal, and perhaps the most interesting of all subjects for conversation. We are all of us, God bless us, born gossipers. Let us all try to be *thoughtful* gossipers. Let us try to avoid the fate of the woman whose figure has been carved on one of the *misereres* in Shakespeare's church at Stratford-on-Avon. This woman was such an incurable gossiper that her tongue hung out of her mouth to a point well below her belt. Her fate, however, was mild in comparison with that of the gossipers in Algernon Blackwood's story. The tongues of these gossipers, you will recall, were turned into tongues of flame and burned holes in everything that their mouths touched.

There is nothing so vicious as evil gossip. On the tongues of thoughtless people gossip may descend to slander, and heaven help those who are the victims of such slander. Evil gossip is the shop-talk of little minds. Those of you who have read Sheridan's *School for Scandal* or Echegaray's *The World and His Wife* are familiar with the effects of vicious gossip.

But on the other hand, *good* gossip is a delight. It pleases those who gossip, those who are gossiped *to,* and even those who are gossiped *about.* For, as André Maurois observes, "men so like to be talked about that a discussion of their faults delights them." If you gossip about people, you make them feel important. You pay them an indirect compliment. Good-natured gossip is indeed the *best* compliment you can pay to people. If gossip may descend to slander, it may also rise to sympathy. If we talk about people, it is because they interest us. We discuss those about whom we try to learn something. The great novelist, Henry James, confessed that he was fond of gossip. "It is through it only," he said, "that we learn about man."

The most interesting of books, like Boswell's *Life of Johnson,* are those that gossip about the great. The most interesting of newspaper columns, like Walter Winchell's or O. O. McIntyre's, are those that gossip about the men and the women who are in the public eye. The most interesting of conversations are those that gossip about everything under the sun.

And this is the chief advantage of gossip as a subject for conversation. For gossip covers all the other subjects. To paraphrase the Latin poet's line which has already been quoted in this book, "I am a man, and therefore I am interested in gossiping about everything that is human."

When you gossip about your friends, however, be sure to emphasize their good rather than their bad qualities. Be more eager to praise than to blame them. For they are sure to hear what you have said about them, and they will repay you by saying like things about you. Gossip, like the earth, travels in a circle. It returns to the place that it started from.

§ 2

DEVELOPING THE RIGHT STYLE

To be a good conversationalist, you must know not only *what* to say, but *how* to say it. In this connection, there are several definite rules that will guide you:

1. *Be mentally quick*. Associate with those who have a nimble mind and an equally nimble tongue. Study them. Try to acquire some of their characteristics for yourself.

Be quick, but not *brutally* quick. The man whose tongue hurts is a fool. There is no greater conversational bore than the fellow who degenerates into a mere "wise-cracker" when he tries to be a wit. We all know him, and we all try to avoid him.

2. *Be civil*. "To be social without being civil," writes Professor Mahaffy, "is not possible."

He who is civil is thoughtful; he who is thoughtful is modest; he who is modest is charming. When you indulge in a conversation, remember not to overemphasize your own importance. There are others present who regard themselves as being equally important. Make them feel that you are aware of their worth.

Some of the world's greatest men are among the most *modest* men. Einstein, for example, is extremely modest. Spinoza, too, was as modest as if he were merely one of the world's humblest lens-grinders instead of being the world's outstanding philosopher. So, too, was Saint Francis. He spoke to the birds in the fields as his equals. And history has rarely seen three more charming conversationalists than Einstein, Spinoza, and Saint Francis.

3. *Be simple.* In other words, be truthful. Truth is always simple. It is only falsehood that is complicated.

Speak the truth simply and directly. Do not lie. The liar may overwhelm his listeners with a false show of brilliance. But they will soon find him out for what he is,—a painted character in an unimportant farce. His struttings are put on only for show. They have no relation to life.

A good conversation should be a mirror of the mind. Show a clear and honest surface to your friends. Admit them to your thoughts without any subterfuges or evasions.

4. *Be unselfish.* On the one hand, do not sit back merely as a listener. Join as a speaker. It is your duty to bear part of the burden of the conversation. Be silent when others have something important to say, and do not be afraid to speak when you yourself have something worth while to contribute. On the other hand, do not monopolize the conversation. A man who does this is always regarded as a bully, and what is worse, as an unmitigated bore.

In observing the rule of alternate speech and silence, remember the good old Greek adage: Nothing too much.

5. *Be dramatic.* Avoid monotony. A monotonous voice and bearing are like the continual drizzling of rain upon the sparkle of a lively conversation. When you talk with your friends, put life into your voice and motion into your body. Don't sound like a train-schedule announcer at a railroad station, and don't sit like a motionless Buddha mouthing a succession of wearisome maxims.

Use gestures. A raising of the brow, a shrug of the shoulder, and a movement of the hand are all good helps in the art of conversation. "How can I talk if you hold my hands?" said the Frenchman. And he was right. A conversation without gestures is dead.

Beware, however, of overdoing the dramatic element in conversation. Don't be monotonous; but, on the other hand, don't be vociferous. Never declaim when you talk to your friends. If there is anybody at a conversation more obnoxious than the dummy, it is the ranter. Gesture, but don't gesticulate. Be dramatic, but don't be melodramatic. Melodrama may be good on occasion in the theater, but it is always out of place in the drawing room.

6. *Be sympathetic.* Give a willing ear to your opponent's point of view. Try to see the subject under discussion from *his* angle as well as from your own. The better you understand each other, the sooner you will reach a common ground of agreement and closer friendship.

Sympathize with others. Respect their points of view. Do not, however, become patronizing. We admire those who regard us as equals, but we despise those who presume to look down upon us. Sympathy includes a warm respect. Patronage includes a cold pity. None of us wants to be pitied.

7. *Be tactful.* This is of supreme importance. It is difficult to define this word, but it is easy to feel what it is. We recognize the tactful man the moment we see him. *Tact* is that peculiar ability to come into contact with others in such a manner as not to hurt their feelings. The tactful person will be able to feel the mental pulse of his audience. He will know when they are irritated, and he will insert just the right word at just the right moment to calm this irritation. He will sense the point where another is eager to throw in a word, and he will enable that person to have his say. He will avoid the anecdote that may hurt anyone. For example, if a man or a woman present has been recently divorced, the tactful man will refrain from any reference to divorce in general. Above all, the tactful man will sense the dangerous moment when a pleasant conversation is likely to turn into an unpleasant argument, and he will switch the subject to something more palatable.

Cultivate tact. It is one of the rarest of social virtues. But it is also one of the most valuable. If you are recognized as a tactful person, you will be a welcome guest wherever good conversations are held.

8. *Be witty.* Wit is a natural gift. We are born either witty or witless. Yet we can all learn to understand a joke, and if we try hard we can all learn to tell one. In order to shine as a person who can say the smart thing at the right time, cultivate a good memory. Or, still better, carry a note-book in your pocket and jot down any clever jest or epigram that you hear. One of my acquaintances makes constant use of such a note-book. Whenever he is invited to a party, he sits down and

selects about five or ten witty passages from the note-book and learns them by heart. He has become so adept at this that he seems to sparkle with *original* and *spontaneous* wit wherever he is invited.

If you follow this method, however, you must beware of repeating yourself. Don't tell the same story in the same place more than once. And don't tell to your friend a story that he has told to you. A boomerang of this kind is very embarrassing. Even Oscar Wilde was once guilty of this social carelessness. Having heard a good story from Whistler, he forgot the source of the story and several months later repeated it to Whistler as his own.

"But, my dear Oscar," laughed Whistler. "Don't you remember? This story is mine!"

For a moment Oscar Wilde was put out. But then his natural wit came to the rescue.

"Oh, you're quite mistaken," he said. "The story is my own. When you first told it to me, it was *tame*. But now, you see, it has a *Wilde* flavor to it."

A joke *well* told arouses the laughter of admiration. A joke *poorly* told arouses the laughter of ridicule. Learn to bring out the point of a joke at the proper time; and then stop. A dragged-out joke is a pitiable thing.

Learn to tell a witty story. But it must be a *good* story, and it must be *well* told. The words must be few, and the sentences brief. Avoid unnecessary detail. Don't get the reputation of Cardinal Richelieu. Speaking of the cardinal's inability to tell a good story, Walpole said: "His listeners laugh *before* they hear his story, which is right, for they surely will not laugh *after* they hear it."

§ 3

ANECDOTE, WIT, AND HUMOR

Season your conversation, but don't *overseason* it, with the spice of anecdote, wit, and humor. An anecdote is an amusing biographical incident. Wit and humor are the expression of the ridiculous element of life. Wit is a sudden flash, an electric spark, a stroke of lightning. Humor is a glowing flame, a steady, smiling warmth.

As a general rule, youth loves wit, middle age is fond of humor, and old age enjoys its anecdotes. It was Professor Babbitt, I believe, who said that old men decline into *dotage* and *anecdotage*.

The above distinctions, however, need not be taken too seriously. The good anecdote, the witty joke and the successful humorous story can appeal to all of us at all ages. No conversation is complete without them. They tease the mental appetite, and they enable us to digest the more serious parts of the discourse.

The following collection of anecdotes and jokes will help you to add zest to your conversations.

Anecdotes

Two boys once decided to play a trick on Charles Darwin. They took the body of a centipede, the wings of a butterfly, the legs of a grasshopper, and the head of a beetle, and glued them together. Putting the strange creature into a box, they took it to Darwin.

"Please, sir," said the older boy, "can you tell us what sort of a bug this is?"

The naturalist looked at the bug and then at the boys.

"Did it hum?" he asked.

"Oh, yes, sir!"

"In that case," declared Darwin, "I would say it's a *humbug*."

* * *

Bill Nye was fond of telling the following story to his friends:

One day, as I was riding in a train, two men sat in front of me. It was obvious that they were strangers to each other.

"P-p-p-pardon me, s-s-sir," said the first stranger to his companion, "b-b-b-b-but is the n-n-next s-s-station S-s-s-s-salem?"

No answer.

"D-d-did you hear me?" asked the first stranger. "I w-w-w-would l-l-like to know if the n-n-n-next station is S-s-s-s-s-salem?"

Again no answer.

About five minutes later the conductor came into the car and called out, "Next station Salem!"

The train came to a stop and the first stranger got off. Whereupon, my curiosity getting the better of me, I turned to the second stranger.

"May I ask why you didn't answer the gentleman?"

The man turned to me and with an innocent smile said, "D-d-d-d-did you w-w-want me t-t-t-to get my b-b-b-b-block knocked off?"

* * *

O. Henry once asked a friend who was a good poker player:

"Tell me, Jim, when you play poker, does a good deal depend on luck, or does luck depend on a good deal?"

* * *

A few years ago John Masefield, the Poet Laureate of England, wrote a book entitled *Odtaa*. When asked to explain the meaning of that title, he said that O-d-t-a-a stood for *One damn thing after another*.

This title, by the way, is said to be the child of that famous philosophical distinction between life and love. "Life," said the philosopher, "is just one fool thing after another: love is just two fool things after each other."

* * *

An amusing story was recently printed in the *Boston Herald* about Roosevelt—not *Franklin* Roosevelt, but *Teddy* Roosevelt. When Teddy Roosevelt came to Heaven, he began to criticize everything in it just as he had criticized everything on earth.

"What you need," he said, turning to St. Peter, "is to re-organize your celestial choir. Get 100,000 new tenors, 100,000 new sopranos, and 100,000 new baritones."

"And what about the bassos?" asked St. Peter.

"*I*," said Teddy Roosevelt, "sing basso."

* * *

Recently a Hindu mystic spoke to a group of Boston ladies. In order to show his familiarity with the English language, he announced the death of his mother in the following scrambled metaphor:

"I regret to announce that my beloved mother, the hand which rocked the cradle, has kicked the bucket."

* * *

A British journalist, in an article on Sir Henry Irving, wrote:

"I was his guest regularly at all Lyceum first nights for a whole quarter of a century. . . . Mr. Irving delighted in the company of third-rate people."

* * *

A young Chinese student came to New York to study at Columbia University. He had the proper credentials, but he was told that he could not enter Columbia until he had learned the language of the country. Accordingly he secured a job on the lower East Side and waited patiently.

A year later he returned to Columbia and announced that he could now speak the language of the country.

But, much to his surprise, the secretary could understand not a word of what he was saying. Turning to one of the students who happened to be in the office, she asked, "Are you able to make him out?"

"Of course," laughed the student. "This isn't English he's talking, it's Yiddish!"

* * *

Artemus Ward said:

"When I am sad, I sing, and then others are sad with me."

* * *

O. Henry occasionally ate in a restaurant that was noted neither for its food nor for its music. When he was asked why he selected this particular restaurant, he replied:

"Because it works two ways: most of the times the food is so bad that I can even stand the music, and the music is so bad that I can even stand the food."

* * *

The great Caruso used to tell this one about himself:

It was about one o'clock in the morning when the hostess requested me to sing for the guests.

"It is too late, madam," I protested. "I should disturb your neighbors."

"Not at all," she replied. "Besides, they poisoned our dog last week."

* * *

Mark Twain was listening to a famous violinist at a private reception. The piece contained some particularly long rests. During one of these intervals, Mark Twain said to the soloist:

"Young man, why don't you play something you can remember?"

* * *

The office-seeker in Washington admitted that he had never heard of Mark Twain.

"What? Never heard of *Tom Sawyer?*"

"Nope, never heard of him."

"Nor *Innocents Abroad?*"

"Nope, never heard of him, neither."

"Nor *Puddin'head Wilson?*"

"Oh, Lord, yes!" exclaimed the office-seeker. "Why, I voted for him."

And then he added sadly:

"An' all the good it done me! He won't even give me a job now!"

* * *

The following anecdote shows that Mr. Somerset Maugham, author of many successful novels and plays, is as adept at turning out a neat compliment as he is at inventing a clever plot for a story:

Mr. Maugham was asked by a Frenchman what he thought of the translation of one of his novels by Mme. Blanchet.

"Since I have read the French version," he replied, "I have the feeling that I translated it very badly into English."

* * *

Jean Paul Richter used to tell a story about the atheist who said, "I don't believe in anything, thank God!"

Puns

A pun is a play on words. Many writers consider punning as the lowest form of humor, and one of them (John Dennis) even goes so far as to say that "a man who would make a pun would not scruple to pick a pocket." I disagree with these critics. It is true that very few things can be so stupid as a stupid pun. Yet very few things can be so clever as a *clever* pun. If not carried to excess, a sprinkling of puns will improve the flavor of any conversation. Some of the greatest men in history, such as Homer, Cicero, Chaucer, Shakespeare, Scott, Byron, Heine, and even St. Paul, were fond of an occasional good pun.

The following list contains a number of puns that have become famous through the centuries.

* * *

The famous playwright, Richard B. Sheridan, paid the following compliment to a Miss Payne:
" 'Tis true I am ill; but I cannot complain,
For he never knew pleasure who never knew Payne."

* * *

I'll *gild* the faces of the grooms withal,
That it may seem their *guilt*.
—*Shakespeare*

* * *

Burke, on being dunned by his tailor to pay at least the interest on his bill, answered that it was not his interest to pay the principal, nor his principle to pay the interest.

* * *

Here lies the tongue of Godfrey Lill,
Which always lied, and now *lies still*.

* * *

When the Shakespearean critic, Charles Knight, died, a wag suggested the following epitaph for him:
"Good Knight!"

* * *

Free verse is the triumph of mind over metre.
—*Life*

* * *

Teacher: Why don't you like our school, Willie?
Willie: Oh, it isn't the school—it's the *principal*
of the thing.   —*London Tit-bits*

* * *

Epitaph on the tomb of the famous attorney, Sir
John Strange:

"Here lies an honest lawyer—that is *Strange.*"

* * *

On the gravestone of a certain Richard Button:

Oh! sun, moon, stars, and ye celestial poles!
Are graves then dwindled into Button-holes?

* * *

Newspaper Headline for the Coronation:

The People Began to Hail, when the King Began
to Reign.

* * *

A witty reviewer called a certain inferior production of *Abie's Irish Rose* "a kosher play filled with
ham actors."

* * *

The following extract, from Thomas Hood's
Faithless Sally Brown, contains a number of clever
puns:

"Oh Sally Brown, oh Sally Brown!
    How could you serve me so?
I've met with many a breeze before,
    But never such a blow."
So sang the hapless sailor lad.
    He stormed and raged and cried.
His head was turned, and so he chewed
    His pigtail till he died.

His death, which happened in his berth,
    At forty-odd befell.
They went and told the sexton, and
    The sexton toll'd the bell.

* * *

JOKES ABOUT DOCTORS

The famous Dr. L——, dean of the Medical College, was appointed private physician to the king. Whereupon he proudly wrote the following notice on the blackboard of his classes:

"Professor L—— informs his students that he has been appointed Honorary Physician to His Majesty the King."

When he returned to his classroom in the afternoon, he found written below his notice this line:

"God save the King!"

* * *

Anatole France was fond of this one:
Family Physician: I congratulate you, M. Bonfils.
Patient (excitedly): Will I recover?
Family Physician: No, I'm afraid not. But you're dying of a new disease, and we are going to name the disease after you.

* * *

The doctor looked at his patient's tongue, felt of his pulse, knocked on his chest, and began:

"Same old story, my friend. Too much confinement. Don't deny it. What you need is plenty of outdoor exercise. Walk, walk, walk."

"But, doctor——"

"Don't argue with me. *I* am the doctor. Take my advice. Walk ten times as much as you do now. That's the only thing that will cure you."

"But my business——"

"That's just the trouble. Your business! Well, change your business, so that you can get a chance to walk more. What *is* your business?"

"I'm a letter-carrier."

* * *

The young man got a severe case of laryngitis, and couldn't speak above a whisper. Passing by the office of the doctor who had just moved into town, he decided to come in and be examined.

He rang the bell. The door was opened by the doctor's young and pretty wife.

"Is the doctor in?" asked the young man in a whisper.

"No, he isn't," the young wife whispered in reply. "Come right in."

* * *

This story is ascribed to Mark Twain. Speaking on one occasion to a group of physicians, he said:

"Gentlemen, there is one disease to which you will never find a remedy. It will be fatal in every case."

"And what disease is that?" asked several of the physicians.

"Life," replied Mark Twain.

* * *

Jokes About Lawyers

It was Mark Hanna, I believe, who used to tell this one about his friend, Attorney J——:

One day, after a heated discussion with the Judge, Mr. J—— deliberately turned his back upon the dignified jurist and started to walk off.

"Are you trying, sir, to show your contempt for the Court?"

"No, your Honor," was the reply. "I am trying my best to conceal it."

* * *

Professor Munro, of Harvard, relates an illuminating incident in a Harvard Law School classroom:

The students were discussing a point of law, when one of the young men stood up and said, "But, Professor, this point may be legal, but it is not just."

"My dear young man," said the professor. "If you are looking for justice, go across the street to the Divinity School. This is the Law School."

* * *

Benjamin Franklin once said that he went through all his money in two lawsuits. He went through *one-fourth* of it in the first case, which he lost, and *three-fourths* of it in the second case, which he won.

*   *   *

When the sick lawyer asked the doctor which side it is best to lie on, the doctor, with a knowing smile, said, "The side which pays you the biggest fee."

*   *   *

This was one of O. Henry's favorites:
"I couldn't serve as a juror, your Honor. One look at that fellow convinces me he's guilty."
"Sh-h! That's the district attorney!"

*   *   *

JOKES ABOUT PREACHERS

"Tell me, Bishop Berkeley, is there a life after death?"
"There certainly is. When we die, we enter upon a life of eternal bliss. But let's talk about something pleasant, instead."

*   *   *

At a recent dinner given in honor of a well-known actor, it was learned, too late, that no minister of the Gospel would be present. Turning in this emergency to the guest of honor, the toastmaster said:
"Mr. B——, since there are no clergymen present, will you kindly say grace?"
The actor rose, bowed his head, and fervently remarked:
"There being no clergymen present, let us thank God."

*   *   *

Mark Twain occasionally attended the services of his good friend, the Reverend Mr. Doane. One Sunday he decided to play a joke on the minister.
"Dr. Doane," he said, "I enjoyed your sermon this morning. I welcomed it like an old friend. I have, you know, a book at home containing every word of it."

"You have not, Mr. Twain!"

"I certainly have."

"Send the book to me! I'd like to see it!"

"I will."

The next morning Mark Twain sent the rector a copy of *Webster's Dictionary.*

* * *

During the sermon a baby began to cry at the top of its voice. The mother rose from her seat and began to carry the baby toward the door.

"Don't go," said the minister. "The baby isn't disturbing me in the least."

"The baby may not be disturbing *you,*" said the mother, "but *you're* disturbing the baby."

* * *

This last story about preachers is an anecdote of Mark Twain's. One Sunday, he said, he went to church and listened to a passionate appeal for funds to save the heathen.

At the end of five minutes he burst into tears and was ready to contribute fifty dollars.

At the end of fifteen minutes, he reduced his prospective contribution to twenty-five dollars.

When the minister had spoken for half an hour, he cut the sum to five dollars.

When the minister had spoken for an hour and the plate was passed around, Mark Twain took two dollars out of it.

* * *

JOKES ABOUT NATIONS

Sandy Ferguson went to London for his honeymoon. When he was asked where his wife was, he explained that he had left her at home, because it was too expensive to take her along.

* * *

An Englishman, an Irishman, and a Scotchman each owed five dollars to a certain man. When the man died, the three decided to pay their debt at once.

The Englishman put a $5 bill into the coffin. The Irishman did likewise. The Scotchman put into the coffin a check for fifteen dollars and took the ten dollars in change.

* * *

The Irish sailor was telling the inquisitive old lady about his adventures:

"An' one foine day, ma'am, I fell into the ocean, an' along came a shark an' grabbed me leg."

"Merciful heavens!" cried the old lady. "And what did you do?"

"Let 'im have me leg, ma'am. I niver argue with a shark."

* * *

Nora, the cook, was engaged to Mike for two years. Finally her mistress got impatient.

"When are you going to be married, Nora?" she asked.

"Indade, mum, an' it's niver at all, I'll be thinkin'," replied Nora sadly.

"Why, what's the trouble?"

"You see, mum, it's like this. I won't marry Mike whin he's drunk, an' he won't marry me whin he's sober."

* * *

The following inscription is to be found in an old Irish cemetery:

"This monument is erected to the memory of James O'Brien, who was accidentally shot by his brother as a mark of affection."

* * *

On Tuesday, the colored maid asked her mistress for permission to attend her fiancé's funeral on Friday.

"But you're not wearing mourning," remarked her mistress.

" 'Tain't time yet. They're hangin' him on Thursday."

* * *

Dr. Sing Lee was the best physician in Chinatown. And he proved it to Wi Wong's satisfaction. Said Wi Wong:

"Me velly sick man. Me get Doctor Sing Song. Takee him medicine. Velly more sick. Me get Doctor Ping Pong. Takee him medicine. Velly still more sick. Me call Doctor Sing Lee. Him busy, no can come. Me get well."

* * *

The Scotch are not the only economical people in the world. The Japanese run them a close second. Two Japanese friends were talking about their fans. "My fan," said Nogu, "has lasted for twenty years. And this is how I managed it: I had it made in four sections, and each five years I opened only one of the sections."

"That is nothing," replied Togu scornfully. "My fan has lasted a lifetime. I open it wide, and hold it motionless under my nose. Then I wave my head."

* * *

Isaac Cohen had written a letter to a former desirable customer who had strayed from the fold owing the Cohen Clothing Emporium a considerable bill. Mrs. Cohen, in passing on the letter, remarked:

"It's a fine letter, diplomatic, and inoffensive, but you should not have spelled 'dirty' with two 't's' and cockroach does not begin with a 'k'."

* * *

Two Jews were sleeping together one night at a New York hotel when one of them got up and began pacing the floor.

"For why you walk the floor?" the other asked.

"Well I owe Rubenstein $100 and I promised to pay him tomorrow, and I haven't got the money," he answered.

"Why don't you come back to bed and go to sleep— let Rubenstein walk the floor."

* * *

Professor Freud cites this as a good example of Jewish humor:

The *schnorrer* (professional beggar) was a regu-

lar Sunday-dinner guest at the home of the charitable
Mr. Epstein. One Sunday he came with a young
stranger, who took his seat at the table together with
the others.

"May I ask who is this young man?" asked the
host.

"He married my daughter last week," replied the
schnorrer, "and I've agreed to support him the first
year."

* * *

Englishman: The British are the promptest payers
of insurance in the world, don't you know. If a man
died tonight, his widow would receive her money by
the first post tomorrow.

Yankee: You don't say? Well, now, see here.
We've got an office on the sixth floor of a sixty-story
building. One of our clients fell out of a window on
the forty-fifth floor. We handed him his insurance
check as he passed our floor.

* * *

Professor Brun, of Harvard, used to tell this one
to his classes:

Frenchman: We've got a remarkable sausage
machine in Paris. We put in a live pig at one end,
and we turn and turn the handle until the sausages
come out at the other end.

Yankee: That's nothing. We've got an even better
machine in Boston. We put in a live pig at one end,
and we turn and turn the handle until the sausages
come out at the other end. Then we taste one of the
sausages; and if we don't like it, we put them all back
into the machine and we turn and turn the handle
backward until the pig comes out alive again.

CHAPTER XI

The Successful Sales Talk

§ 1

PREPARATION

THE BEST SALES TALK, like the best radio interview, always sounds spontaneous; and it sounds spontaneous because it is so carefully prepared. "A real salesman," wrote the head of a big insurance company, "is one part talk and nine parts preparation." In New York there is a certain business man who is famous for his gruffness to would-be interviewers. It was a standing joke among the reporters that anybody who tried to interview the grouchy old Mr. D—— would "get his nose snapped off for sticking it into other people's business."

One day the old-timers thought they would play a joke on a cub reporter. They told him to get a story out of Mr. D——. The cub reporter said he would get it in a month.

And, sure enough, at the end of the month he got it.

"How did you do it?" asked the older reporters in amazement.

"Easily enough," said the cub reporter. "Before I went to see him, I learned all about *his* business; and when I saw him, I minded *my own* business." He had actually spent an entire month in learning the complete story of the man's life. When he came to interview him, he was so full of the subject, and he was able to speak about it so familiarly and so sympathetically, that Mr. D—— was highly flattered and opened himself up completely to the young man.

This young cub reporter later became Mr. D——'s private secretary.

In order to sell any article, from an interview to an apartment house, you must prepare yourself to *know* your subject. Suppose you try to sell a radio to a customer who is using

188

another make. You must know not only your own radi/
his. Get him to talk about it. Ask him to point out all its goo
qualities. Try to sympathize with him. In this way you
will have gained his confidence. Then, if you really know
his radio, you will be able to point out wherein it falls short
of his ideal; and if you know your own radio, you will be
able to show wherein yours comes nearer to his ideal.

The better you know your own article and all the competitive articles in the field, the more fairly and therefore the more
convincingly you can talk to your customer. Don't condemn
your rival's product. To do so would show your ignorance of
it. There must be *some* good features about it, or else it
wouldn't be in the market. Point out those good features. And
then, when you have done this, point out wherein your own
product has *still better* features.

Know your product and the products of your rival companies. But even *that* is not enough. Know how to sell your
product to your customer, and how your customer in turn can
sell it to *his* customers. This is very important. When you
deliver the goods, you must also try to deliver some ideas for
distributing the goods. It isn't enough to sell a case of canned
goods to a grocer. Show him how he can *dispose* of that case.
In order to do that, you must know not only your product and
the rival products, but the complete market for these products
and the possible ways of extending it. Such men as Ford,
Lamont, and Schwab are successful because they know their
field and their goods. And the best men trained under them
are the men who have best learned to know their field and
their goods.

One of the young salesmen for a silk hosiery manufacturer
unloaded too big an order on a customer. When the bill fell
due, the customer refused to pay it. Instead, he offered to return the goods. Whereupon the sales manager decided to do
something about it. He knew his goods, and he knew the field
for it. He had tested his company's stockings, and he had
learned from his tests that he could make a spectacular demon-
stration of their strength. Accordingly he asked the dealer to
inform his customers that on a certain day, at 10 o'clock in
the morning, they would see something interesting in front of
his store.

At the appointed time, there were several hundred people there. And what they saw was certainly interesting. A truck was tied to a Ford by means of a pair of stockings, and the truck was towed around the block without causing the slightest injury to the stockings.

By noon of that day the dealer had disposed of his surplus stock, paid the bill, and ordered a larger stock of hosiery from the same manufacturer.

One of the best salesmen in Massachusetts is a "name" broker. That is, he acts as an agent for those mail-order companies who rent out the names of their customers to other mail-order companies. When he comes into your office to get an order, he does not talk to you about selling names. Instead, he gives you a keen analysis of your business, and he shows you how you can improve it by circularizing the names of such-and-such a company. So thorough is his knowledge of your problems that you feel confident in taking his advice. This man spends all his spare time in studying the business of those people whom he tries to get as his customers.

There is an insurance salesman in Cleveland who is a regular Walter Winchell so far as his prospective customers are concerned. He knows their lives as intimately as he knows the lives of his brothers and his sisters. And, as a result, he can get their confidence as if they actually *were* his brothers and his sisters. He can give each client the precise reason for taking out a particular type of insurance, and he is easily one of the most successful insurance salesmen in the country.

The first requisite for a good sales talk, therefore, is knowledge. A clothing manufacturer recently outlined twelve interesting facts about his goods. He found, when he made a check-up on his salesmen, that they mentioned on an average only five of these facts to their prospective customers. Because of their lack of knowledge, or their carelessness in *using* their knowledge, they lost many sales.

But, you will ask, how can you acquire the necessary knowledge? The answer is: by reading, and by inquiring. Read all the literature you can get on your subject—general books, the pamphlets of your own company, the pamphlets of your rival companies, and the trade journals in your line. And ask questions. Consult your boss, your manager, the factory foreman, the star salesman—in fact, everybody from whom you can learn. Try to do as Socrates did. Socrates, as you know, was a perpetual question mark. He asked more questions, perhaps, than any other man in history, and he probably *knew* more than any other man in history. And, incidentally, he was one of the best salesmen in history. He sold an article which the world has been enjoying for over two thousand years. What was that article? His personality.

A good salesman sells his personality. Like Socrates, he knows how to talk. He has mastered his subject, and he has *organized it into a logical story*.

This *organization* of your knowledge is the next important step in the preparation of your sales talk. Arrange your arguments in your own mind and then write them down on paper. Suppose, for example, you are trying to sell a new Children's Encyclopedia to mothers. There are already plenty of good Children's Encyclopedias on the market. How are you going to present your own set in such a light as to make it appear outstanding? First, by pointing out those features which are common to all encyclopedias but which are more adequately treated in your own encyclopedia. Second, by pointing out those features which are to be found *exclusively* in your own encyclopedia. Third, by summarizing all these features in an appropriate slogan.

Suppose, now, that you are familiar with all the sets in the field. Your procedure, then, will be to arrange in your mind, and to set down on paper, the following outline for an effective sales talk:

A. *Common Features*.

1. The work is authoritative. Give a list of the outstanding scholars who have collaborated in the preparation of this set, as well as a list of well-known educators who have endorsed it.

2. The work is written in a simple and graphic style—a style which children can *understand* and *enjoy*. Prepare specific examples to prove this point.

3. This set is profusely illustrated, and the illustrations are up to the minute. Prepare a portfolio of these illustrations to show to your prospective customer. Include in this portfolio

such striking illustrations as are not to be found in any of the other encyclopedias.

4. Each volume contains a complete index. This index will enable the child and the parents to find the necessary references without any difficulty or loss of time.

5. The printing is clear, the type is large and the paper is of good quality. Thus the set is easy and pleasant to read. Have, in your portfolio, a specimen page to show to your customer.

6. The binding has been designed by famous artists. Give their names and their background. Always try to cite important names. There is nothing that impresses people quite so much as the authoritative assertion that the famous Mr. or Mrs. So-and-so has had a share in the preparation of your product.

B. *Exclusive Features.*

1. The method followed in this set is the question and answer method. This method will arouse the curiosity of the children, and also of the parents. Prepare a set of questions to ask the prospective customers. Let these questions be popular, yet difficult to answer. Point out the fact that each of the questions which you have prepared is answered on such-and-such a page.

2. Your set contains a unique study guide for children prepared by Professor X——, Dean of the M—— State Normal School for Teachers. Show how this study guide has been designed to meet the latest methods in education.

3. The set contains the condensations of the hundred best books for children—drama, fiction, biography, and poetry. In this encyclopedia, therefore, the children are able to meet the best creative minds of the centuries.

4. The set includes a complete outline of history, of literature, of science, of music, and of art. Each of these outlines is *biographical* instead of *chronological*. The children are thus enabled to become acquainted with living personalities rather than with dead dates.

5. One of the features of this set is a vocational guide. This guide, prepared by the well-known educator, Dr. Y——, may do much to start your child on the right road to happiness and success.

C. *Slogan.*

The old system of education stressed the three R's. This set, based upon the *new* system of education, while not neglecting the three R's, emphasizes the three H's—the education of the Head, the education of the Hand, and the education of the Heart.

The above outline may be varied to sell anything at all—from encyclopedias to shirts. The same principles will apply in every case. Your sales talk should include (1) the features shared in common with competitive articles, (2) the exclusive features, and (3) the slogan. No two salesmen will prepare exactly the same kind of talk, since no two minds are exactly alike. Yet every salesman who wants to be successful should prepare *some sort* of effective talk based upon his *thorough* knowledge of the *entire* field which he is trying to cover. A spontaneous sales talk is rarely, if ever, effective. It is just as fatal to try to arrange your *thoughts* in front of your customer as to try to arrange your *collar and tie*. Come in to your prospect's home or office with your body and mind *completely dressed.*

§ 2

PRESENTATION

When you have prepared the outline of your talk, you have merely the skeleton. Your next move is to dress it with the flesh of a simple and sincere style. Avoid exaggerations and flowery expressions. Your sales talk is not a declamation; it is a conversation. Much of what has been said in our chapter on the art of conversation applies equally well to the art of successful selling. There is this difference, however: a good conversation may wander leisurely from one subject to another; a good sales talk, however, must stick to one subject. It must deal with the article which you are trying to sell.

In order to stick to your subject, memorize your talk after you have written it down. A good many companies prepare a stereotyped sales talk for all their salesmen, thus saving them the trouble of preparing their own individual talks. This method has its disadvantages as well as its advantages. A talk which does not originate with you cannot express your own personality. When you present another man's ideas, your manner is bound to be cold, however eloquent your words. You will very likely fall into that sing-song style so common to the untrained and unintelligent canvassers who come to your back door to sell you patent medicines and shoe-laces and razor-blades. This sing-song, phonographic method of presenting a sales talk will succeed in selling only one thing—sleep. Avoid it as you would the plague. Even when you have prepared your own sales talk, you are in danger of falling into a sing-song, especially if you have memorized it word for word. Try to memorize the *gist* of your speech, not the *words*. For you must never deliver the same sales talk twice. Your customer will ask you questions that may lead you off the trail. If you stick to one set speech, you are very likely to fumble around and lose your way. Furthermore, different points in your speech will have to be emphasized when you talk to different sorts of people. A speech that will sell an encyclopedia to the wife of a shoe-maker, for example, will fail utterly if presented to the wife of a college professor. A young man attempted this very thing in the city of Cambridge a few months ago. He tried to sell a dictionary to the wife of Professor G——, of Harvard University. He had learned his sales talk only too well, but not any too wisely.

"Madam," he said, "I offer you a dictionary that is brief, and complete, and simple. It is not for the highbrows, but for people like you and me. When your husband comes home at night, he sits down to read the paper. Suppose he runs across a word he doesn't understand. Here's just the dictionary to help him. No involved explanations—no complicated derivations—just plain, ordinary, average words for the average man."

Mrs. G—— was amused, but disinterested. She politely told the young man to select his customers and his language with greater care in the future.

To deliver a good sales talk, therefore, you must first learn your talk, and then *unlearn* it. A great psychologist once said that there are three stages in our mental development: the first stage, when we are simple through ignorance; the second stage, when we become complex through the process of learning;

and the third stage, when we become simple again through knowledge. The salesman who has never prepared his talk belongs to the first group; the salesman who has prepared and memorized it, belongs to the second group; the salesman who has prepared and learned and digested it so thoroughly that he can use or discard any part of it at will, belongs to the third group. He is the most successful salesman.

But before you can deliver your talk, you must attract the attention of your customer. There are several simple ways in which you can do this:

1. Dress well, but not too loudly. Let your clothes give you an air of modesty and of prosperity. If your clothes are garish, you will be looked upon as a blusterer. If they are shabby, you will be set down as a failure. In neither case will you gain a respectful hearing.

2. Excite the customer's curiosity, if he appears disinclined to give you a hearing. When you come in to see a customer, his mind is usually not on your goods, but on his own affairs. It may therefore be necessary to startle him out of his own sphere of thought and into yours. Here are a few examples of unusual methods employed by unusual salesmen:

a. Mr. B—— represented a line of unbreakable glassware. Whenever he went into a prospect's office, he would let fall, as if by accident, one of his pieces of unbreakable glass. The prospective customer would jump from his seat in alarm, and when he saw that the glass fell harmless to the floor, he would be ready to listen to the salesman.

This sort of trick, by the way, dates back over two thousand years. That old master-salesman of Rome, Marcus Porcius Cato the Elder, wanted to induce his countrymen to declare war against Carthage. One day, as he began a speech in the senate, a number of figs fell, as if by accident, from one of the loosened folds of his toga. When some of the senators picked them up and admired their size and their beauty, he casually remarked that they grew in Carthage, and that the Romans could get possession of them by conquering the city.

Cato succeeded in selling the idea to the Romans.

b. A young man tried to sell an insurance policy to John Wanamaker. "My time," said Mr. Wanamaker, "is worth two dollars a minute." The young salesman, taking a bill out of his pocket, said quietly: "Very well, Mr. Wanamaker, I'll have ten dollars' worth of your time."

c. An advertising salesman carried in his pocket a trick pencil that twisted into all sorts of shapes when anyone tried to write with it. If a prospect was inattentive, he would pretend a similar inattention and begin to write in a notebook with his trick pencil. The customer's curiosity would be aroused by the funny gyrations of the pencil, and in this way his interest in the salesman would be restored.

d. A young bond salesman walked into the office of Mr. Macdonald, a testy old Scotch bookbinder. The old man sat writing at his desk and didn't even take the trouble to say *how do you do* to the young fellow. For a few moments the salesman looked at the bookbinder, and then spoke out in a tone of command:

"Mr. Macdonald, wake up and live!"

The old fellow looked up angrily. "Don't be impertinent, young man! I'm very *much* alive!"

"Fine! Then you're the very man I want to speak to! I've got a live proposition for live men."

The salesman succeeded in making a substantial sale of bonds to the old bookbinder on that day.

3. Begin your sales talk by asking a couple of questions. People love to answer questions, or to have them answered *for* them. Curiosity is one of the commonest of human traits. First ask a question that your customer can answer. It will give him a glow of pleasure and a sense of superiority. Then ask him a question that he *can't* answer. It will make him turn to you for instruction. Let this second question be a *leading* question. Let it lead directly to the article you are trying to sell. You have now excited his curiosity and aroused his interest. You are ready for the main argument.

Your main argument, let us repeat, should be *simple* and *sincere*. And it should also be *personal*. Try to present your product from your customer's point of view. That is all he is interested in. He doesn't care about you and your desire to sell. He cares only about himself and the advisability of his buying. Transform that advisability into a necessity. Show him how it is to *his advantage* to buy. Always use the pronoun *you*, never the pronoun *I*.

Don't do all the talking. Your customer also may want to say something. Let him have his say; and when he is through, try to apply his argument to your advantage. If you have memorized a stereotyped speech, you will not be able to do this. Your arguments should be *based* upon a prepared speech, but they should be flexible enough to depart from it whenever necessary.

A good salesman is a good listener as well as a good talker. There is one great advantage in letting your customer have his say. Sooner or later he is bound to show a weakness in his argument, and then you can jump into the breach and clinch your own point. A well-trained quarterback on a football team will occasionally employ the very same method. He will allow the opposing team to take the lead in order that he may take advantage of the other fellows' mistakes.

Don't, however, make your customer see that you are waiting for his mistakes. Don't look incredulous, or supercilious, or patronizing when he is doing the talking. Look sympathetic. Make him feel that what he is saying is worth listening to. He will then feel that what *you* are saying is also worth listening to.

Don't interrupt your customer in the middle of his argument. This will only irritate him and lose you a possible sale. It is poor tact and poor salesmanship to break into the train of a man's thoughts when he is trying to explain them to you. Be fair to your customer as you want him to be fair to you. For sales conduct, as well as for human conduct, there has yet been devised no better formula than the Golden Rule.

Speak in a moderate voice. Don't be too assertive. Don't give your customer the impression that you know everything and that he knows nothing. Be modest. Feed his vanity. Assure him of his wisdom. Create in him the impression that *because* of his wisdom he will be able to see the merits of your proposition. Act the gentleman rather than the bully. A *pat* on the shoulder is always better than a *chip* on the shoulder.

Encourage your customer to ask questions. Be sure that he clearly understands every point in your argument before you go on to the next point. Your customer may be timid about asking questions. He may possibly feel that to do so would be to display his ignorance. Dissipate any such notion on his part. Make him feel that if a point is not clear to him, it is not his fault but yours. Never say to him, "You don't understand." Always say, "I haven't made myself clear."

Look squarely at your customer when you talk to him or when you show your samples to him. Never look at your samples. Show him that you are primarily interested not in your samples, but in him. Try as far as possible to harmonize your thoughts with his. Show him, throughout your talk, that you are anxious to see *his* point of view, that you want *him* to be satisfied, and that you are trying to make the sale for *his* sake. For that is what he himself is after: his own satisfaction and his own profit.

And this takes us to our next point—persuasion.

§ 3

PERSUASION

People are interested in those things which will bring them satisfaction or profit. Every article that you sell must produce one or both of these results. In order to persuade your customer, therefore, you must show him how the buying of your article will benefit him. You must make him *want* your article. How can you best do it? In three ways: (1) by sticking strictly to the truth; (2) by showing that important people have *indorsed* your article; and (3) by showing that important people have *bought* your article.

1. Tell the exact truth to your customer. Don't exaggerate. Some sales executives will disagree with this principle. They maintain that exaggeration will sometimes startle your customer into listening to you. Yes, but it will also startle him into thinking that you are a clever liar. He may listen to you, true enough, but he will listen to you as an entertainer and not as a salesman. He may enjoy your clever talk—we all enjoy hearing a good lie—but he will have no confidence in your article. He will regard both you and your product as fakes.

It is better to understate your case than to overstate it. Too glowing a description rarely brings conviction. Never allow your customer to get the feeling that what you say is too good to be true. Never put too high a value on your own goods and too low a value on your competitor's goods. Don't knock. When your customer hears you knock the other fellow's product, he will conclude that there must be something the matter with your own product. If you have something really good to sell, you can afford to pay a mild compliment to your competitors. It's bad policy to say, "Mr. B's soap is very poor. Now just look at *my* soap." It's much better to say, "Mr. B's soap is very good indeed. But just look at *my* soap." Your fairness to your competitor will arouse conviction in your sincerity and confidence in your product.

This principle was well illustrated by Benjamin Franklin —the man, you will recall, who succeeded in selling our American Revolution to the French. Franklin admitted that as a young man he had been prone to exaggeration and vindictiveness in his arguments. This attitude of his, he said, had proved very costly to him. But a Quaker friend cured him of this bad habit. He stopped exaggerating his own side and abusing the other side. "I soon found the advantage of this change in my manner," he wrote . . . "The modest and truthful way in which I presented my views procured for them a readier reception . . . To my new tactics I think it principally owing that I had early such weight with my fellow citizens when I proposed new institutions, or alterations in the old . . . For I was but a bad speaker, never eloquent, subject to much hesitation, and my choice of words hardly correct in language— and yet I carried my points."

These very words of Franklin illustrate the principle which he is trying to explain. Franklin was *not* a bad speaker; he was *not* subject to much hesitation; and his choice of words as a rule was *quite* correct. But the entire passage carries all the more conviction because of these modest understatements.

In trying to persuade your customer, don't confuse understatement with indecision, modesty with timidity, or truthfulness with dulness. As a matter of fact, you can never be so dynamic as when you tell the truth in a moderate voice. We see this principle clearly enunciated in the Old Testament. The prophet tells us that the Lord speaks to us, not in the whirlwind, and not in the thunderbolt, but in the still small voice. We find this same still small voice so beautifully effective in the *Sermon on the Mount.*

Cultivate the quiet but confident tone. A confident tone is never dull; it is always convincing. Put color into your voice, but let the color be soft and harmonious. Enthusiasm? By all means! But no exaggeration. Don't be argumentative. Be persuasive. Tell your customer nothing but the truth, and *prove* that you are telling him nothing but the truth.

2. You have now reached the point where your customer believes in you. He is ready to admit that you yourself are convinced of the value of your article. It is now up to you to clinch the sale. Show him that other people are also convinced that you have the right article at the right value. In other words, you are ready for your testimonials. The more authoritative the testimonials, the better. Don't show these testimonials on a printed circular. They are not very effective when presented in that way. A printed word looks cold. It does not reveal the personality of the author. Carry your testimonials with you in their original form. Bind them into a portfolio, and keep them well indexed for ready reference. Show your customer the *actual letter* which you have received as an endorsement of your product. This letter, with its firm name at the top, and with the author's signature at the bottom, is like a personal talk from that man to your customer.

Testimonials are of the utmost importance. Yet they represent a danger which you must be careful to avoid. Nobody likes to read a succession of letters, some of which may possibly be long and not particularly interesting. Many an "almost" sale has been lost through an unskillful presentation of testimonials. Don't ask your customer to wade through every letter and to find for himself the few passages that are likely to interest him. Select these passages yourself. *Surround them with a red line.* This has a double advantage. The passages thus marked off in red will not only attract your customer's attention, but will seem doubly important because they stand out so strikingly from the rest of the letter. Red, you know, is an arresting color. When you turn the pages of your portfolio, and your customer sees one red circle after another, each one containing a boost for your product, he becomes more and more convinced that he wants to buy it.

But you must arrange your letters in such a way that the strongest endorsements come last. Guide your customer's

interest to a climax. Some salesmen make the mistake of starting with a strong testimonial and ending with a weak one. This
leads to an anticlimax, a loss in interest, and very likely a lost
sale.

An advertising salesman for a national magazine uses the
red-circle testimonials to good advantage. He has prepared
not one portfolio of letters, but several. He has a portfolio
for jewelers, another for publishers, a third for automobile
dealers, a fourth for candy manufacturers, and so on. When
he calls on a customer, he has the right portfolio ready for
use at the psychological moment. He is a walking encyclopedia
of facts and figures—especially figures. And his testimonials
invariably prove his case by means of figures. Thus, when he
calls on a jeweler, he shows him a group of convincing testimonials from other jewelers who have used the columns of his
magazine with profitable results. These results are tabulated
somewhat as follows:

Date of Insertion	Space	Cost	Returns
March 24, 1937	½ page	$800	$1927.48

These figures are better than any verbal argument. They
prove to the prospective client that a rival advertiser has
more than doubled his outlay on a single insertion. A magazine with such a *pull* must be a very good magazine indeed in
which to advertise. Time and again the clever salesman has
used his well-arranged and well-tabulated testimonials to verify
his sales talk and to sign up a new customer.

Many salesmen have tried a similar trick and failed. And
their failure has been due to a very definite reason: they used
general rather than *particular* arguments. They said to their
prospective client: "Mr. Smith, several of our advertisers
have more than doubled their advertising outlay on a single
insertion in our magazine." And that was all they said. They
made a vague statement which fell upon deaf ears. They did not
give any concrete figures or show any specific testimonials.

To clinch a sale, you must prove your point by means of
facts and figures. And these facts and figures will best convince your customer if presented in the form of endorsements.
Especially if these endorsements come from those who not
only *approve* your article, but *use* it.

3. Show that other people have *bought* your article. The greater the number of these people, and the greater their importance, the better. There is no stronger sales argument than a proof of actual sales. Everybody loves to buy what everybody else is buying. If you try to get a ticket for a play, and the tickets are all sold, you will be doubly anxious to see that play. If you hear of a book that has sold 100,000 copies, you will be curious to buy and to read it even though you may know that it is mere trash. There is a magic in numbers. Most of us like to be part of the crowd. A successful product becomes not merely a necessity, but a habit. A few years ago the captain of a transpacific liner offered a prize to the first passenger who would finish reading a novel that was the best seller at the time. At the end of the voyage, nobody came forward to claim the prize. For nobody had read the book beyond the first hundred pages. And yet almost every passenger had *bought* the book. Why? Because they had all been impressed by the sales figures.

You can best sell a popular line by talking figures. And—this is important—you can best sell an *unpopular* line by talking figures. It is an effective argument to say that 100,000 people have bought your article. It is an equally effective argument to say that you are selling your article to *only a few* people, since you are catering to a *discriminating* public. This implied flattery will please your customer and very likely get you the sale.

Don't let the fact that you are handling a poor seller discourage you. A clever sales talk, based upon the *discriminating* argument, and bolstered by the names of people who have bought from you, will turn a *poor* seller into a *good* seller. This sort of thing has been done over and over again—notably in the case of Jack Michaelson. This young man sold shoe leather to cobblers. The grade was good, but the price was almost prohibitive. At first Michaelson was discouraged, since he could make no headway. But he was an unusual salesman. Though no student of psychology, he subconsciously worked upon the scientific principle that if you act as if you *can't* fail, you are certain *not* to fail. With this mental attitude he approached his customers. He made a study of the situation. He learned, by means of careful tests, that his leather lasted longer than several other grades of leather then popular among cobblers. He took the trouble to go to the homes of people and to find out how well or how poorly their repaired shoes were wearing. Then he compiled convincing statistics, based upon actual cases with actual names. By means of these statistics he was able to prove that in the long run his leather cost the public *less* than most of the so-called cheaper grades. It was a long and difficult fight. Little by little, however, he was able to convince one after another of the cobblers. He flattered their vanity. He called them the *aristocrats* of the cobbling fraternity, because they were among the *few* who realized that it paid *them,* and that it paid *their customers* to get the better grade of leather at a higher price. He prepared a slogan : *A higher price at the start, but a lower price in the end.*

In less than two years, Michaelson became the most successful leather salesman in his state. Today he is the president of one of the three biggest tanneries in the country.

It is therefore immaterial whether your line is popular or unpopular, whether it costs little or much, whether your customer thinks that he can afford it or feels that he cannot afford it. A well prepared sales talk, skillfully presented, and persuasively documented, will generally produce the results.

Final Warning

When you have secured the sale, don't overstay your welcome. Many a sale has been lost because the salesman talked too much after the customer was ready to order. Don't try to oversell your article. To *oversell* means to *unsell.* Finish your talk, get your order, and *go!*

CHAPTER XII

Public Speaking

§ I

ACQUIRING SELF-CONFIDENCE

THE LATIN POET, Ennius, once said that he would rather fight in three battles than give birth to a single child. Whereupon a companion remarked: "I would rather give birth to three children than deliver a single speech."

The best of us, however brave we may be in other respects, are cowards when it comes to making a speech. Even the most successful orators and actors experience a tightening of the throat when they face an audience. Sarah Bernhardt said that every appearance on the stage was an ordeal to her. To the average person who attends a dinner it is almost like pronouncing a death sentence if you ask him to make a speech.

Yet the art of public speaking can be taught to almost anybody. There is only one rule to master, and you can become a pleasing, if not a perfect, public speaker. This rule is— *develop your self-confidence.*

How can you acquire self-confidence? By constant practice. You are afraid of facing an audience. You feel caught, as it were, in your mental pyjamas. You have very little to say, and very few words in which to say it. Your ideas and your vocabulary seem to have become frozen somewhere in the back of your mind where you cannot get at them and thaw them out. We have all experienced this feeling at some time or other. We simply don't know how to face a crowd.

Very well, then, let us learn to do so by facing ourselves. I mean this literally. *Practice speaking to yourself*—in the mirror. Do this for a few minutes every day. Be your own audience. Watch your facial expressions; observe your gestures; listen to your voice; criticize yourself severely; don't face others until you are ready to face yourself and to say frankly that you have done a satisfactory job.

It is immaterial, at the start, what speech you make to yourself in the mirror. It may be your own composition, or a selection from somebody else's speech. But practice it faithfully. Imagine that you are speaking not to *one* image, but to *several* images—several strangers. In other words, become your own audience, your own critic, and your own teacher.

Pay special attention to your gestures, your tongue, and your voice.

1. Avoid ungraceful and violent gestures. Don't strut, and don't use your arms like the arms of a windmill. Don't be over-anxious to make an impression. This over-anxiety will only make you ridiculous. Be calm—but not *too* calm. It is just as fatal to *underdo* your gestures as to *overdo* them. When you hold out your hand or open your palm, show that there is life in you. Don't act like a rheumatic. Let your body, like your voice, express your conviction and your confidence. Be leisurely, but emphatic. Use, in your gestures, not only your hands, but other parts of your body—if you can learn to do so gracefully. A humorous lighting up of the eye, an appropriate contraction of the muscles of the face, a shrug of the shoulder, a slight inclination of the trunk—all these may prove to be as eloquent as your words. Don't attempt these subtler gestures, however, unless you are certain that you have pretty good control of your muscles. Try, above everything else, to be natural. Cultivate poise. Let your motions be easy, rhythmical, and well-coördinated. Shift your position occasionally, but not too often. In short, let your gestures display good manners, but never let them descend to a vulgar show of *mannerisms*.

2. Train your tongue to speak easily. You know the story of Demosthenes, who trained himself by putting pebbles into his mouth. An equally effective method is to put tongue-twisters into your mouth. The tongue is an unruly and clumsy tool. But it can be subdued by patient exercise. The following tongue-twisters will give you the necessary exercise:

The sea ceaseth and it sufficeth us.

* * *

She sells sea-shells down by the sea-shore.

* * *

Some shun sunshine, some shun rain.

* * *

Peter Piper picked a peck of pickled peppers;
A peck of pickled peppers Peter Piper picked;
If Peter Piper picked a peck of pickled peppers,
Where's the peck of pickled peppers Peter Piper
    picked?

* * *

Sister Susie's sewing shirts for soldiers.

* * *

The Zarathustran sit-down striker seized six seething scissors and seven sizeable sizzling zithers.

* * *

Pronounce each of the above tongue-twisters very slowly. Then increase your pace little by little until you can rattle them all off in ten seconds. When you can do this without making a single mistake, you have your tongue under pretty good control. And you are then ready for the next step in your training—the cultivation of your voice.

3. Develop a voice that is clear, strong, flexible, and soft. Learn to use it without effort. Speak slowly, deliberately, and easily. In order to speak well, you must learn to breathe correctly. Practice breathing. Take a good, deep breath before each group of words that you wish to speak aloud. Let the breath penetrate the deepest recesses of your lungs. Practice this sort of thing until it becomes natural. When you are ready to make a public speech, you must no longer give much thought to your breathing. If you have practiced it long enough and intelligently enough, it will take care of itself.

When you speak, keep your throat open and relaxed. Too many speakers make the mistake of opening their mouths and shutting their throats. The result is a squeaky voice. There are too good ways of opening the throat: begin to swallow or to yawn. Practice this until you have acquired a resonant, round, and flexible tone.

Place your tongue in the front roof of your mouth, and not in the back roof. In this way you will acquire clearness and volume. A "throaty" voice is one that is projected from a position too close to the throat, where it is so cramped that it has no chance to expand and ring.

Accustom yourself to *listen* to your voice. When you speak into your mirror, don't be merely your spectator. Be your audience, too.

Practice reading poetry and prose aloud. All sorts of poetry and prose. In this way you will develop all sorts of modulations in your voice. Try the following passages:

For the conversational tone—

> The man that hails you Tom or Jack,
> And proves, by thumping on your back,
>   His sense of your great merit,
> Is such a friend that one had need
> Be very much his friend indeed
>   To pardon or to bear it.

For the resolute tone—

> The star of the unconquered will,
>   He rises in my breast,
> Serene, and resolute, and still,
>   And calm, and self-possesst.

For the reflective tone—

> Tomorrow, and tomorrow, and tomorrow
> Creeps in this petty pace from day to day
> To the last syllable of recorded time;
> And all our yesterdays have lighted fools
> The way to dusty death.

For the elevated tone—

> The poet's eye, in a fine frenzy rolling,
> Doth glance from heaven to earth, from earth
>   to heaven;
> And as imagination bodies forth
> The forms of things unknown, the poet's pen
> Turns them to shapes, and gives to airy nothing
> A local habitation and a name.

For the optimistic tone—

Give us, oh, give us, the man who sings at his work! He will do more in the same time—he will do it better—he will persevere longer. One is scarcely sensible of fatigue when he marches to music. The very stars are said to make harmony as they revolve in their spheres.

For the fervid tone—

I held it truth, with him who sings
To one clear harp in diverse tones,
That men may rise on stepping-stones
Of their dead selves to higher things.

For the sincere tone—

You know I say
Just what I think, and nothing more nor less,
And when I pray, my heart is in my prayer.

For the angry tone—

I impeach Warren Hastings of high crimes and misdemeanors.

I impeach him in the name of all the Commons of Great Britain in Parliament assembled, whose parliamentary trust he has betrayed. . . .

I impeach him in the name of the people of India, whose laws, rights, and liberties he has subverted, whose properties he has destroyed, and whose country he has laid waste and desolate. . . .

I impeach him in the name of human nature itself, which he has cruelly outraged, injured, and oppressed in both sexes, in every age, rank, situation and condition of life.

For the sympathetic tone—

And beyond that lies the darkened chamber of labor that only rises to toil and lies down to rest. It is lifted by no hope, mellowed by no comfort; looks into gardens it created, and up to wealth which it has garnered, and has no pleasure thence; looks down to its cradle—there is no hope . . . And gaunt labor says, "I don't ask pity, I ask for justice."

For the humane tone—

> Abou Ben Adhem (may his tribe increase)
> Awoke one night from a deep dream of peace
> And saw within the moonlight of his room,
> Making it rich and like a lily in bloom,
> An angel writing in a book of gold.
> Exceeding peace had made Ben Adhem bold,
> And to the presence in the room he said,
> "What writest thou?"—The vision raised its head,
> And, with a look made of all sweet accord,
> Answered, "The names of those who love the
>   Lord."
> "And is mine one?" said Abou. "Nay, not so,"
> Replied the angel.—Abou spoke more low,
> But cheerfully still, and said, "I pray thee, then,
> Write me as one who loves his fellow-men."
>
> The angel wrote and vanished. The next night
> It came again, with a great wakening light,
> And showed the names whom love of God had
>   blessed—
> And, lo! Ben Adhem's name led all the rest!

For the scornful tone—

> The right honorable gentleman has called me an "unimpeached traitor." I ask him why not "traitor" unqualified by an epithet? I will tell him; it was because he durst not. It was the act of a coward, who raises his arm to strike, but has not the courage to give the blow. I will not call him villain, because it would be unparliamentary, and he is a privy councillor. I will not call him fool, because he happens to be Chancellor of the Exchequer. But I say, he is one who has abused the privileges of Parliament and the freedom of debate, by uttering language which, if spoken out of the House, I should answer only with a blow.

For the courteous tone—

> How sweet and gracious, even in common speech,
> Is that fine sense which men call Courtesy!
> Wholesome as air and genial as the light,
> Welcome in every clime as breath of flowers,

It transmutes aliens into trusting friends,
And gives its owner passport round the globe.

For the religious tone—

If we work upon marble, it will perish; if we
work upon brass, time will efface it; if we rear
temples, they will crumble into dust; but if we work
upon our immortal minds, if we imbue them with
principles—with the just fear of God and our
fellow-man—we engrave on those tablets something which will brighten to all eternity.

For the sincere and simple tone—

Be simple, unaffected; be honest in your speaking
and writing. Never use a long word when a short
one will do . . . Where a short word will do, you
always lose by using a long one. You lose in clearness, you lose in honest expression of your meaning; and in the estimation of all men who are
competent to judge, you lose in reputation for
ability.

The only true way to shine, even in this false
world, is to be modest and unassuming. Falsehood may be a very thick crust, but in the course of
time truth will find a place to break through.

Write as you would speak; speak as you think
. . . The truly wise man will so speak that no one
will observe how he speaks.

This last passage from the pen of William Cullen Bryant
is a perfect guide for the public speaker. A simple style, a
soft voice, and a modest manner—these are the three corner-
stones upon which to build the pyramid of a good speech. One
of the greatest orators in history, Marcus Tullius Cicero, gave
the following advice to a student who wanted to become a good
speaker:

"To acquire self-confidence, and to win the confidence of
your audience, it is necessary to develop a soft voice, a modest
countenance, and a simple manner of speaking . . . This
method is especially valuable in those speeches in which you
are trying to influence a fair-minded judge . . . Energetic
oratory is not always desirable; more favor is to be gained
by a gentle demeanor, a soft voice, and a simple style."

§ 2
INFORMAL TALKS

We are called upon, at one time or another, either to deliver an informal talk or to introduce an informal speaker.

When you introduce another speaker, be brief. Don't make a long speech yourself. It is discourteous to your guest speaker. He will most likely resent it; and your audience, too, will be displeased. Make no elaborate eulogy about the speaker. It will embarrass him and put him at a disadvantage. Nobody likes to hear his own funeral oration before he is dead.

Be sure you know all the requisite facts about the speaker you are introducing. Don't be like the toastmaster at a recent dinner who tried to introduce a speaker about whom he knew very little. He began the introduction with a clever joke about divorce. Imagine his surprise and his embarrassment when he learned that the man whom he had introduced had recently gone through a very unpleasant divorce and was quite sensitive on this subject.

Avoid, in your introduction, such trite expressions as:

"It gives me great pleasure to introduce——"
"We are indeed fortunate to have——"
"Mr.—— needs no introduction."

Begin the introduction, if possible, with an anecdote about the person you are introducing. If you cannot *create* such an anecdote, try to *adapt* one for the occasion. Let us, for example, imagine that you are introducing a friend who can stand a little joke at his expense, provided the joke is rounded off at the point, so that it tickles the victim instead of stinging him. I have heard this sort of introduction at a recent class dinner. The toastmaster was introducing a prominent attorney to his classmates:

"Gentlemen," he said, "the next speaker has told me a good story about himself. Whether or not the story is true, I shall leave it for you to decide. Here is the story: One day this young man was speaking, so he told me, to a convention of his colleagues.

When he was halfway through with his speech, he looked at his audience and said—'My friends, I hardly know how to modulate my voice from now on. If I speak too softly, the people in the back rows won't hear me. If I speak too loudly, the people in the front rows will wake up. Now I want all of you to hear me, and yet I don't want any of you to be deprived of your sleep. What shall I do?'

"Whereupon someone in the audience remarked, 'Just keep on talking natural-like, and in ten minutes we'll all be asleep.'

"Gentlemen, I shall now introduce to you the young man who has told me this story about himself. Is it a *true* story? Personally I don't believe it. For the man who told it to me is a modest man, and a very good speaker, and a *lawyer*. Where a clever lawyer *lies,* you know, *nobody* can sleep.

"Seriously, though, it has been my good fortune to hear this young man on many occasions. And every time I've heard him, I have been roused to new thoughts, new emotions, and new enthusiasms.

"Gentlemen, it is now our good fortune to hear one of the most brilliant of our classmates—the Honorable Daniel Robinson!"

* * *

Sometimes, when you have several speakers to introduce, it is best to climax the introduction of the last and principal speaker with the mere statement: "And now, ladies and gentlemen, Dr. Leland Bowers!" This is especially effective when the last speaker is famous, so that no specific compliments are necessary.

When you introduce a speaker, it is very important to know just when to stop. Say no less and no more—especially no more—than is necessary to make the desired effect. There is a greater danger in saying too much than in saying too little. Several months ago, at a medical banquet, the toastmaster made the mistake of saying just a little too much. When he came to the last speaker, he introduced him as follows:

"And now comes the moment for which we have all been waiting so eagerly. Ladies and gentlemen, Professor Kenton!"

Although the toastmaster was unaware of the fact, his first sentence had contained an implied insult to the previous speakers. The last speaker was tactful, however, and he gracefully atoned for the toastmaster's blunder with the words:

"Ladies and gentlemen, *my* eager moments came when I listened to the other speakers. Indeed, they acquitted themselves so splendidly that whatever I may have to say will come, I am afraid, as an anticlimax."

* * *

When you introduce a speaker who is universally known, the proper way to introduce him is merely to mention his name or his office. For example:

Ladies and gentlemen, Professor Einstein!
Ladies and gentlemen, the President!
Ladies and gentlemen, the President of the United States!

A toastmaster's job, you see, is a difficult and a delicate one. It requires special talents, one of the most important of which is tact.

This quality of tact is equally important whether you introduce another speaker or make your own speech.

Be tactful. Think of the other fellow's feelings. An informal talk is intended primarily to entertain. Do your share in creating good fellowship. Avoid being either a rowdy or a bore.

Tactfulness means quick thinking. Learn to think quickly on your feet. An informal talk requires rapid organization. Learn to organize your thoughts *as you talk*. Practice this for several minutes every day. Jot down a number of subjects, and talk extemporaneously on each of these subjects for ten minutes. Then, when you have acquired a sufficient measure of ability in doing this sort of thing, try the following game among the members of your family or your friends: Let each one jot down a subject on a piece of paper. Fold these papers and put them into a hat. Then let each one in turn take out one of these papers at random and speak for ten minutes on the subject indicated on that paper. Try it. I have seen it produce excellent results over and over again. As an example of the kinds of

subjects to select for this exercise in extemporaneous speaking,
consider the following:

Is Gandhi a Failure?
The Traffic Problem
What Is Genius?
The Crime Wave
The Future of Aviation
The Modern Boy
The Modern Girl
The Modern Parent
Intercollegiate Sports
College Fraternities—A Benefit or a Menace?
Capital and Labor
The Supreme Court
The Constitution
Democracy and Dictatorship
Can Dictatorship Happen Here?
The Movies—How to Improve Them
The Homeliest Man I Know
A Man Is Known by the Company He Keeps
Are Kings Outmoded?
Is This Age Irreligious?
Modern Transportation
Discuss Browning's passage:

"God's in His Heaven,
    All's right with the World."

Prejudice
Do People Think Enough?
Do People Play Enough?
Do We Live Too Rapidly?
A Healthy Mind in a Healthy Body
Divorce
Television
Spring's Message
Hitch Your Wagon to a Star
The Ten Greatest Men Today
The Ten Greatest Men in American History
The Ten Greatest Men in World History
How to Improve My City
How to Improve My Home
How to Improve Humanity
Our Leisure Hours—How to Spend Them

Gossip
Strange Hobbies
The Future of Exploration
My Favorite Authors
My Favorite Composers
My Favorite Artists
Why So Much Insanity Today?

Should your informal talk be serious or humorous? That depends upon your personality. Remember that the average audience enjoys a good thought as well as a good laugh. Long anecdotes are out of place in a short informal talk. A brief joke or epigram, however, will snap an audience out of its inattention and put it into a receptive mood. In Chapter X you have seen a number of brief jokes. These can be made to fit well into an extemporaneous talk. Following is a list of epigrams that will add sparkle and fire to your talk:

I

Epigrams of Unknown Authorship

A bad custom is like a good cake, better broken than
  kept.

* * *

A candle lights others and consumes itself.

* * *

The qualities rare in a bee that we meet
  In an epigram never should fail;
The body should always be little and sweet,
  And a sting should be left in its tail.

* * *

The best time to marry: when you're young, later;
  when you're old, never.

* * *

A closed mouth catches no flies.

* * *

A Tyrant's Epitaph
Lie heavy on him, earth! For he
Laid many heavy loads on thee.

* * *

A crank is a little thing that makes revolutions.

* * *

A degenerate nobleman who boasts of his ancestors
is like a turnip. The best part of him is under-
ground.

* * *

Knowledge, when wisdom is too weak to guide her,
Is like a headstrong horse that throws his rider.

* * *

Seven wealthy towns contend for Homer dead,
Through which the living Homer begged his bread.

* * *

The pleasures of youth are but flowers of May;
Oh, let me live well, though I live but a day.

* * *

Though men have many faults,
    The women have but two:
There's nothing good they say,
    And there's nothing right they do.

* * *

It's a very good world that we live in,
To lend, or to spend, or to give in;
But to work, or to beg, or to borrow,
It's a heck of a world, full of sorrow.

* * *

The law doth punish man or woman
That steals the goose from off the common,
But lets the greater scoundrel loose,
Who steals the common from the goose.

* * *

If four play whist,
    And one looks on,
They make blunders,
    He makes none.

* * *

Why should we work for posterity? Posterity has
done nothing for us.

* * *

Here's a toast to poverty! It sticks by us when all
our friends forsake us.

* * *

Haste makes waste. When you are in a hurry, dress
slowly.

* * *

A wit said of Franklin D. Roosevelt that "by going
a little more to the left, he came a little nearer to
the right."

* * *

A man of words and not of deeds
Is like a garden full of weeds.

* * *

The best remedy against adversity is patience.

* * *

When the stomach is full, the head is empty.
—*An Arabian Proverb*

II

Epigrams of Famous Authors

How often do sudden fortunes ruin young men! . . .
I should like to be ruined.
—*Artemus Ward*

* * *

Steal a loaf of bread, and you go to jail; steal a
railroad, and you go to Parliament.
—*George Bernard Shaw*

* * *

We are all as God made us—only a good deal worse.
—*Cervantes*

* * *

The Athenians govern the world; I govern the
Athenians; my wife governs me.
—*Themistocles*

* * *

He has a right to criticize who has a heart to help.
—*Abraham Lincoln*

* * *

To be useful is the only way to be happy.
—*Hans Christian Andersen*

* * *

Good Americans, when they die, go to Paris.
—*Thomas Gould Appleton*

* * *

The greatest of all sacrifices is the sacrifice of time.
—*Plutarch*

* * *

Proverbs are short sentences from long experience.
—*Cervantes*

* * *

A physician is a man who pours drugs of which he knows little into a body of which he knows less.
—*Voltaire*

* * *

To young men I have but three words of advice— Work, work, work.
—*Bismarck*

* * *

If Cleopatra's nose had been a little shorter, the whole face of the world might have been changed.
—*Blaise Pascal*

* * *

We love people not for what they can do for us, but for what we can do for them.
—*Tolstoy*

* * *

Nothing great was ever achieved without enthusiasm.
—*Emerson*

* * *

It is much easier to be critical than correct.
—*Disraeli*

* * *

Too few words obscure the sense. So do too many words.

—*Horace*

* * *

Be not simply good; be good for something.

—*Thoreau*

* * *

Is banter permissible in extemporaneous speaking? Sometimes, yes. Good-natured banter is not out of place among friends, or even among friendly enemies. At a dinner of Harvard and Yale students the Harvard toastmaster made the following toast:

> "Here's to my Yale friends. They have many faults, to be sure, but on the whole they're too good to be damned."

> Whereupon the Yale toastmaster stood up and said:

> "And here's to my Harvard friends. They have many virtues, to be sure, but they're too damned to be good."

* * *

Don't laugh at your own jokes. Let others do the laughing. One of the most successful of American after-dinner speakers, Artemus Ward, used to regard his audiences with a look of innocent surprise whenever his jokes sent them into gales of laughter. Some humorists, like Fred Allen, can laugh at their own jokes and do so gracefully. This is a rare talent, however. Try, if possible, to imitate the style of Artemus Ward rather than that of Fred Allen.

When you are through with your joke, however, assume a pleasant face. An informal talk, remember, is intended primarily to amuse rather than to instruct. The best informal talks are after-dinner speeches. When people have eaten well, they don't like to think. Their blood is in their stomachs, not in their heads. Help them, with your talk, to digest their food. In an after-dinner talk, sad subjects, and to a certain extent, even *serious* subjects, are taboo.

§ 3

FORMAL SPEECHES

The informal speaker is an entertainer. The formal speaker is an instructor. Do not, however, carry this distinction too far. Every good entertainer is an instructor, and every good instructor is an entertainer. Even your formal speech must be simple, natural, and palatable.

The formal speech must not only instruct, but it must convince. In order to convince others, you must be thoroughly convinced yourself. And this brings us to a phase of public speaking which, I believe, requires a careful overhauling. I mean the school and the college debate. It is a mistake, I think, to ask youngsters to uphold a side in which they do not believe. If a young man believes ardently in democracy, it is not right for his teachers to ask him to prepare a convincing speech against it. This preparation may train him to be a good hypocrite; it will not train him to be an honest advocate of his beliefs. A debater should be trained to be, above all things, truthful.

This applies to all speakers. Don't waste your time trying to be clever about subjects which are not close to your heart. Sincerity is more important than cleverness. In a formal speech, as well as in an informal talk, honesty is of paramount importance.

The primary object in a formal speech is to impart honest information. You are a teacher, and your listeners are your scholars. Teach them what you know, and convince them that what you teach them is genuine. A formal speech is a serious matter. You are spreading information among a mass of people. You never can tell how far-reaching this information may be. A single speech may be the cause of untold good or of incalculable harm.

This is a day of popular lectures. Never before in the history of the world has the man of ideas been able to present them to so vast an audience. The classroom, the club, and the radio have made the modern world ear-minded. The formal speech, therefore, is a great factor in our present-day education. Most of us have a special knowledge of some subject, or a special point of view. And, if we can present this subject or point of view in a simple and honest and convincing manner, the world is ready to listen to us.

Suppose you are an army officer, or a writer, or an insurance salesman, or a farmer, or an engineer, or a food expert, or a doctor. You possess a wealth of information with which you can make your audience richer. Your speech to them will be a public benefaction. You and I are living in a day of adult education. We are constantly educating one another, making the private knowledge of each the common knowledge of all. Every group has its lectures, delivered either by an expert outsider, or by a member of the group. And this last procedure is a step in the right direction. It is rapidly becoming the ambition of almost every one of us—and a very good ambition it is—to be a public speaker at least in our little circle.

The best training for this is first to become a *private* speaker. The college student who wants to become an expert oarsman is first taught to row in a wherry. Then, when he has attained sufficient skill in handling this simpler kind of boat, he is allowed to go into a scull. In the same manner, if you want to make a good *formal* speech, practice at first by making *informal* speeches.

For some years it was my privilege to attend the meetings of a mutual benefit society. The membership consisted of workingmen and small businessmen. I watched those men, week after week, stand up and speak on matters that deeply concerned them. I saw new members of the society trying to make their first informal speech. I noted their embarrassment, their reddened faces, their stammering tongues, their clumsy efforts to find the right word and the right phrase. I saw them make their informal speeches a month later, a year later, and I was amazed at the improvement. Some of them, as a result of this sort of informal practice, became excellent formal speakers. I heard them at conventions, where they delivered, as delegates, the wishes and the views of their society. They spoke simply, fluently, and honestly, and the other delegates listened to them attentively and were convinced. These speakers knew what they wanted, and they had learned, through faithful practice, how to express their wants. And they carried their point!

The formal speech is, in some ways, easier than the conversation or the informal talk. When you converse, or when you talk informally, you are probably conflicting with the desires of others to talk. They are therefore impatient with you. They are anxious to have you get through with your talk so that they may get their own chance. But when you come prepared to make a formal speech, your audience comes equally prepared to listen to you. All they expect of you is for you to present your material simply, entertainingly, and honestly.

Let your formal speech be simple. Use ordinary words. If you are a doctor or a lawyer or an engineer, avoid technical terms, unless you happen to speak to a group of your own profession. Don't use involved sentences. Don't try to appear too learned. An audience will fall asleep if you attempt to impress it with sentences that are "pinnacled dim in the intense inane."

Arrange your material, as well as your sentences, in a simple and logical order. In the short time allotted to you for your speech, you can give to your audience only a small part of your knowledge. Select this part carefully, so that it will not be a jumble of unrelated facts. Suppose you are a doctor. If you are talking to a group of college men, you will present certain phases of your knowledge. You will give the young men such facts as will interest them in connection with their particular hygienic problems. You will not drag in any such facts as might appeal to middle-aged women or old men. This advice is rather obvious, and yet it is surprising how frequently a speaker will disregard it in delivering a public lecture.

Suit your talk to the emotional need and the mental capacity of your audience. Therein lies simplicity.

Begin at the beginning, and end at the end. In writing, this is not always sound advice. In his excellent essay on style the Latin poet Horace advised the writer to jump into the middle of a subject. This may be good for the writer, but not for the speaker. To jump into the middle of a speech would confuse an audience. You are taking your listeners on an excursion into a field of knowledge familiar to you but unfamiliar to them. Take them along the easiest paths into the most interesting spots. Don't compel them to follow you in leaps and bounds from one obscure place to another.

Begin your speech with a definition of any unfamiliar terms that you may have to use in the course of your speech. Dr. James J. Walsh, formerly Dean of the Fordham Medical School, is one of the most successful of contemporary speakers. One of the chief reasons for his success is that he is constantly defining terms. He takes his words and his phrases apart and he shows you *why* they mean *what* they mean. His subject may deal with abstract science or medieval philosophy, but his talks are always clear and illuminating. For he always remembers to define his terms.

Define your terms. Prepare the way for a complete understanding of your subject. Outline the subject; divide it into sections; number these sections. For example, if you are going to speak on the subject of *Strikes,* you may introduce your talk somewhat as follows:

"There are three important angles from which we may consider the question of strikes: (1) their effect upon labor; (2) their effect upon capital; and (3) their effect upon the general public.

"I shall discuss these three angles in their regular order."

This sort of introduction supplies your audience with a map of your entire speech. Together you will be able to travel from beginning to end, without anyone at any time losing his way.

The introduction of a speech is difficult, but the conclusion is even more difficult. Many a speaker, like Tennyson's brook, goes on and on and on, for the simple reason that he doesn't know how to stop. A good end is very important—more important, indeed, than a good beginning. Your audience will judge your speech by the concluding words. The *last* sentence is the *lasting* sentence. It will linger longest in their minds. Therefore you must conclude with a punch. Your anecdote, your joke, and your epigram can best serve you at the end of a speech, especially if they can be made to fit gracefully into the framework of your own discourse.

Don't bring your speech to a sudden stop. It's like suddenly jamming your brakes while traveling at 50 miles an hour. It will jolt your listeners and leave them with a sense of discomfort. Lead gradually up to your final sentence. Let your voice take on a more impressive tempo. Warn your audience, by your manner, that you are about to conclude. And then, when your audience is properly keyed up, speak your last sentence slowly and distinctly. A good way to end a formal speech is with a quotation from some well-known poet. Many people dislike poetry. Yet everybody is impressed with an apt quotation that is well delivered at the psychological moment.

There is one kind of speech—the inflammatory speech—in which the foregoing advice does not apply. What must you do when you make a speech of that nature? Two things.

First, if you want to make an inflammatory speech—don't. An intelligent public speaker should instruct the mind, not arouse the passion. As we become gradually civilized, we depend more and more upon *education,* and less and less upon *agitation.* A ranting speaker is nowadays regarded as an object of ridicule.

Second, if an unusual occasion arises where you *must* make an impassioned speech in a just cause, work the speech up to a climax. Instead of *lowering* your voice and *retarding* your tempo, *raise* your voice and *accelerate* your tempo. Let the last sentence be a ringing climax—a trumpet-call to action.

* * *

The following quotation from Wendell Phillips is a good example of the effective ending:

> The third charge brought against us is that we form trades unions. To be sure we do . . . We say to the mills of Lowell, who have turned us out of doors, "We'll starve you into submission." Well, "it's a narrow contest. It's an unjust, it's a cruel, it's an avaricious method." So it is. Where did we learn it? Learned it of capital, learned it of our enemies.

A lawyer, pleading for a man who was on trial for his life, concluded his speech with this apt quotation from Shakespeare:

> The quality of mercy . . .
>   . . . is twice blest;
> It blesseth him that gives and him that takes;
> It is enthroned in the hearts of kings;
> It is an attribute to God Himself;
> And earthly power doth then show likest God's
> When mercy seasons justice.

When Franklin D. Roosevelt made his last radio campaign speech on the night before the presidential election in 1936, he concluded most dramatically with this quotation from the Bible:

> What doth the Lord require of thee
> But to do justly, to love mercy,
> And to walk humbly with thy God?

OTHER EXAMPLES OF GOOD BEGINNINGS AND GOOD ENDINGS

A

Beginnings

Oliver Cromwell's Speech at the Opening of the First Protective Parliament:

> Gentlemen,—You are met here on the greatest occasion that, I believe, England ever saw; having upon your shoulders the interests of three great nations with the territories belonging to them; and truly, I believe I may say it without any hyperbole, you have upon your shoulders the interests of all the Christian people in the world. . . .

* * *

Napoleon's Address to the Army at the Beginning of the Italian Campaign:

> Soldiers,—You are naked and ill-fed! The government owes you much and can give you nothing. . . . It is my design to lead you into the most fertile plains of the world. Rich provinces and great cities will be in your power; there you will find honor, glory, and wealth. . . .

* * *

Victor Hugo's Oration on the Centennial of Voltaire's Death:

> One hundred years ago today a man died! He died immortal, laden with years, with labors, and with the most illustrious and formidable of responsibilities—the responsibility of the human conscience informed and corrected. He departed amid the curses

of the past and the blessings of the future. . . . He was more than a man—he was an epoch!

* * *

Henry Ward Beecher's Oration at the Raising of the "Old Flag" at Fort Sumter, April 14, 1865:

On this solemn and joyful day we again lift to the breeze our fathers' flag, now again the banner of the United States, with the fervent prayer that God may crown it with honor, protect it from treason, and send it down to our children with all the blessings of civilization, liberty, and religion. Terrible in battle, may it be beneficent in peace. . . .

* * *

Daniel Webster's Bunker Hill Monument Oration:

This uncounted multitude before me, and around me, proves the feeling which the occasion has excited. These thousands of human faces, glowing with sympathy and joy, and, from the impulses of a common gratitude, turned reverently to heaven, in this spacious temple of the firmament, proclaim that the day, the place, and the purpose of our assembling have made a deep impression on our hearts. . . .

* * *

Chauncey M. Depew's Speech at the Unveiling of the Bartholdi Statue of Liberty in the New York Harbor:

We dedicate this statue to the friendship of nations and the peace of the world.

The spirit of liberty embraces all races in common brotherhood; it voices in all languages the same needs and aspirations. The full power of its expansive and progressive influence cannot be reached until wars cease, armies are disbanded, and international disputes are settled by lawful tribunals and the principles of justice. . . .

* * *

Ingersoll's Oration on Humboldt:

Great men seem to be a part of the infinite—brothers of the mountains, and the seas.

Humboldt was one of these. He was one of those

serene men, in some respects like our own Franklin, whose names have all the lustre of a star. He was one of the few, great enough to rise above the superstition and prejudice of his time, and to know that experience, observation, and reason are the only bases of knowledge.

He became one of the greatest of men in spite of having been born rich and noble. . . .

* * *

Bryan's Speech on the Cross of Gold:

It would be presumptuous, indeed, to present myself against the distinguished gentlemen to whom you have listened if this were a mere measuring of abilities, but this is not a contest between persons. The humblest citizen in all the land, when clad in the armor of a righteous cause, is stronger than all the hosts of error. I come to speak to you in defense of a cause as holy as the cause of liberty—the cause of humanity. . . .

B

Endings

Patrick Henry's Speech Delivered at the Virginia Convention, March 23, 1775:

. . . . It is in vain, sir, to extenuate the matter. Gentlemen may cry, Peace, Peace—but there is no peace. The war is already begun! The next gale that sweeps from the earth will bring to our ears the clash of resounding arms! Our brethren are already in the field! Why stand we here idle? What is it that gentlemen wish? What would they have? Is life so dear, or peace so sweet, as to be purchased at the price of chains and slavery? Forbid it, Almighty God! I know not what course others may take; but as for me, give me liberty or give me death!

* * *

Danton's Speech on the Defense of the French Republic:

. . . . The tocsin we shall sound is not the alarm signal of danger; it orders the charge on the enemies of France. To conquer we have need to dare, to dare again, always to dare! And France will be saved!

* * *

Napoleon's Speech at the Beginning of the Russian Invasion:

. . . . Among the Russians there are no generals in fighting against whom I can gain any glory. All I wish is to win the victory with the least possible bloodshed. My soldiers are my children.

* * *

Henry Ward Beecher's Oration at the Raising of the "Old Flag" at Fort Sumter:

. . . . To thee, God of our Fathers, we render thanksgiving and praise for that wondrous providence that has brought forth from such a harvest of war the seed of so much liberty and peace.

We invoke peace upon the North. Peace be to the West. Peace be upon the South!

In the name of God we lift our banner and dedicate it to peace, union, and liberty, now and forever more.

* * *

Henry Clay, Denouncing Andrew Jackson, April 30, 1834:

. . . . Sir, the advisers of the President, whoever they are, deceive him and themselves. They have vainly supposed that, by an appeal to the people, and an exhibition of the wounds of the President, they could enlist the sympathies and the commiseration of the people—that the name of Andrew Jackson would bear down the Senate and all opposition. They have yet to learn, what they will soon learn, that even a good and responsible name may be used so frequently, as an indorser, that its credit and the public confidence in its solidity have been seriously impaired. They mistake the intelligence of the people, who are not prepared to see and sanction the President putting forth indiscriminate charges of a violation of the Constitution against whomsoever he pleases, and exhibiting unmeasured rage and indignation when his own infallibility is dared to be questioned.

(Note: This speech of Clay's is entitled, interestingly enough, *Dictators in American Politics*. Observe the surprising modernity of the tone. It was delivered against Jackson in 1834. Change the name of the President, and it sounds like a speech that might have been delivered against Roosevelt by his political opponents in 1937.)

* * *

Daniel Webster's Bunker Hill Monument Oration:

. . . . Our proper business is improvement. Let our age be the age of improvement. In a day of peace let us advance the arts of peace and the works of peace. Let us develop the resources of our land, call forth its powers, build up its institutions, promote all its great interests, and see whether we, also, in our day and generation, may not perform something worthy to be remembered. Let us cultivate a true spirit of union and harmony. In pursuing the great objects which our condition points out to us, let us act under a settled conviction and a habitual feeling that these twenty-four States are one country. Let our conceptions be enlarged to the circle of our duties. Let us extend our ideas over the whole of the vast field in which we are called to act. Let our object be our country, our whole country, and nothing but our country. And by the blessing of God may that country itself become a vast and splendid monument, not of oppression and terror, but of wisdom, of peace, and of liberty, upon which the world may gaze with admiration, forever.

* * *

Abraham Lincoln's First Inaugural Address:

. . . . I am loth to close. We are not enemies, but friends. We must not be enemies. Though passion may have strained, it must not break, our bonds of affection. The mystic cords of memory, stretching from every battlefield and over this broad land, will yet swell the chorus of the Union when again touched, as surely they will be, by the better angels of our nature.

* * *

Chauncey M. Depew's Speech at the Unveiling of the
Bartholdi Statue of Liberty:

. . . . I devoutly believe that from the Unseen and
the Unknown two great souls have come to partici-
pate in this celebration. The faith in which they died
fulfilled, the cause for which they battled triumphant,
the people they loved in the full enjoyment of the
rights for which they labored and fought and suffered, the spirit voices of Washington and Lafayette
join in the glad acclaim of France and the United
States to Liberty Enlightening the World.

* * *

Ingersoll's Speech at His Brother's Grave:

. . . . He who sleeps here, when dying, mistaking
the approach of death for the return of health, whispered with his latest breath: "I am better now."
Let us believe, in spite of doubts and dogmas, and
tears and fears, that these dear words are true of all
the countless dead.

And now to you who have been chosen, from
among the many men he loved, to do the last sad office for the dead, we give his sacred dust. Speech cannot contain our love. There was, there is, no greater,
stronger, manlier man.

* * *

Ingersoll's Oration on Humboldt:

. . . . The angel of history added another name to
the starry scroll of the immortals.

The world is his monument; upon the eternal
granite of her hills he inscribed his name, and there
upon the everlasting stone his genius wrote this, the
sublimest of truths,

"The Universe is Governed by Law!"

* * *

Victor Hugo's Oration on Voltaire:

. . . . Let us stop the shedding of human blood.
Enough, despots! Barbarism still exists. Let philosophy protest. Let the eighteenth century help the nine-
teenth. The philosophers, our predecessors, are the

apostles of truth. Let us invoke these illustrious phantoms that, face to face with monarchies thinking of war, they may proclaim the right of man to life, the right of conscience to liberty, the sovereignty of reason, the sacredness, the blessedness of peace! And since night issues from thrones, let light emanate from tombs.

* * *

All the foregoing beginnings and endings are so effective because they are so simple and so sincere. The great orators knew how to introduce themselves and bow themselves off without the blare of trumpets. Their speeches were successful because they had learned just how to start and just when to finish. And, if *you* learn to begin and end right, *your* speeches, too, will be successful. A speech well begun is half done; and, no matter what blunders you may make in the body of your speech, a speech well ended is completely mended.

When you have successfully mastered the beginning and the end, your next step is how to present the body of your speech. Here, too, you must be guided by the principle of simplicity. Let your speech flow along like a limpid brook, without any sudden turns or twists or cataracts of oratory. Plan out the order in which you want to bring home your points—one, two, three, four—and deliver your speech in that order. Begin with the least important and end with the most important. Lead up to a climax. It is a mistake to have a weaker argument follow a stronger. The order should be the other way around. Suppose you want to discuss the wisdom of adopting a dictatorship for the United States. You do not believe in such a dictatorship. You think its adoption in this country would be a disaster. You will therefore advance your argument against this measure somewhat as follows:

   I. Introduction.
  II. The measure is unwise.
      A. It is contrary to our political philosophy.
      B. It is contrary to our political precedents.
      C. It has been disapproved by eminent authorities.
 III. The measure is impractical.
      A. It has failed wherever it has been tried.

IV. The measure is unnecessary.
    A. It would *not* solve our problems.
    B. Our present form of government *can* and
        will solve our problems.
V. Conclusion.
  A dictatorship for the United States, therefore, is
unwise, impractical, and *unnecessary.* It would be, in
short, a *tragedy.*

One of the best examples of the simple and sincere and
therefore highly effective speech is Thomas Jefferson's First
Inaugural, entitled *Democracy Defined.* Let us first outline
this speech, and then quote it in full:

Outline

I. Introduction.
    A. Jefferson thanks the public for his election.
    B. He expresses his fear that he is unworthy
        of the honor.
    C. He asks the other branches of the gov-
        ernment to co-operate with him.
II. Definition of the *Democratic Principle.*
    A. The will of the majority should rule.
    B. The rights of the minority should be pro-
        tected.
    C. Political intolerance, like religious intol-
        erance, should be abolished.
    D. Democracy is the world's best hope.
III. The necessity of establishing a wise and frugal
   government,—
    A. To give freedom to the individual.
    B. To protect labor.
IV. Jefferson's aim as President.
    A. To dispense equal justice.
    B. To maintain peace.
    C. To support the state governments.
    D. To uphold the Constitution.
    E. To guard against revolution by a peaceful
        correction of abuses against the
        people.
    F. To abide by the decisions of the majority.
    G. To maintain a strong militia.

   H. To subordinate the military to the civil
     authority.
   I. To practice economy.
   J. To pay all debts.
   K. To encourage agriculture and commerce.
   L. To maintain the freedom of religion, of
     the press, and of the people.
   M. To continue the principle of impartial
     trial by jury.
  V. Conclusion.

The Complete Speech

Friends and Fellow-Citizens: Called upon to undertake the
duties of the first executive office of our country, I avail myself
of the presence of that portion of my fellow-citizens which is
here assembled, to express my grateful thanks for the favor
with which they have been pleased to look toward me, to declare a sincere consciousness that the task is above my talents,
and that I approach it with those anxious and awful pre-
sentiments which the greatness of the charge and the weakness
of my powers so justly inspire. A rising nation spread over a
wide and fruitful land, traversing all the seas with the rich
productions of their industry, engaged in commerce with nations who feel power and forget right, advancing rapidly to
destinies beyond the reach of mortal eye; when I contemplate
these transcendent objects, and see the honor, the happiness,
and the hopes of this beloved country committed to the issue
and the auspices of this day, I shrink from the contemplation,
and humble myself before the magnitude of the undertaking.
Utterly, indeed, should I despair, did not the presence of many
whom I here see remind me that in the other high authorities
provided by our own constitution I shall find resources of wisdom, of virtue, and of zeal on which to rely under all difficulties. To you, then, gentlemen, who are charged with the sovereign functions of legislation, and to those associated with you,
I look with encouragement for that guidance and support
which may enable us to steer with safety the vessel in which
we are all embarked, amid the conflicting elements of a
troubled world.

During the contest of opinion through which we have passed.

the animation of discussions and of exertions has sometimes worn an aspect which might impose on strangers unused to think freely and to speak and to write what they think; but this being now decided by the voice of the nation, announced according to the rules of the Constitution, all will, of course, arrange themselves under the will of the law, and unite in common efforts for the common good. All, too, will bear in mind this sacred principle, that though the will of the majority is in all cases to prevail, that will, to be rightful, must be reasonable; that the minority possess their equal rights, which equal law must protect, and to violate which would be oppression. Let us then, fellow-citizens, write with one heart and one mind; let us restore to social intercouse that harmony and affection without which liberty, and even life itself, are but dreary things. And let us reflect, that, having banished from our land that religious intolerance under which mankind so long bled and suffered, we have yet gained little, if we countenance a political intolerance as despotic, as wicked, and capable of as bitter and bloody persecutions. During the throes and convulsions of the ancient world, during the agonizing spasms of infuriated man, seeking through blood and slaughter his long-lost liberty, it was not wonderful that the agitation of the billows should reach even this distant and peaceful shore; that this should be more felt and feared by some and less by others; and should divide opinions as to measures of safety; but every difference of opinion is not a difference of principle. We have called by different names brethren of the same principle. We are all Republicans: we are all Federalists. If there be any among us who would wish to dissolve this Union, or to change its republican form, let them stand undisturbed as monuments of the safety with which error of opinion may be tolerated, where reason is left free to combat it. I know, indeed, that some honest men fear that a republican government cannot be strong; that this government is not strong enough. But would the honest patriot, in the full tide of successful experiment, abandon a government which has so far kept us free and firm, on the theoretic and visionary fear that this government, the world's best hope, may, by possibility, want energy to preserve itself? I trust not. I believe this, on the contrary, the strongest government on earth. I believe it the only one where every man, at the call of the law, would fly to the standard of the law, and would meet invasions of the public order as his own personal concern. Sometimes it is said that man cannot be trusted with the government of himself. Can he, then, be trusted with the government of others? Or have we found angels in the form of kings to govern him? Let history answer this question.

Let us, then, with courage and confidence pursue our own federal and republican principles; our attachment to union and representative government. Kindly separated by nature and a wide ocean from the exterminating havoc of one quarter of the globe; too high-minded to endure the degradations of the others; possessing a chosen country, with room enough for our descendants to the hundredth and thousandth generation; entertaining a due sense of our equal right to the use of our own faculties, to the acquisitions of our own industry, to honor and confidence from our fellow-citizens, resulting not from birth, but from our actions and their sense of them; enlightened by a benign religion, professed, indeed, and practiced in various forms, yet all of them inculcating honesty, truth, temperance, gratitude, and the love of man; acknowledging and adoring an overruling Providence, which, by all its dispensations, proves that it delights in the happiness of man here and his greater happiness hereafter; with all these blessings, what more is necessary to make us a happy and prosperous people? Still one thing more, fellow-citizens—a wise and frugal government, which shall restrain men from injuring one another, shall leave them otherwise free to regulate their own pursuits of industry and improvement, and shall not take from the mouth of labor the bread it has earned. This is the sum of good government; and this is necessary to close the circle of our felicities.

About to enter, fellow-citizens, on the exercise of duties which comprehend everything dear and valuable to you, it is proper you should understand what I deem the essential principles of our government, and consequently those which ought to shape its administration. I will compress them within the narrowest compass they will bear, stating the general principle, but not all its limitations. Equal and exact justice to all men, of whatever state or persuasion, religious or political; peace, commerce, and honest friendship with all nations, entangling alliances with none; the support of the State governments in all their rights, as the most competent administrations for our domestic concerns, and the surest bulwarks against anti-republican tendencies; the preservation of the general government in its whole constitutional vigor, as the sheetanchor of our peace at home and safety abroad; a jealous care of the right of election by the people; a mild and safe correction of abuses which are lopped by the sword of revolution, where peaceable remedies are unprovided; absolute acquiescence in the decisions of the majority, the vital principle of republics, from which is no appeal but to force, the vital principle and immediate parent of despotism; a well-disciplined militia, our best reliance in peace and for the first moments of war, till regulars may relieve them; the supremacy of the civil over the military authority; economy in the public expense, that labor may be lightly burdened; the honest payment of our debts, and sacred preservation of the public faith; encouragement of agriculture, and of commerce as its handmaid; the diffusion of information and arraignment of all abuses at the bar of the public reason; freedom of religion, freedom of the press, and freedom of person, under the protection of Habeas Corpus; and trial by juries impartially selected. These principles form the bright constellation which has gone before us, and guided our steps through an age of revolution and reformation. The wisdom of our sages and blood of our heroes have been devoted to their attainment; they should be the creed of our political faith: the text of civic instruction; the touchstone by which to try the services of those we trust; and should we wander from them in moments of error or of alarm, let us hasten to retrace our steps and to regain the road which alone leads to peace, liberty, and safety.

I repair, then, fellow-citizens, to the post you have assigned me. With experience enough in subordinate offices to have seen the difficulties of this, the greatest of all, I have learned to expect that it will rarely fall to the lot of imperfect man to retire from this station with the reputation and the favor which bring him into it. Without pretensions to that high confidence you reposed in our first and greatest revolutionary character, whose pre-eminent services had entitled him to the first place in his country's love, and destined for him the fairest page in the volume of faithful history, I ask so much confidence only as may give firmness and effect to the legal administration of your affairs. I shall often go wrong through defect of judgment. When right, I shall often be thought wrong by those whose positions will not command a view of the whole ground. I ask your indulgence for my own errors, which will never be intentional; and your support against the errors of others, who may condemn what they would not, if seen in all its parts. The approbation implied by your suffrage is a great consolation to me for the past; and my future solicitude will be to retain the good opinion of those who have bestowed it in advance, to conciliate that of others by doing them all the good in my power, and to be instrumental to the happiness and freedom of all.

Relying, then, on the patronage of your goodwill, I advance with obedience to the work, ready to retire from it whenever you become sensible how much better choices it is in your power to make. And may that Infinite Power which rules the destinies of the universe lead our councils to what is best, and give them a favorable issue for your peace and prosperity.

* * *

To summarize in a few words the necessary qualifications for a good speech, and to show that those elements which have the best human appeal remain pretty much the same in every generation, let us end this chapter with a few lines on public speaking written by the eighteenth-century poet, Dr. Leifchild:

> Begin low, speak slow;
> Take fire, rise higher;
> When most impressed,
> Be self-possessed;
> At the end wax warm;
> And sit down in a storm.

CHAPTER XIII

The Art of Letter Writing

§ 1

GENERAL RULES

EVERY LETTER is the mirror of a personality. Dress your letter, like your person, neatly, harmoniously, and correctly.

1. Use a paper of good quality. A shabby sheet of paper, like a shabby suit of clothes, is obnoxious.

2. Select the right shade to express your personality. Blue is somber. Pink is cheerful. Brown is staid. Gray is conservative. Cream is luxurious. White is frank. When you receive a letter, you subconsciously form a definite picture of the sender from the color of the paper. This first impression will have much to do with your final reaction to the letter. Spend some time and thought on the color of your paper. It is worth while.

3. Use an envelope of the same color and the same quality as the letter. A blue letter in a brown envelope or a gray letter in a white envelope creates an unfavorable impression. It gives the person who receives your letter the feeling that your personality and your thoughts are out of harmony—in other words, that you are a scatterbrain. The same holds true if you put a costly letter into a cheap envelope, or vice versa.

4. During a period of mourning, it is customary to use paper with a black border.

5. For social letters, have your street address printed, or still better, if you can afford it, engraved, at the top and in the centre of the first page. Some people have the desire and the daring to *stand out* from the crowd. Accordingly they select an unconventionally conspicuous place for the printing of their street address. Or else, they try to attract attention by

printing some impertinent motto on their letter-head. This may be clever; but the persons who do this are generally set down as *queer*. If you wish to be so regarded, you may follow their example. But if you prefer to be formal and correct, have your street address at the *top* and in the *centre*.

6. For business letters, more latitude is permitted. The firm name and the address may be printed in any number of designs, and either in the centre, at the left, or at the right. The form and the position depend entirely upon the wishes of the owner and the skill of the artist.

7. A social letter should never be typewritten. It smacks too much of professionalism.

8. A business letter should not be hand-written. It smacks too much of amateurishness.

9. Try to keep your lines straight. A letter with lines slanting either upward or downward produces an unfavorable impression.

10. Whether your letter consists of two or of three or of four pages, it is best to write these pages *consecutively,* and to number each page. Some authorities will tell you to criss-cross your pages, thus: 1-3-2-4. It is not wise to do this, however. In writing a letter, bear in mind the convenience of the person to whom it is addressed. Make it as easy and as logical as possible for that person to follow you. Criss-crossing the pages of a letter is like doubling back every once in a while upon your own tracks when you take a walk with a friend. Let the pages of your letter be arranged like the pages of a book. This is the only *natural* and *sensible* way.

11. Do not crowd your letter. Have plenty of margin at the top, at the bottom, and on both sides. And try, for courtesy's sake, to use a legible hand. It is an insult to your friends to compel them to read a poor handwriting. In letter writing, as well as in conversation, the first and most important requisite is thoughtfulness.

12. Your letter should be divided into five parts:

The Date
The Salutation
The Body
The Conclusion
The Signature

§ 2

SOCIAL LETTERS

1. An Informal Invitation to a Dear Friend:

Boston, August 7, 19—

My dear Jane:
    What are you planning for the week-end? If you have nothing better to do, why don't you come to Ogunquit? I'm having a few friends at my bungalow there; and, needless to say, the party will be incomplete without you.
    Do come, Jane. *You* know that *I* know that *everybody* knows that you will be the life of the party.

Expectantly yours,
Helen Williams

In the above letter, please note the following points:
In the date—commas after the city and the day of the month.
In the salutation—the word *dear* is written with a *small*, and not with a *capital*, letter. At the end of the salutation there is a colon.
In the body of this informal letter—the style is unconventional and chummy and warm. It is a letter written, so to speak, in a lounging gown.
In the conclusion—the word *yours* is written with a small letter.

* * *

2. An Informal Answer to the Informal Invitation:

15 Lane Park
Brighton, Massachusetts
August 9, 19—

Dear Helen:
    Your invitation is as welcome as it is generous. I shall certainly accept it. Thanks—a million.

Ever devotedly yours,
Jane Benton

In this letter please note that every word in the conclusion with the exception of the first word is written with a small letter.

* * *

In the dating of a letter, it is best to use no abbreviations. The names of cities, of states, and of months should be written out in full. Thus:

> Boston, Massachusetts,
> January 15, 19—

Some people prefer to write the date at the end, instead of at the beginning, of the letter. This is permissible. Example:

> Melrose, New York

My dear Mrs. Johnson:
>   We are to have an informal bridge party on Monday, April 9, at 8 P.M. Please be sure to come. We need your charming presence and your clever playing. You will be particularly glad to know that I have invited the Badgers. They, too, like myself, are anxious to have you with us.
>   I do hope you can come.
> > Cordially yours,
> > Anne C. Winston

January the fifth.

Note: If the date is at the top of a letter, it is generally indicated by figures; if at the bottom, it is written out in full.

In the salutation, you may abbreviate the following words: *Mr., Mrs.,* and *Dr.* Do *not,* however, abbreviate such words as *Captain, Professor, Admiral,* and *General.*

3. A Semi-formal Letter:

My dear Reverend Smith:
   Our Sisterhood would be happy to have you talk to us at our regular Wednesday meeting. Our President, Mrs. Peterson, has suggested that you give us a review of Dr. Brown's *Biography of Cotton Mather.* If you prefer, however, to select your own subject, we shall be only too happy to abide by your wishes in the matter.

The meeting, as you know, is to be held at my home.

Will you kindly advise us whether you can come. We hope you can, as we are all eager to hear one of those talks which are always so stimulating and illuminating.

Very sincerely yours,
Mrs. Grace D. Hall

The Reverend John D. Smith,
375 Arlington Street,
Winchester, Rhode Island.

In the above semi-formal letter, the name and the address of the recipient are written in the lower left-hand corner of the page.

* * *

When you close an informal or semi-formal letter, avoid such old-fashioned expressions as *Thanking you in advance for your courtesy, Trusting to hear from you at once, Hoping you are in good health,* etc. These are no longer considered good form.

There are many fitting words with which you may conclude a social letter. Your choice will depend upon your personality, as well as upon the degree of familiarity that you may wish to express. Here are a few of the accepted closing expressions:

Sincerely yours
Yours sincerely
Very sincerely yours
Yours very sincerely
Cordially yours
Affectionately yours
Devotedly yours
Lovingly yours
Yours as ever
Always fondly yours
Heartily yours
Really yours

A splendid old gentleman used to conclude his letters with the words *Vigorously yours.* He is dead now—he died at the age of 91—but his personality is alive and vigorous in the memory of his friends to this very day.

4. A Formal Social Letter:

27 Myrtle Street
Boston, March 21, 19—

Colonel Joseph M. Hardy,
2034 Riverway Boulevard,
Springfield, Pennsylvania.

Dear Sir:
You do not know me, and perhaps you may think it impertinent of me to write to you. But I feel compelled to do so in order to tell you how much I have enjoyed reading your article on *National Defense* in last week's issue of *The Contemporary Review*. I only wish there were in this country more men with your vision and your social and political outlook.

I trust it may some day be my good fortune to meet in person a gentleman who so adequately and so nobly expresses my own views about our national needs.

Respectfully yours,
John Doe

Note: The term *Respectfully yours* is used only in formal letters, or in business letters, in which an inferior is addressing himself to a superior. It is never to be used in informal letters exchanged between persons of equal social rank.

5. The Signature:
Very intimate letters are signed in the first name only. Where the degree of intimacy is not quite so great, it is permissible to sign the first and the middle name with the last name omitted, or the first and the last name with the *middle* name omitted. Thus

Harriet Muriel
or
Harriet Tobin
but not
Harriet Muriel Tobin or *Harriet M. Tobin*

When an unmarried woman writes to a stranger, she signs her name as follows:

Very truly yours
(Miss) Josephine D. Bradford

A married woman or a widow, when writing to a stranger, signs her name as follows:

Very truly yours,
Estelle B. Thompson
(Mrs. Frank L. Thompson)

In formal letters, the following rules should be observed:

1. Have your letter printed or engraved or handwritten—never typewritten.

2. Use a white or cream paper—no other colors.

3. Write in the third person.

4. Spell out all numbers.

5. Give full details. If you invite anyone, mention the date, the hour, the place, and the occasion for the invitation.

6. Invitations should have no salutation at the top, and no signature at the bottom.

7. Every formal invitation requires an answer.

Examples

A. A Formal Invitation—Printed:

Dr. and Mrs. Walter F. Gilbert
request the pleasure of
Professor and Mrs. John W. Smith's
company at dinner
on Sunday evening, the twenty-fifth of October
at eight o'clock
205 Garden Street

In the above invitation, please note that the names of the invited persons are to be written in ink.

B. A Formal Invitation—Written:

Mrs. Walter F. Gilbert requests the pleasure of Professor John W. Smith's company at dinner on Sunday evening, the twenty-fifth of October, at 8 o'clock.
205 Garden Street
October Eighteenth

C. Formal Acceptance :

Professor John W. Smith accepts with pleasure the kind invitation of Mrs. Walter F. Gilbert to dinner on Sunday evening, the twenty-fifth of October, at 8 o'clock.

24 Walker Street
October twentieth

D. A Formal Regret :

Professor John W. Smith regrets extremely that a speaking engagement in Detroit prevents his accepting Mrs. Walter F. Gilbert's kind invitation to dinner on Sunday evening, the twenty-fifth of October.

24 Walker Street
October twentieth

When you decline an invitation, it is not necessary to mention the hour. When you accept it, however, be sure to mention the hour in order to verify it.

§ 3

BUSINESS LETTERS

The Individual Letter

The purpose of every business sales letter is to sell something : either to sell your services to some firm, or to sell your goods to the public.

If you are trying to sell your services—that is, to get a job— your letter must have the following qualities :

1. Neatness. A neat letter will please the eye and open the mind of the recipient. Many an application for a job is thrown into the waste-basket because of its slovenly appearance. Your letter reveals your personality. Let it convey the mental picture of a careful and refined personality whom the recipient will be pleased to meet.

2. Clearness. Tell the employer who you are ; give him your age, your nationality, your religion, your education, and your experience. Let him get a clear and complete picture of you. Avoid any misunderstandings. The employer knows just ex-

actly what sort of man he wants. Let him know from your first letter whether or not you are that man.

3. Conciseness. Don't be long-winded. Very few business-men have the time to read a long letter. Give the employer all the necessary information in as few words as possible. A social letter may be rambling; a business letter should come quickly to the point.

4. Human interest. When you apply for a job, you are try-ing to further the interest of a human being—yourself. Tell the employer something about your life, your ambitions, your dreams. Establish a contact of mutual sympathy. In a few care-fully selected sentences, try to reveal a living personality to your prospective employer.

5. Coöperation. Don't ask for a job. Ask for an opportunity to prove your worth. Show the employer that you are ready to give as well as to take. Prove it by citing a specific instance in which you can help. Try, in other words, to sell to the em-ployer not only your hands, but your brains. Don't write, "I'm looking for a job." Say rather, "I think I've got a plan to in-crease your business." This sort of approach will get you a hearing, since every employer is interested in increasing his business.

6. Courtesy. Be polite. Don't write with a chip-on-the-shoulder attitude. It is wise to tell the employer, in a quiet way, that you will be an asset to his business; but it is fatal to try to give him the impression that his business has just been waiting for your arrival. The employer is looking for a worker, not a boss. Too cocky a style in a letter of application is just as bad as too modest a style.

7. References. More important even than the tone of your letter is the list of your references. Enclose your references with your letter. The employer will be much more impressed by what others say of you than by what you say of yourself. A good letter of application should *begin* and *end* with references.

The following letter was written to an investment broker:

> At the suggestion of Professor B——, I am writ-ing to apply for a position in your company. I am 22 years old and just out of college. I am a member of the First Congregational Church, of which my uncle, the Reverend Dr. S——, is the minister.

Frankly, I know nothing about the practical side of the stock market. I have, however, made a thorough academic study of it at college under Professor B——, and I think I can learn the practical side of it in a short time. At least, I mean to try, as I am fascinated by it and am eager to make good. And I know that if I am so fortunate as to become associated with your splendid firm, I will make good.

It may interest you to know that my father is a physician. Personally I am acquainted with quite a number of well-to-do doctors. These people are good prospects for an investment broker. Should I get this position, I will begin with them. And—if you will pardon my presumption—I *know* I can bring you some business from the very start.

The initial salary is of little consequence to me. What I am particularly concerned with is to show you what I can do.

I am enclosing several references. I trust you will find the time to look them over.

May I hope for a favorable answer to this application?

Respectfully yours,
John C——

The above letter is clear, concise, personable, coöperative, and courteous. And it contains the necessary references. It shows just the proper degree of confidence. It is neither too modest nor too aggressive. The young man who wrote the letter got the job.

* * *

When you have secured your job, you become a member of the organization. You will now have occasion to write all sorts of business letters: adjustment letters; letters of acknowledgment; sales letters; and collection letters. In order to write the proper kind of letter in every case, you must learn the two important elements of every business letter. These two elements are: (1) the layout; and (2) the substance.

1. The layout. Your letter should conform to the accepted standards. Do not be eccentric in your layout. The reader of your letter wants to do business with solid and sensible people,

not with faddists or Bohemians. You are a practical and honest businessman. Show it in your letter.

The business letter today is as a rule typed on stationery of the standard size, 8½ by 11 inches. Leave plenty of white space all around the letter. If your letter is short, type it in a slender column down the center of the page. A letter consisting of ten narrow lines looks much more attractive than a letter consisting of five wide lines. A short and wide letter gives the reader the same unpleasant impression as a short and fat person. Your whole letter should form a box of the same shape as the paper on which it is written.

A short letter should be double-spaced. Long letters are generally single-spaced.

The heading of the letter consists of the name of the recipient, his firm, his address, and the repetition of his name, as follows:

> Mr. John Price
> The Thompson-Waring Company
> 125 Beach Street
> Springdale, Vermont
>
> Dear Mr. Price:

Notice the space between the fourth and the fifth lines. Notice also the absence of punctuation at the end of the first four lines. This is the generally accepted practice at the present time.

When you are writing to a firm instead of an individual, you use the following heading:

> The Thompson-Waring Company
> 125 Beach Street
> Springdale, Vermont
>
> Gentlemen:

If you want to call your letter to the special attention of a member of the firm, you write your heading as follows:

> The Thompson-Waring Company
> 125 Beach Street
> Springdale, Vermont
> Attention: Mr. John Price
>
> Gentlemen:

The first line in the body of your letter may or may not be indented—thus:

Mr. John Price
The Thompson-Waring Company
125 Beach Street
Springdale, Vermont

Dear Mr. Price:
     Thank you for your letter of April 21. We shall be happy to fill your order, etc.

Mr. John Price
The Thompson-Waring Company
125 Beach Street
Springdale, Vermont

Dear Mr. Price:
Thank you for your letter of April 21. We shall be happy to fill your order, etc.

The signature of the letter consists of the name of the firm writing the letter, the individual signing it, and his official title. The name of the individual is written in ink. The rest is typewritten. Example:

THE PLYMPTON COMPANY, INC.
Judson Brown
Sales Manager.

Note that the name of the firm is typed in capital letters. Sometimes the name of the individual is typewritten immediately under the signature, thus:

THE PLYMPTON COMPANY, INC.
Judson Brown
Judson Brown, Sales Manager.

This is a good practice where the signer's handwriting is hard to read.

2. Assuming that the layout of your letter is in accordance with accepted standards, your next problem is to look after the substance. Almost every business letter, remember, is a sales letter. Its secondary purpose may be to adjust some-

thing, to acknowledge a communication or an order, or to collect a bill. In every one of these cases the primary purpose is to *sell* goods or good will.

Adjustment Letters

Suppose you are writing an adjustment letter. Your customer is displeased. His order has not received the proper attention, or the goods have arrived too late or in imperfect condition. You have lost his good will. It is your business to regain it, by writing him a letter that is courteous, patient, and thoughtful. Explain that his grievance is a just one; that you do not blame him for his dissatisfaction; that you thoroughly understand his position and that if you were in his place you would act exactly as he is now acting. The customer is always in the right. At least, he loves to be told that he is. Agree with him in whatever complaint he may make, and you will generally find that he will run out of complaints and become a satisfied customer.

When you receive a letter of complaint, answer it promptly. A delay is certain to breed suspicion and may possibly result in a lawsuit.

Be patient. Don't lose your temper. Explain the situation calmly and clearly. No matter how angry you may feel at your customer's complaint, do not show your anger in your letter. Be courteous: first, last, and always.

The following is a satisfactory letter of adjustment:

> We are sorry to learn from your letter of the 9th that several of our hats have proved unsatisfactory. The fault is entirely ours. Here is how the situation arose:
> Our shippers are instructed to lay aside all imperfect goods. Apparently, however, one of our new shippers misunderstood our instructions and carelessly allowed a few imperfect hats to slip into your shipment.
> Thank you for calling the matter to our attention. We are giving strict orders to the manager of our shipping department never to allow this sort of thing to happen again.
> Will you kindly return the imperfect hats so that

we may send you a credit slip at once? And we beg to assure you that there will be no recurrence of this inadvertent and regrettable error.

Letters of Acknowledgment

Closely allied to a letter of adjustment is a letter of acknowledgment. When you answer a complaint, you try to *retain* a customer's good will; when you answer an inquiry, you try to *gain* it. Clearness, thoughtfulness, and a desire to please the new customer are the ingredients that make such a letter successful. This will be discussed more fully in our section on sales letters. For the present let us consider one type of acknowledgment which is a sort of *anticipated* adjustment. It is the acknowledgment of an order which you may not be able to fill promptly. This sort of letter requires tact. In addition to thanking your customer, you must give him the unpleasant information that he will have to wait for his goods, and you must also overcome in advance whatever objections he is likely to raise.

In a letter of this nature, you must (as always) think of your customer's problems. Don't tell him what a loss it will be to you if he cancels the order. He is not interested in that. Tell him, rather, what a *gain* it will be to *him* if he *waits* for the order. Try to prove to him that the delay means superior workmanship, better goods, and bigger profits in the long run.

Sales Letters

Letters of application, of adjustment, and of acknowledgment should generally be short. This, however, does not hold true of sales letters. In a sales letter you can afford to be just as long as you can manage to be interesting. The proof of the pie is in the eating. Some of the most successful sales letters have been two or even three pages long. A long letter that multiplies words is a failure. But a long letter that multiplies *ideas* is a success. If you try to sell anything by mail, you must give not only an *interesting* but a *full* description of your article. This cannot be done in a few words.

The sales letter is an inexpensive form of advertisement. You can send out a thousand letters, using a one-cent stamp, for about $25 or $30. A one-cent stamp, experience has shown, is usually just as effective in securing mail-order sales as a three-cent stamp. If you select your lists carefully—and there are good list brokers who will help you to do that—you can reach 10,000 prospects at the small expense of $250 or $300. And the chances for profitable returns are good—provided your letter is well-written.

There are, of course, other factors which determine the success or failure of a mail-order sales letter. For example:

1. A sales letter should be mailed at the proper season. The best months for mail-order sales have been found to be from October to April. The other months are too warm, and too many people are away on their vacations, for a mail-order sales campaign to be effective.

2. A sales letter should be mailed to reach the prospect on the right day. The first day of the week and the first day of the month are bad days for the arrival of mail-order letters. On the first day of the week people are busy trying to make up for the time lost over the week-end; and on the first day of the month people are worried over their bills that have fallen due. A sales letter should reach a prospect when he is mentally relaxed.

3. A sales letter, to be effective, should be one of a series. A single visit from a salesman is not enough. The same holds true of a single letter. Get your customers to know your letters intimately, just as you want them to know your salesmen intimately.

4. Time your series of letters just as you would time the visits of your salesmen. If you send out only two letters, a month is a reasonable interval between the two. If you send out more than two, mail them about three weeks apart. In laying out your schedule, you must remember two things: first, that the entire mail-order season is short; second, that before you send out a new letter you must allow yourself plenty of time testing out your field in the regular mail-order season. Be sure that you time your series of letters carefully. It has happened again and again that a good sales campaign came to a premature end because of poor timing. Never begin your sales campaign too late in the fall. You will find that you have come to the end of the season before you are half through.

5. Test out your field before you go into any expensive

campaign. The spring and the summer months are a good testing season. If your returns are satisfactory in a small spring
or summer test, the chances are that they will also be satisfactory in the larger campaign later on. Don't waste precious
time testing out your field in the regular mail-order season. Before you have had a chance to tabulate the results of the test,
the time for the campaign will have passed by.

A warning is necessary at this point. The returns on a test
are almost always a little better than they are going to be on
your entire campaign. Bear this in mind when you try to figure
out the possible total receipts on your campaign.

6. It is a good plan to test out two, or three, or even four
letters simultaneously. Experience has shown that even the
cleverest campaigner can never tell in advance just which one
of his test letters will produce the best results.

The above six factors deal with the mechanics of mail-order
advertising rather than with the technique of mail-order letter-
writing. Let us now consider this technique:

1. A good sales letter should have the proper salutation.
When you send out several thousand letters at a time, it is
rather difficult and expensive to fill in the name of each
prospective customer. Various "fill-in" devices have been invented. A great many successful mail-order letters, however,
have a general salutation without any name at the head of
the letter.

Here are some of the salutations used in successful mail-
order letters within recent years:

> Dear Reader:
> Dear Public Speaker:
> Dear Club Member:
> Good Morning!
> How About *This* Opportunity!

Most of the successful sales letters use the simple salutation,
Dear Friend. Occasionally you may find a person who will be
offended at such a salutation. A company that tried to sell fountain pens through the mail received the following curt note
from one of the prospects:

> "I am *not* your friend, and I will ask you not to
> pester me with any more of your letters."

This reaction, however, is rare. As a rule, there is a personal note of mutual sympathy established in such a salutation. After all, the majority of us *do* want to be friendly. A sales letter addressed *Dear Friend* generally gets a favorable hearing, even if it does not always produce a sale.

2. A good sales letter should have a proper conclusion. Here, too, as in the salutation, try to put a note of respectful familiarity, of whole-hearted enthusiasm, or of genuine goodwill into your message. Among the successful conclusions used in recent sales letters are the following:

> Yours most sincerely
> Cordially yours
> Heartily yours
> Really yours

Remember that the end of a good letter is the beginning of a good order.

3. A good sales letter must be well organized. It must *introduce, induce,* and *produce.* That is, it must introduce your product, induce the prospect to listen to your arguments, and produce the sale. Generally speaking, these are the three main parts of a sales letter.

A

Introducing Your Product

In order to introduce your product, you must first capture your reader's attention. This is a difficult thing to do, and all sorts of ingenious devices have been tried with which to pry open the closed mind of the prospective customer. Like a sales talk, a sales letter should begin by startling the reader. Touch upon something that vitally interests him. Suppose you are trying to get customers for your summer camp in the White Mountains. You may begin your letter somewhat as follows:

> Dear Sports-Lover:
> Lost River beckons. Echo Lake is waiting for the sound of your merry shout. Mount Washington is challenging you. Summer is here and eager to welcome you. And so is the management of the Massawatomee Camp.

If you are trying to sell automobile insurance, you may begin with a striking bit of statistics:

Dear Friend:
Do you know that last year the cost of automobile accidents amounted to the amazing figure of $750,-000,000? Three quarters of a billion!

If you are offering a new car to a prospect who owns an old car, you may use the following approach:

Dear Friend:
Last year my friend Bill Jones, of 79 Preston Street, Southbridge, spent $329 in repairs on his 1934 car. An extraordinary case? Well, ask *your* friends who own second-hand cars. Or, still better, try to check up on the repairs of your own car for the past twelve months.

If you want to sell an endowment policy, you may begin thus:

Dear Friend:
How would you like to retire at 55? And live without worry for the rest of your days?

A dealer who tried to sell a new kind of oil for automobiles started his sales letter as follows:

Greetings, Friend Motorist!
Your car, like yourself, needs a spring tonic after the hard winter. Our X—— Motor-Oil will supply that tonic.

B

INDUCING YOUR CUSTOMER TO CONSIDER YOUR PRODUCT

All the foregoing opening paragraphs are likely to interest the prospective customer. After you have *gained* his interest, you must now try to *retain* it. You must translate his interest into a desire to buy. This desire can best be aroused by means of pictures. Print a striking picture of your article on the circular that accompanies the letter. Or else, picture some scene or idea that will create an appetite for the article. But, in addition to that, make the language of your letter pictorial.

Paint for your prospective customer the benefits and the pleasures to be derived from the purchase of your product. Create in him a mental image that will "make his mouth water."

Use concrete language. Let there be action in your story. If you sell a fountain pen, or an automobile tire, or a refrigerator, or anything else for that matter, don't merely *describe* your article. *Show it in action.* And show it in an action in which your prospect is likely to be interested. In other words, instead of writing about your article, write about the prospect's pleasure in *using* that article. Make the letter personal. Appeal not only to the mind of your prospect, but to his emotions as well.

In this part of the letter it is a good idea to use facts and figures and testimonials. These inducements, if skillfully woven into the argument, will bring conviction to the customer. He will be ready to give serious consideration to your article.

C

Producing the Sale

Your next step is to get your customer to make out the order blank. You have now come to the last and most difficult part of your letter. In the earlier part of your letter you have overcome the indifference of your customer. It is now necessary for you to overcome his inertia. Most people are too lazy to bother about signing and mailing an order blank. "Why do it today?" they will say to themselves. "Tomorrow or the day after tomorrow will be just as good." This is an attitude that is fatal to the sale of your article. You must overcome this attitude. You must put an urge into the end of your letter. The customary and most effective urge is to use some sort of expression as the following:

Get this pen at once. The supply is limited.
Order at once. After 5 days the price will go up.
If you order within three days after you receive this letter, you will get a beautiful premium—a silver-plated cigarette-case.
To the first 500 people ordering this set of books, we are giving a beautiful self-filling fountain pen. These pens are going *fast,* so order your set *at once.*

A common device nowadays is to send your article on a five-day or a seven-day approval basis. This undoubtedly increases the orders, but it means the return of many units, a large proportion of which may be spoiled. It also means that a proportion of the units that you send out will never be returned or paid for. Yet veteran mail-order companies have found that a return privilege, with all its disadvantages, is likely to pay out in the end.

SPECIMEN SALES LETTERS

The following letters, reprinted here by permission, have produced profitable sales. Note how in every case the letter first arouses interest, then translates this interest into a desire, and finally impels this desire into an order.

1. A Letter from the American Institute of Finance:

DID YOU MAKE THESE BIG PROFITS ON UTILITIES?

Earlier this year, when pessimism on the utilities was most extreme, the American Institute of Finance recommended a $1,000 commitment in low-priced utilities which was worth $5,000 when we advised acceptance of profits.

The recommendation provided for the purchase outright of 500 shares—100 shares each of American Superpower at 50¢, then 3¼; Am. Power & Light at 1½, then 9⅜; Columbia Gas at 3½, then 13½–14; Electric Bond & Share at 3½, then 20; and United Gas at 1, then 4½.

The Institute recommended the purchase of that group in the following emphatic and unmistakable language:

"Is the public as wrong on public utility holding company stocks now as in 1929? . . . We warned against speculation in public utility stocks in 1929. Recognizing existing difficulties, as speculations we cannot help but recommend them now as strongly as we warned against them six years ago."

This has been incomparably the greatest opportunity during the current rise and the best speculative opportunity in the stock market since 1929.

ANOTHER LOW-PRICED OPPORTUNITY!

The Institute has recommended a low-priced specialty selling around 10 which we believe has good 1936 possibilities. This stock sold at 93 the last boom.

This new recommendation will be immediately available to those now entering enrollments.

Faithfully yours,
H. G. Gomperts
For the Institute

In this letter, note how the writer startles the reader into attention by the heading; how he transforms this attention into interest by citing the figures of what this company *has* done and *can* do for its customers; and how he fans this interest into a desire to act by stating that *you,* as a subscriber, may get an *immediate* chance for profit if you enroll *now.*

In the same envelope with this letter came a circular with the following heading:

350% PROFIT
IN 5 MONTHS!

DID YOU EVER SEE A
BETTER OPPORTUNITY THAN THIS?

A separate order blank accompanied the letter and the circular.

2. A Letter from Delane Brown, Incorporated:

Dear Friend:

Are you one of the many folks who agree that there is nothing quite so good for breakfast or supper as a tasty, tempting dish of broiled or fried SHAD ROE and bacon?

Will you let me send you—at my risk—six full 7½ oz. tin of fancy WHOLE shad roe, all ready to heat and serve whenever you want it, in or out of season?

Because good shad roe is something that nearly everyone likes, yet is so impossible to obtain out of season, I have made it a year 'round dish—a treat that you may enjoy at any time—as often as you wish and at a price that enables you to serve it, not as an occasional luxury, but as a regular and delightful family dish or as a surprising out-of-season treat when you have guests.

So certain am I that you will be more than pleased with my shad roe that I will gladly send it ON AP-PROVAL, without a penny in advance. All I ask is that you open one tin and serve the roe for break-fast, dinner or supper. Then, if you feel that this delicious dish is not worth repeating; if you are sure you won't find yourself "hankering" for another ap-petizing plate of it—just send the five unopened tins back to me at my expense and that ends the matter, at no cost to you. Otherwise, your check for only $3.65 in ten days squares the account.

But that's not all! I am not only going to provide you with the finest shad roe you ever tasted, but right in the same package, with my compliments, I am going to send you a grill-skillet, a handy and practical kitchen utensil that is to shad roe what a griddle is to pancakes. There is a picture and description of this new and useful device on the inside pages of this let-ter. Try it! You'll say it's the greatest thing you ever saw for cooking shad roe, bacon, fish, steaks and chops, without smoke or unnecessary odors. It's my gift to you for the privilege of introducing my deli-cious shad roe into your home.

Because my limited supply of shad roe won't last long, I must ask that you let me hear from you at once. Send no money now unless you wish to. The enclosed card requires no postage stamp; just sign it and mail it today! Your tasty, tempting shad roe, and the grill-skillet for cooking it, will be shipped the very day I hear from you.

Yours sincerely,
Delane Brown

This letter covers the first page of a four-page folder. The paper is a rich cream; the firm name and the writer's name are in red; and the body of the letter is typewritten in brown ink. The second and the third pages contain printed matter of a pictorial and appetizing nature, as well as striking illustrations of a plate of shad roe and a skillet with slices of bacon frying in it. Altogether, this is an effective piece of mail.

3. A Letter from The Commentator:

Dear Reader:

Because your name is included on a selected list of those we should prefer to have as our Charter Subscribers, we invite you to receive the next six monthly issues of The Commentator at the special introductory price of only $1.00. The regular price is $3.00 per year—25¢ a copy.

All modern newsstand records for a *new* 25¢ magazine were broken by our February issue when the first edition of 200,000 copies was almost entirely *sold out* immediately after publication.

See for yourself why *every page* of The Commentator assays "BEST SELLER!" A quick glance at the list of "top popularity" contributors on the enclosed folder should tell the story. Here is the very apex group of thinkers, writers, and coiners of wit whose ideas are "white hot" with modern significance. Among all who speak, these are the voices tuned most precisely for the ears of achieving, keenly functioning minds.

Like dull acquaintances, the tepid magazines of yesterday have lost your interest and mine.

I am associated with John B. Kennedy, H. V. Kaltenborn, and Hawthorne Daniel, as editors of this bright new success in the field of monthly journalism.

The Commentator, *pocket-size,* pithy, brief, and provocative, is as modern as the wit and will of the day commands it MUST be. No subject, no fact of public value—and no *illuminating side* of any topic can be TABOO in this frank, informative, strenuous, and diverting publication.

The impact of The Commentator will gladden those of stocky mental stature who abominate stodgy tea-time essays, and order their *facts* straight and crusading, man-sized—their *fun* in healthy, hilarious portions. It is for those already in tune with today's tempo for tomorrow's life. When you read it, as eagerly as we know you will, your conversation should be two jumps ahead of the rest of the group, wherever you are!

Each month it will bring you at least 30 original articles of "front-page" import—128 double-column pages on things of current predominance about which you MUST know. The solemn, serious, casual, tragic, comic sides of men, events, problems, will be discussed by none but the most capable and entertaining interpreters of modern life.

The Commentator is $3.00 per year, and after its initial campaign for Charter Subscribers it may no longer be available at the six months for the $1.00 price which we now invite *you*, on our preferred list, to enjoy.

We tell you sincerely that your name has been included at this time because of its special significance to us as a Charter Subscriber. We have segregated a known and selected group of readers, preferred as first subscribers. With this key group at the start, the merits of the magazine will be discussed in the right circles by people whose opinions are respected. For that reason we offer *you* this initial reduced price of $1.00 for six months' issues.

Accept our invitation NOW. Just fill in your complete address on the convenient form enclosed. No postage stamp is needed. Drop it in the mail in the envelope provided herewith.* You may either enclose $1.00 now or we will send you a bill later—just as you prefer.

Sincerely yours,
Lowell Thomas

Editor, THE COMMENTATOR

*If you send the dollar NOW *with* your order, thus saving us the clerical operations of billing, we will reciprocate the favor by sending an additional copy—and you will then receive *seven* issues for $1.00.

The effectiveness of this letter is based upon three factors: a good description of the contents of the magazine; a concrete summary of the outstanding writers connected with it; and a flattering allusion to the importance of the prospective subscriber.

4. A Letter from Maxwell Droke, Publisher:

Greetings, Blithe Spirit!

Is your gang a bit fed up on bridge? Do they groan when you sit down at the piano? Are they rather so-soish at the suggestion of an evening of dancing?

Do you want to put new life into your next party?

Well, here's how—and HOW! Present A NIGHT AT THE OP'RY HOUSE, featuring "Glamorous Gladiola, or Gee, How She Loved a G-Man!" Here's a super ultra colossal epoch of love, mystery, adventure, romance, mystery, love, adventure, mystery, romance, and, and—oh, yes—love.

The whole show comes completely in a handy box. Requires no preparation. You could put it on in the middle of the Sahara Desert, but perhaps the sheiks and some of the less discerning of the camels might not appreciate the subtle humor. On second thought, your own living room is probably a better bet. A NIGHT AT THE OP'RY HOUSE requires four characters. (If you want to make it a stag affair, any 200-pound male can take the part of a Glamorous Glad and treble the fun.) The package includes separate scripts for each character; a black moustache for Nicodemus Gnashtooth, the Villain; a rube beard for Cornelius Crabtree, the Father; a—but hold on! To catalog the "props" would reveal too much of the plot. You can depend on it, though, they're hilarious.

That eminent gagster, Frank Ryan (you see his stuff in *Sat Eve Post, Esquire, Ballyhoo, Judge, et al*) wrote the sketch and designed the properties. And a right swell job he's done, too.

You simply lift the lid, distribute the parts—and the show is on. In this case, *lack* of practice makes perfect. Rehearsal is fatal. This is a show for hams. It's part of the game that each character must *read* his lines from the script book. The clumsier the performance, the more fun it will be for all concerned.

The whole play—from the opening line to the final gag—is one huge, uproarious laugh. Audience and players will unite in declaring that there hasn't been so much fun hereabouts since that time Uncle Theophilus got his whiskers caught in the door of the old base-burner stove. And for your part in introducing the new game, you'll be voted the cleverest host of this or adjacent seasons.

So certain are we of your complete satisfaction that we unhesitatingly offer this Guarantee, brand new in the entertainment field:

> If *A NIGHT AT THE OP'RY HOUSE* *doesn't convulse your audience, pack up the* *whole shebang, ship it back to us, and your* *money will be refunded, practically on the* *wings of the wind!*

The price? Only $1.50, complete and postpaid. Order NOW—and be ready for the next gathering of the gang!

Really yours,
R. L. Gaynor
for MAXWELL DROKE, Publisher

P. S.: May we have the names of a few congenial friends who might be interested in this unique parlor play? (See back page for handy form.)

This letter very cleverly plays upon three human emotions: the desire to be amused; the desire to amuse; and the desire to show off. The tone is personal and the approach familiar. The appearance of the letter is in keeping with the style. The body of the letter is typed in black, and five cartoons, scattered over the pages of the letter, are printed in red. An excellent letter.

5. A Letter from the Literary Guild:

Your Gift Certificate Enclosed
Entitles You to a Free Copy of
THE HUNDRED YEARS
a $3.00 Book!

Dear Friend:

You have been elected to full membership in the Literary Guild of America for one year. Here is your Membership Certificate and an interesting outline of the privileges and savings you can enjoy as a Guild Member. You now need only sign and return the Membership Certificate card to put your membership

into immediate effect and to receive the beautiful
GIFT volume.

The same card will bring you at once, ABSO-
LUTELY FREE, a copy of Philip Guedalla's latest
book, THE HUNDRED YEARS. Here the history
of the last hundred years unfolds in a panorama of
exciting pictures. In a clear and colorful manner,
Guedalla shows the interesting course of events by
which the world came to its present state. It is a
stimulating and valuable work by one of the greatest
of modern historians. We want you, as a new member, to have this new book as a *gift* from the
Guild.

Your membership will entitle you to the full services of the Guild—including many special NEW
features that have already been enthusiastically received by thousands of older members. Now, more
than ever before, the Guild provides the most satisfactory and most economical method of obtaining
the books you want to own. Guild service has been so
greatly expanded that it has become practically a
necessity to its 110,000 members.

As a member of the Literary Guild you now receive all of these advantages:

1. *You Receive the Monthly Selection Service*
   You may choose from *two selections* each
   month—the best fiction, or the best non-
   fiction; or you may take both if you desire.
2. *You Get the Special Price of* $2.00 *on All
   Guild Selections*
   You save an average of 50% on the Guild
   Selections you take. You pay no more than
   $2.00 for any Guild selection even if it is a
   $3, $4, or $5 book.
3. *You Take the Guild Selection only if You
   Want It*
   You may choose your own books in any
   month when the Guild selections do not appeal to you, or you need not take any book
   when you so desire.
4. *You Do Not Take a Book Every Month*
   You may buy as few as four books a year to
   retain full membership.

5. *Free Bonus Books Twice a Year*
> You share in FREE "Bonus Books" (value $2.50 to $5.00) distributed twice a year by the Guild. (See enclosed brochure for full particulars.)

6. *A Year's Free Subscription to "WINGS"*
> You receive a free subscription to "WINGS" —the monthly literary magazine published for Guild members.

You will find additional features of great value in the enclosed announcement.

IMPORTANT: The cost of raw materials for the manufacture of books *is being advanced* 30%. The Guild, however, guarantees to protect members against any increase in the price of Guild Selections for one year. It is to your advantage, therefore, to join the Guild now before it becomes necessary to withdraw this guarantee.

Since the record of the Literary Guild during the past four years has definitely established the fact that free membership is the most convenient, satisfactory and economical method of purchasing the outstanding new books of ALL publishers, why don't you sign and return the enclosed membership certificate without delay? THE HUNDRED YEARS, Guedalla's fascinating and colorful history of modern civilization—now a best seller—will be sent to you at once, FREE, as soon as the Guild receives your card.

> Sincerely yours,
> John Beecroft
> Chairman, Membership Committee

This letter is psychologically and commercially sound. It *starts* and it *ends* with the most important item—the offer of a FREE book to those who subscribe. People love to get something for nothing. The body of the letter is equally strong. It not only gives a *general* account of the service it offers, but it enumerates six *particular* reasons why the reader of the letter should subscribe. It is well designed to fulfill the three requirements of a sales letter—it *introduces* the product, it *induces* the reader to want to buy, and it *produces* the sale.

Collection Letters

The collection letter is the most difficult and the least successful of all business letters. There are two reasons for the difficulty: a collection letter must be insistent, and it must be polite. It takes a delicate balancing of psychological values to produce a letter that is polite enough to retain the good will of your customer and at the same time insistent enough to secure his check. And there are two reasons for the failure of many collection letters: the debtor either is shiftless, or he hasn't the money.

And yet, in spite of these difficulties, good collection letters have been written and are being written all the time. A collection letter, more than any other type of business letter, should have the personal touch. If your customer is a grouch— and who isn't a grouch when he owes money?—try to smooth down his ruffled feathers. If he is shiftless, try to appeal to the better side of his nature. If he is poor, try to help him by making the payments easy. But, in every case, insist upon what is due you. Don't give your customer the impression that you're an "easy mark." Once you give him that impression, he will pay his debts to everybody else before he pays them to you.

Don't send out routine collection letters. Even if you have to mail several thousand statements every month, put a personal note into these statements. *And don't let your delinquent accounts grow cold.* The longer you allow them to run, the less chance you have of collecting them. Don't be afraid of pestering your customer with frequent reminders. He may growl at you, but the fact remains that he will pay those accounts that are the most insistent.

Appeal to your debtor's sense of humor and his sense of honor. A well-worded humorous letter will frequently collect a bill. And the same is true of a letter reminding your customer that as an honest man he certainly means to pay his debt. Even a shiftless debtor will want to be regarded as a man of honor.

If all your statements and all your appeals have failed, your next step is to send a threat letter. Don't do this, however, unless you mean to follow up your threat with legal action. Tell your delinquent debtor in a few curt words that if you

do not receive a check by such and such a date, you will turn
the account over to an attorney for collection. Try, however,
to avoid any such threat letters. If your other collection letters have been well-worded and well-timed, you will rarely
be obliged to resort to the final threat.

Specimens of Successful Collection Letters

The following letter, reprinted by permission, was prepared by the Direct Mail Associates, Inc. It was recently
awarded a gold medal by the Dartnell Corporation:

> What would YOU do if you had an account like
> this?
> It isn't large . . . by itself . . . but how a group of
> them can count up! And when they are for small
> amounts like this, how hard it is not to lose all your
> legitimate profit—and more—on collection expense!
> We were glad to extend open account terms to
> you—and although this has run far beyond the usual
> 30 days, isn't it true that we've been fairly decent
> about waiting this long for our money?
> There, in a few short lines, is our whole case. We
> don't want to be unpleasant. Most certainly we don't
> want to subject you to annoyance by turning over this
> little bill to a collection agency.
> We want your good will. We'd like to count you
> among our preferred customers. I cannot believe that
> you want us to suffer a loss because of our good faith
> in sending your order without cash in advance.
> So I am enclosing an addressed envelope that needs
> no postage, and I am appealing to you to use it—this
> moment—to send the small sum owing to us.
> Please!

The following series of seven collection letters, also re-
printed by permission, was prepared for the Huntington
Laboratories by Professor Alta Gwinn Saunders, of the
University of Illinois:

1.

GOOD MORNING!

There's no use going into a long story about why
we want our money. Our customers are good busi-

ness men . . . they know all the reasons as well as we do . . . and these customers, we have found, are the right type.

From past experience we know that we can depend on them to "pay up" except in some unusual emergency.

That's why we're not at all bashful about reminding you that your account with us is a little overdue. It's dated ———, and it amounts to $———.

Won't you send us your check today?

Thanks; we'll surely appreciate it.

Sincerely,

HUNTINGTON LABORATORIES, INC.

2.

GOOD MORNING!

It has been our experience that nonpayment of an account is more often due to an oversight than to refusal or inability to pay. This, we believe, is true in your case.

Will you be good enough to check your invoice on this account? If the amount listed below agrees with the "balance due" on your invoice, will you send us your check today?

We are quite sure that you appreciate the reasonableness of our request.

Sincerely,

HUNTINGTON LABORATORIES, INC.

Amount due: $———.

3.

GOOD MORNING!

It is not surprising now and then to find the names of some of our very best customers appearing temporarily on our past due record. As you know, your account has been owing since ———.

You must be experiencing some difficulty of which we are not informed.

The purpose of this letter is to request, if you are not in a position to let us have payment by return mail, that you let us know about your problem and your intentions, so that we can agree on some plan satisfactory to both of us.

With kindest regards,

HUNTINGTON LABORATORIES, INC.

Amount due: $——.

4.

GOOD MORNING!

This letter concerns our mutual interest—your credit account with us. Despite the fact that we have written you on ——, ——, and —— without receiving a reply, we are still confident that it is your earnest desire to take care of this obligation. But you are making it mighty hard for us to continue in that frame of mind.

You are well thought of in our organization, and we greatly value the orders which you have given us. As business men and executives, however, we cannot be expected to be satisfied with your account.

An unpaid account will cause friction sooner than anything we know of, and we certainly don't want friction between your firm and ours. May we suggest the way to prevent it?

Mail us your check today!

Sincerely,

HUNTINGTON LABORATORIES, INC.

Amount due: $——.

5.

Gentlemen:

No doubt you feel, as we do, that continual requests which produce no results are tiresome.

For —— weeks we have been writing you about your account of —— which is as yet unpaid. We have confidence in your integrity and we believe that you intend to pay your account in full, but we cannot continue any longer simply making requests for payment.

What our next step will be is entirely up to you. We sincerely hope that our reason for writing you again will be to say: "Thanks for the check," and not to warn: "We're going to force collection."

Which will it be? We are willing to wait just —— days for your decision.

Sincerely,
HUNTINGTON LABORATORIES, INC.

6.

PRESIDENT'S OFFICE

Gentlemen:

This morning, our collection manager suggested to me that we turn your account over to Dun's. He placed before me copies of the —— letters which were sent you since ——.

I do not wish to authorize such action before taking up the account with you personally. You understand that I want to give you every opportunity to settle your account without reporting it to Dun's.

To speak frankly, I am inclined to think you have some good reason for not writing to us. I shall retain this correspondence on my desk ten days to give you an opportunity to send your check or to tell us what to expect.

You must realize that this debt is a matter of real importance to you. Please let me hear from you.

Sincerely,

Amount due ——.

7.

Gentlemen:

Take $7.50 out of your cash register. Now put it in your pocket.

Know what it is? That's what we have saved you through refusing so far to sue for the amount you owe us. It is what the court imposes on all unsuccessful litigants.

But—if you want to keep that $7.50 we saved you, you must send your check for $—— without delay. Our attorney has your account, but because we still have faith in human nature, we are not allowing him to serve you with papers for another ten days.

Very truly yours,
HUNTINGTON LABORATORIES, INC.

Notice how the pressure in the above letters increases gradually from the first to the last. Each one is a little more insistent than the one before it. The first letter is just a polite and friendly request for payment. The second letter reminds the customer that the request for payment is *reasonable*. The third letter is a friendly hint that the sender expects either a payment or an explanation. The fourth letter is a mild threat that if the customer doesn't pay at once, he will lose his credit. The first four letters, you will note, are headed with the words —*Good Morning!* This heading is dropped in the last three letters. The fifth letter puts the matter squarely up to the debtor. It says, in effect, "Do you, or don't you, want to be *forced* to pay?" Yet this alternative is carefully and tactfully worded in such a way as to produce results without giving offense. The sixth letter comes directly from the president of the company. It contains a broad hint that the account, if not paid within ten days, will be turned over to Dun's. The seventh and last letter is a firm demand for payment, plus a concrete reminder that a payment *now* will save the debtor a definite sum of money *later on*. To summarize the seven ascending notes in a successful series of collection letters:

First Letter: *Please pay.*
Second Letter: *Be reasonable.*
Third Letter: *Explain your delinquency.*
Fourth Letter: *Save your credit.*
Fifth Letter: *Pay willingly, or else*——
Sixth Letter: *If you don't pay at once*——
Seventh Letter: *Our attorney will collect at YOUR expense.*

CHAPTER XIV

Writing for Income

§ I

GENERAL REMARKS

YOU WANT TO WRITE FOR PROFIT. How can you go about it? By remembering and applying this simple rule: *Have something interesting to say, and say it in an interesting manner.*

1. In order to have something interesting to say, you must learn to be an individual, and not part of the crowd. Look at life through your own eyes. No two visions are exactly alike. The trouble with most of us is that we don't try to see and interpret things for ourselves. We take the other fellow's word for it. If you want to be a writer, develop your own vision and your own thought. Every successful writer enables us to see life through spectacles of a new color. That is why we read him. It is always a thrilling adventure to see the world in a new light. Develop your originality. Create a pair of magic glasses for your reader, and he will sit at your feet and put gold into your pocket.

One of the most successful of modern writers is Sir James Jeans. This popular writer on astronomy is so successful because he is so individual. He transforms the stars of the heavens into something new and magical and exciting. His books take you on an adventure such as you have rarely experienced before. You have often looked at the stars, to be sure, but you have never really *seen* them until you have examined them through the enchanted glasses of this author's personality.

Thousands of scholars have written about philosophy. An indifferent world has glanced at their books and thrown them away. But then there came a poet who undertook to write a *Story of Philosophy,* and the world eagerly absorbed his book.

272

Dr. Will Durant *had something interesting to say* about philosophy. He looked upon it with a new pair of spectacles. In the first place, he presented the *philosophers* to us. In this way he brought philosophy down to earth and into our homes. He enabled us to meet the creators of the world's greatest thoughts. He made them concrete and lovable and alive, men of flesh and blood, subject to *our* weaknesses and disappointments, seeking *our* paths of salvation, and giving wings to *our* hopes and aspirations. In the second place, Dr. Durant gave a new and concrete form to their philosophy. He tore away the veil of obscurity which had concealed these precious thoughts, and he displayed them in all their glittering colors. He thus turned an old and dull spectacle into something new and thrilling. He accomplished this miracle by throwing upon philosophy the searchlight of an individual personality.

We have all been compelled to study history in the public schools, and most of us have been bored. But along comes a historical novel like *Quo Vadis,* or *Anthony Adverse,* or *Gone with the Wind,* and history is suddenly illuminated for us. The authors of these books have taken old truths and exhibited them in new colors. This is the secret of their success.

In September, 1936, at the Harvard Tercentenary celebration, there was a display of fireworks on the Charles River. Tens of thousands of people came to see it. Many of them were familiar with the scenery at that spot—the winding river, the bridges, the Weld Boat House, the college dormitories on the Cambridge side of the river, the Harvard Business School on the Boston side, and the Stadium in the background. Under ordinary conditions it is a pretty enough landscape, but there is nothing breath-taking about it. Under the multiple lights of the fireworks on that September night, however, it was a spectacle never to be forgotten. During those few minutes the spectators beheld, not the familiar river and college, but a magical stream flowing past enchanted palaces. For a brief and breathless moment an old scene had been transformed into something gloriously new. A touch of unusual color had changed a commonplace etching into a masterpiece.

The successful writer's pen does for the story or the poem or the drama what the outburst of colored flame did for Harvard on the tercentenary celebration.

Have you ever observed an ordinary piece of quartz under the ultra-violet ray? If you have, you will remember the cry of astonishment that escaped your lips at the wonder of it all. A piece of stone transformed into a liquid fire of colors such as you have never seen under ordinary light. If you want to be a successful writer, exhibit your subject under the ultra-violet ray. The reader is sick of the old lights. He wants something new.

To return to the figure of the eye-glasses. Go into a Woolworth store and buy half a dozen pairs of glasses of different colors—red, pink, blue, gray, green, and brown. Then go into any place you know well and look at it through the six different pairs of glasses. You will see, instead of *one familiar* place, *six unfamiliar* places, each one amazing in its individual beauty. *This* is the sort of effect you must produce upon your reader if you want his admiration and his patronage—and his checks. Give him the treat of a fresh outlook upon a life that otherwise would be tiresome and drab.

Some writers, in their attempt to be unique, will exhibit a subject not only under a new light, but from a new angle. Try to walk down the street on stilts. You will see a scene quite different from what you have observed when walking on your feet. You are now able to look over the heads of people. Your vision is no longer obstructed. Both your eye and your judgment have become improved. You can see not only moving individuals, but streams of motion. You can, to a much greater extent than before, estimate the aim and the direction of the movement. In other words, if you raise yourself *above* the crowd, you can see *better* than the crowd. And you can impart to others the results of your own better vision.

You may obtain the same results if you look down upon a moving crowd from a window. You can best observe a parade in the street if you have secured a position *above the level of the street*. The higher the window, the wider but the less distinct becomes the horizon. From a high window you will see more of the parade, but less of the details. Looking down from a hill or from an airplane, you will get even a more extended view of mass movements. But the more you try to rise above your fellows, the less intimate will become your view of their individual traits.

The successful writer, then, will try to raise his head above the crowd, but he will keep his heart on a level with his fellows.

The angle from which you may view life does not always depend upon the *height* of your outlook. Sometimes it depends upon the *position*. If you lie down on your side, you see a new world. The furniture and the faces of the people in your bedroom assume shapes and dimensions different from those observed in the upright position. When you lie flat on your back, you see quite an extraordinary sort of world. Try it sometimes in the country. Look up at the light sifted through the needles of a pine-tree, or at the birds flying overhead. The spectacle will give you physical angles and mental images to which under normal conditions you are a stranger. The bed-ridden writer and the contemplative writer, whose world is observed from a lying-down position, are quite different in their philosophical outlook from the healthy and active writer.

If you decide to be a professional writer, examine life from a unique position. But let it not be *too* unique. Some writers, in their effort to be different, will assume a most grotesque position from which to contemplate the human comedy. There is a tendency, among a few of the more extreme modern writers, to stand (figuratively speaking) on their heads. The world from this angle will appear topsy-turvy. A world like this may be funny to a few, but to most of us it gives a dizzy headache. The upside-down writers try to cater to what they call the *Intelligentsia*. If you want to make a living with your pen, don't write for the *Intelligentsia*. They have rich imaginations but poor pockets.

To be a successful writer, then, you must learn to look at life in a new light, and you must acquire the knack of examining it from a new angle. A *new* but *sensible* angle. In this way you will have stored up a fund of worth-while information. *You will have,* in other words, *something interesting to say.*

2. Your next step is to learn to *say it in an interesting manner.* The most successful writers, from Homer down to our present-day Nobel prize winners, have had an interesting style. The verb *to interest* means *to engage the attention,* or *to arouse the curiosity.* If you want to be a professional writer, you must develop a mode of expression that will arouse the curiosity of

your reader. When you offer a book to a publisher, or an article or a story to an editor, you invite him to take a stroll with you through the garden of your thoughts. Lay out these thoughts in such a manner as to pique his curiosity and to keep it alive throughout the stroll. If you let go for a moment, you lose him. If you succeed in holding him tense and satisfied to the end, you will win his coöperation and his check.

A good style is one that arouses curiosity at the beginning, maintains it throughout, and satisfies it in the end. To use a rather homely but apt figure, a well-written work provides the reader with a good mental sneeze. Maintain the tickle from the beginning to the explosion. Don't let the sneeze become aborted at any point in the middle. An unfinished sneeze is very disappointing, but a sneeze that ends in a hearty climax and subsequent relief is one of the real pleasures of life. If your literary work can supply such a mental excitement with such a satisfactory relief you may be sure of a steady audience. This is true whether you are writing a poem, a story, a drama, a biography, or a magazine article. Your style must arouse a mental desire and a mental relief.

What are the elements of a good style? They are honesty, simplicity, brevity, clearness, coherence, vividness, and fire.

A good style must be honest. Whatever you write, let it express your own convictions. A dishonest style, like a counterfeit coin, will never ring true. Shakespeare wrote that if you are true to yourself, you cannot be false to other men. This is good advice for every writer. Write what you honestly believe in, and you will find that your readers, too, will believe in it. Say what you think yourself, and not what you think that others want you to think. The greatest writers are the most honest thinkers. The most successful writers today—Sinclair Lewis, Theodore Dreiser, Edna Ferber, Pearl Buck, Robert Sherwood, and Sherwood Anderson, to mention only a few, are the writers who have honest convictions and give an honest expression to these convictions. Honest writing does not necessarily mean propagandistic writing. Indeed, propaganda may often be dishonest. To write honestly, it is not necessary to "plead a cause" or to "deliver a message." A book with a message is generally dull. An honest writer is not a preacher who delivers a sermon, but an artist who tries to tell the truth.

If you want to succeed as a writer, always tell the truth as you see it. Don't try to be clever. Try to be honest.

A good style must be simple. Simplicity is the twin sister of honesty. If your style is honest, the chances are that it will be simple. "Oh, what a tangled web we weave, when first we practice to deceive!" A *deceptive* style is a *complicated* style. It is the mirror of a confused mind, a mind in which the sense of values has become distorted—in short, a mind that *cannot think straight*. If you think straight and write straight, you have the foundations of a good style. Your reader nowadays demands honesty and simplicity in your writing. His world has become so complicated that he is confused. He wants a guide who can show the simple way. This explains the success of the so-called *outline books*. The authors of these books have learned the simple way of teaching the complicated problems of life. They translate difficult thoughts into short words and easy phrases. Long words are dull; short words are alive. Moreover, a style that has too many long words does not sound genuine. It gives you the impression that the author is trying to show off. It makes you feel that you are reading a man who understands the dictionary better than he understands life.

Avoid the affectation of long words. Don't impose upon your reader. Be simple.

The third essential of a good style is brevity. A good way to develop brevity in your style is to practice writing telegrams. In a telegram you are compelled to express a complete idea in the fewest possible words. This is precisely what the good writer does with all his literary work. The day of the novelist with the long words and the long sentences is gone. Henry James wouldn't have much vogue today. The tempo of life is too fast. The mind accustomed to airplane speed cannot tolerate a "horse-and-buggy" pace. As a matter of fact, the mind has always traveled faster than the body. The greatest writers have always been the writers with the speediest style. With their simple words and their brief phrases they hurry the mind of the reader along on the wings of imagination. The most universally remembered passages in Homer, in Shakespeare, in the Bible, in Dickens, in Emerson, in Stevenson, are the passages that move the most rapidly. And the quality that gives them their rapid motion is brevity—brevity in word, in phrase, and in sentence.

A good style, in addition to being honest, simple, and brief, must be clear. A clear style is a style that is simple and brief. It avoids *obscure* words and *long* words. It doesn't wander along like a winding river; it flies, like an arrow, straight to the point.

There is very little distinction between honesty, simplicity, brevity, and clearness. An honest style is a simple style; a simple style is a brief style; and a brief style is a clear style. Start with an honest approach, and you will very likely attain the other three essentials. Remember that if you want to be a successful writer, you must cater to a large public. Many of your readers may in general be just as intelligent as yourself, but they will probably be more or less ignorant of your special field of knowledge. You are therefore their teacher. Explain yourself clearly. Don't use the language of a specialist. Use the everyday language of the man in the street. The clearer your style, the wider your public.

An honest, simple, brief, and clear style, in order to be further effective, must also be coherent. It must stick together. There must be a golden thread of unified thought that binds sentence to sentence and paragraph to paragraph. There must be, so to speak, a blood-relationship between the sentences and the paragraphs of a composition. Let no strangers intrude. They spoil the harmony of the family circle. If your style can be unscrambled and then put together again into a different order, it lacks coherence. A coherent style is a style in which every word, every phrase, every sentence, and every paragraph has been put into the one and only fitting place.

A good style coheres by means of connective words and phrases. Here are a few of the more common connectives:

and	therefore
also	formerly
besides	for my part
furthermore	thereupon
likewise	in the meantime
accordingly	although
above all	under these circumstances
hence	granted

indeed	on the contrary
to be sure	at the same time
it is true	as a matter of fact
in fact	in the first place
at all events	in the second place
after all	in all seriousness
at any rate	briefly
at least	in other words
for that matter	incidentally
however	in conclusion
on the other hand	to continue
nevertheless	to sum up

A coherent style is a group of words harmoniously connected into a congenial family. Always aim for this sort of harmony in your style.

The sixth essential of a good style is vividness. Your article or story or poem must present a concrete and living picture to the imagination. Vividness does not necessarily mean description. Long descriptive passages, as a matter of fact, are fatal to a good style. People don't like to spend much time on descriptions, either in their conversation or in their reading. Yet a graphic word or phrase, or sentence, or even an entire paragraph, if not too long, puts life into a style. Be careful, however, not to waste much time in describing *still life*. Always try to describe *life in motion*.

"The skillful describer," writes Professor Shipherd in his *Manual for College Composition*, "can set us breathingly in the very presence of moving scenes." That is the beauty of a vivid style. It transports us to a charming scene and enables us to live and breathe there. It makes us *part* of that scene. It admits us to citizenship in the imaginative world of the artist. It makes us feel that we belong there. In fact, it virtually transforms us into artists. When we read an unusually vivid style, we feel the author's emotion so intensely that we share it with him. We become *co-creators* with him. The vivid imagination of the writer puts life and fire into the imagination of the reader.

Fire—this is the last and most important essential of a good style. Carlyle writes of Dante's style that it is "of a vividness as of *fire* in a dark night." A style that has fire—some call it gusto or verve or just plain *it*—illumines and warms the dark recesses of the reader's mind. If you have fire, you have all the other essentials of a good style. You have honesty, for dishonesty lurks in dark places. You have simplicity, for a complicated style is like a tangle of brushwood without any air-holes; it can't catch fire. You have brevity, for brief words can easily burst into flame. You have clearness, since fire illumines everything. You have coherence, for fire can melt and blend even a disjointed style into consistency. And you have vividness, since vividness and fire are almost synonymous. A *vivid* object, as you know, is a *living* object (from the Latin *vivere, to live*); an object that has been touched into life by the divine flame.

A great ancient writer on style, Longinus, said that the most perfect style is that which has been kindled by the divine fire of the gods. An equally great modern writer, Jonathan Swift, summarized the essentials of a good style in a much more prosaic but somewhat more practical formula. "Proper words in proper places," he said, "make the true definition of style."

§ 2

FICTION

A

Short Stories

You are a writer who is trying to make a living by the pen. You have a store of good thoughts, and you have developed a good style. In other words, you feel that *you have something interesting to say* and that *you can say it in an interesting manner*. You have selected the short story as your medium for success. Very well, how are you going to go about it?

The best answer to this question is: work, work, work! Write fifty stories before you expect to sell one. If this sounds like hard work, remember that Fannie Hurst wrote *a hundred* stories before she made a sale. It's a rocky road to literary success, but try it and see what fun it is! That is, if you have the courage. It is just as important to have the courage as it is to have the talent. Many a brilliant young writer drops by the wayside because he lacks the hardihood to go on and on against all kinds of obstacles. Don't give up. Don't ever allow your ink or your patience to run dry. You never can tell. Your very next story may be the one to start you off on a successful career. Bernard Shaw wrote for five years before he sold his first manuscript. A young man who wants to be a physician is willing to devote seven or eight or even nine years to his training before he receives his first fee. A young man who wants to be an author should be willing to undergo an equal apprenticeship and an equal degree of suffering.

It is no easy thing to learn the art of short-story writing. No easier, in fact, than to learn the art of medicine or surgery. It takes time and patience and practice. Before the doctor undertakes to heal the body, he must be thoroughly familiar with its anatomy. Before you undertake to sell a short story, you must be familiar with *its* anatomy.

What is a short story? Thousands of teachers have tried to define it, yet no one has quite succeeded. It's like trying to define *life*. You readily recognize it when you see it, but you don't know just what it is. Perhaps as good a definition as any is this: *The short story is a short drama in narrative form.* Like a drama, it must have characters, a plot, and a climax. These three elements have been well summarized in the formula: "Boy meets girl; boy loses girl; boy finds girl." There is a tendency among certain writers at present to write stories without either a plot or a climax. They begin nowhere, ramble along obscurely for a few pages, and then end nowhere. These stories are written for the *Intelligentsia,* and they are published in the *arty* magazines that don't pay for contributions. But you want to write for profit. Don't, therefore, use these stories as models. A formless story is not necessarily a work of art, and a popular story is not necessarily a bit of trash. Shakespeare, you know, wrote his plays to *sell* them, and he tried his best to make them popular. The same holds true for practically every famous dramatist and novelist and short story writer.

Your short story, if it is to find a market, must be popular. It must conform to the standard requirements. It must have characters, a plot, and a climax.

CHARACTERS

First of all, your story must have characters. These characters must be interesting, or else your readers wouldn't care to know anything about them. A good way to begin a story is to make a striking statement about one of the characters—something that will arrest the attention. Present your characters as living personalities. Make them individual. Show their little tricks of speech and action. Picture their appearance, their walk, their mannerisms, the intonations of their voice, the peculiarities of their thoughts—in short, the hundred and one little details that enable us to tell Tom, Dick, and Harry apart when we meet them in the street.

O. Henry, the master story-teller of them all, could take a character out of his page and set him down in your room, so vivid was he in the handling of the details. Time and again I've heard people exclaim, when reading about an O. Henry character, "Why, I know *that* person!" That's the sort of thing for you to aim at. Make your character the sort of person your reader has met and recognizes when he reads about him in your story. Create interesting characters, and your story is half sold.

If you have a group of interesting characters, you have a plot. "The characters," writes Booth Tarkington, "make their own plot." Take the stories of Kipling, of Mark Twain, of Ernest Hemingway, of Somerset Maugham, of Bernard de Voto, or of Ben Hecht. Though different in many ways, they have one thing in common. They collect a group of characters who are interesting enough and diversified enough to weave their own plot.

The young writer often asks: "Where can I find the characters for my stories, and how can I make them life-like?" The answer is: "Do what Fannie Hurst and O. Henry and hundreds of other successful story writers like them did." Fannie Hurst began to sell her stories in a large way when she began to write about the Jewish characters that she knew best. O. Henry wrote about the shop girls and the bank tellers and the drug clerks whom he met and conversed with in the streets and the offices and the stores of New York. The successful short story writer talks to his acquaintances and takes mental notes of them. He studies them in and out of their natural surroundings. They become his text book. He reads their faces and their minds. He observes them curiously, intelligently, sympathetically. He allows no detail of their speech or their manner or their dress to escape his attention. He learns to *know* his characters before he presents them to his readers.

Some writers prepare biographical sketches of the characters whom they plan to put into their stories. An author has no business to write about a character unless he is familiar with his entire life. When you select a character for your story, trace his career, in your mind, from beginning to end. This is necessary even when you are planning to introduce but a single incident of his life. This one incident must be colored by the man's entire personality and background. We understand a man's actions only when we know the man.

Know your characters. The best writers have failed when they have tried to depict characters whom they have not known. This was true of George Eliot when she tried to write about the Jewish Zionist, Daniel Deronda. This was true of Dickens when he put the strange character of Fagin into *Oliver Twist*. This is even more true of our modern novelists and short story writers who try to picture Chinese and Japanese and Hindu characters about whom they know very little.

The writer of short stories has a greater task than the novelist in making his characters lifelike. His job is to show the whole by means of one of the parts. It is like trying to depict the ocean in a pail of sea-water. The short-story writer must exercise the greatest care in the selection and the treatment of his details. His technique must be clear and precise and swift. He has only from one thousand to ten thousand words in which to produce his effect. He is not able, like the novelist, to draw his characters leisurely, to turn them around, as it were, and to present a three-dimensional portrait of them. He must come quickly to the point.

There are certain definite ways in which this can be done. You can master the art of short-story characterization if you practice long enough and hard enough. Here is how it can be done:

1. *Draw* your character; don't *talk* about him. Let *him* do

the talking. The novelist can sometimes afford to philosophize about his characters; the short-story writer, never.

2. Select one or two striking points about your character—preferably one—in order to illustrate a central idea. Then weave your entire story around this central idea. Omit everything that does not throw some light upon it. Study the stories of Poe, of Conan Doyle, of de Maupassant, and you will see how strictly they adhere to this principle. Poe, indeed, carried the idea of the single effect to the extreme. In such stories as *The Tell-Tale Heart, The Black Cat, The Murders in the Rue Morgue,* and *The Pit and the Pendulum,* he not only selects a single trait of character, but in each case he emphasizes and intensifies this trait to such an extent that the characters become abnormal and the stories verge on the melodramatic. The tendency nowadays is to tone down this sort of effect. The modern short-story writer has turned from melodrama to drama. But the best of the present-day writers still adhere to the singleness-of-purpose principle in depicting the characters of their short stories.

Select a single trait of character to present in your short story. But let it be a *dominant* and *universal* trait. Let the ruling passion of your leading character arouse a responsive chord in the ruling passion of your readers. Otherwise your appeal will be limited. The following emotions have the most universal appeal: romantic love; parental love; love of duty; love of mankind; patriotism; revenge; forgiveness; friendship; loyalty; pride; courage; sacrifice; devotion.

Take a character who will exhibit one of the above emotions, and then make the character individual. Show how he will react in his own way to this emotion, and you have the nucleus of a good story.

3. Reveal your character in a crisis. You have no time, in a short story, to develop his dominant trait. It must come as a flash of lightning out of the dark. This means that your story must be a compact unit. It should cover a short time, and, if possible, it should be enacted in a single place. There have been brilliant exceptions to this rule. One of the greatest of stort stories, *Roads of Destiny,* takes the reader over an entire lifetime and through any number of scenes. But it took a master like O. Henry to turn the trick. As a general rule, the best

stories are those whose action covers the shortest time. Until you have become an expert, you will do wise to adhere to this rule. In this way you will find it easiest to reveal your character speedily and effectively in a single crisis.

How to Portray a Character

There are three ways in which you may portray a character. You may do it by means of description, analysis, action.

1. Description is important. Your reader must see your character in order to understand him. He must see the inner person as well as the outer person—the mind as well as the body. The reader wants to know not only what the character looks like, but also what the character thinks. And if the character happens to be a person who doesn't think much, you must tell that, too, to your reader. All this should be done as briefly as possible. In writing short stories, you must be thrifty with your words. Some writers have learned the trick of presenting a complete picture in a single sentence. Notice, for example, the following description from Leonard Merrick's *The Tale That Wouldn't Do:*

> "But she was very pretty—nothing to find fault with, excepting that she hadn't a brain."

Sometimes it is wise to depict a character indirectly. Don't tell what the character looks like, but describe the impression produced by the character upon the other people in the story. This technique, if well handled, is very effective. In Homer's *Iliad* we are not told how Helen looks, but we are allowed to overhear a conversation between some of the old wise men of Troy. Helen, you will recall, was a Greek queen who eloped with a Trojan prince. The Greeks, in revenge, made war on Troy. One day, as the Trojan elders were complaining about the hardships of the war, Helen happened to pass by. They looked at her, and one of them remarked to his companions: "I can now see why we're fighting this war. It's certainly worth while!"

This trick is used to excellent effect in Galsworthy's *Forsyte Saga.* In this book Galsworthy spends very little time in describing Irene, but he devotes a great deal of time to telling about the effect that Irene produces upon others. This is done with such skill that you get a most vivid picture of her appearance and her personality.

A common device among some authors is to put themselves into the background and to let the characters describe one another. This, of course, can be best accomplished by means of dialogue. If you want to adopt this method, be sure that your dialogue is brief and crisp and vivid. Let me caution you once more,—avoid long descriptions. Try to scatter your descriptive phrases or sentences over the story. Don't bring them together into one long paragraph. Use what Professor Blanche Colton Williams calls the "flash-light method" of description.

2. In addition to *describing* a character, you may *analyze* him. Show his mental processes, and give the motives for these processes. Some writers, in order to become efficient psychologists, have had themselves psycho-analyzed. They have done this on the assumption that you cannot know others until you know yourself. Whether or not you may care to do so in your own case is a question for yourself to decide. This, however, is important: Learn something about psycho-analysis if you want to write intelligently and acceptably about modern life. You must acquire the skill not only to *analyze* the minds of your characters, but to *psycho-analyze* them. This does not mean that you must dig down too realistically into the cellar of their subconscious. If you resort to the psycho-analytic method in your writing, be sure that your treatment is scientific and artistic and restrained. An ill-digested knowledge of Freud will make you appear ridiculous as a writer. Yet an intelligent understanding of his work is necessary if you want to be in tune with the times. When you write about modern people, you must use the modern technique in analyzing their thoughts.

The analysis of a character's thoughts, like the description of his features, should be brief. Here, too, it is wise to use the "flash-light method." A brief illuminating glimpse into the inner recesses of his mind is most effective. Ring Lardner was a master of this method. So, too, was Kipling, although he knew nothing about psycho-analysis when he wrote his stories. The most successful short-story writers have learned this trick of brevity in the analysis of their characters. "There is only

one rule," wrote Robert Louis Stevenson, "and that is to
omit." If you want to see what a master can do in the way
of analysis through omission, read any of the stories of Jack
London.

Be sparing of your psychological details. Even if your story
is a story of character rather than of plot, don't devote too
much space to analysis. Give just as much space as is necessary
to reveal the character and to put him into action—no less
and no more.

3. When you have adequately described and analyzed your
characters, you must set them in motion to weave their story.
Your characters will be best revealed through their *actions,*
especially in emergencies. A story, in other words, should reveal characters in a dramatic crisis. Maxim Gorki, in his
famous story, *Makar Chudra,* describes and analyzes two
gypsies, the beautiful and high-spirited Radda and the handsome and imperious Loyko. Radda is the daughter of the old
gypsy chief, Danila. "Words cannot describe this Radda. One
might, perhaps, express her loveliness by means of the violin,
but he alone could do it who knows the violin as he knows his
own soul. . . . Many a brave young heart did she ruin. Ye
gods, how many!"

Then the author goes on to illustrate her high spirits in one
or two brief but striking incidents. Within the first few hundred words we see and know and love this wild gypsy.

Gorki is now ready to introduce us to the next character,
Loyko:

> "One evening we were sitting and listening. Music
> floated over the steppe. It was a wonderful music.
> It set the blood in our veins afire! . . .
> "And it came nearer and nearer. And suddenly a
> horse steps out of the darkness, and upon this horse
> sits a man playing on a fiddle . . .
> " 'Ah, Loyko, it is you!' cried Danila joyously.
> "That, then, was Loyko Zobar. The ends of his
> mustache hung way down over his shoulders; his eyes
> glittered as the bright stars, and the very sun was
> mirrored in his laughter, so help me God!"

Loyko's handsome face and commanding personality capti-
vate everybody—with the exception of Radda. She is too proud

to yield, and he is too determined to give her up. And both of
them are passionate gypsies, as untamed as the steppes on which
they live. Here is a case where the characters themselves have
created the situation for the author. The inevitable happens.
When the crisis comes, the author reveals them in action—in
this instance, a most tragic action. Radda compels Loyko to
grovel at her feet before all the gypsies who have looked up to
him as a god. Loyko yields to her command; and then, like an
infuriated god, he buries a dagger in her heart.

> "And Radda drew the knife out of her heart,
> threw it aside, pressed a lock of her black hair to the
> open wound, smiled, and spoke up loudly and clearly:
> " 'Farewell, Loyko! I knew it would end like this!'
> ... And with these words on her lips she died.
> "And Danila, the father of Radda, picked up the
> dagger that Radda had cast aside and looked at it for
> a long time. His lips quivered. Radda's blood was still
> warm upon the knife, and it was so sharp and
> crooked! Then Danila approached Zobar and
> plunged the knife into his breast, just over the heart.
> For he was, after all, the father of Radda, was this
> old soldier, Danila.
> " 'Well done!' cried Loyko in a ringing voice.
> And then he sank down at Radda's side and his soul
> followed hers out of the world."

* * *

The above outline of Makar Chudra will give you but a
vague idea of the skill with which the author has interwoven his
description, his analysis, and his action in order to reveal
the characters of his story. Read the whole story as a model
of good characterization. Gorki had lived with the gypsies, he
understood them, and he knew how to bring them to life
with the magic touch of his pen.

The success of a story depends to a great extent upon the
skill with which the author describes the action of his characters at the critical moment. Sometimes a story deals with a
character who is incapable of action. The crisis comes, but
the action does not come off. Even a situation of this kind can
be turned into a poignant drama in the hands of a skillful

author. Katherine Mansfield, in her *Life of Ma Parker,*
describes a timid old washerwoman who has had more than
her share of hard luck. She has lost her husband and seven
of her children. Her days and her nights are spent in drudgery
and in a helpless daze as to the meaning of it all. And then
comes the final blow. Her grandson dies. On the day after
the funeral she comes to clean the flat of the literary gentleman for whom she works every Tuesday. As she goes on
with her work, dusting, washing, sweeping, and bending her
rheumatic old figure in agonies of pain, she surveys her life
and a wave of self-pity overwhelms her. She is ready for the
climax of the story—a good cry that will relieve her feelings.
She finishes her work and goes out into the street. Oh, for a
good long cry!

> "But where? Where? She couldn't go home; her
> sickly daughter Ethel was there. It would frighten
> Ethel out of her life. She couldn't sit on a bench any-
> where; people would come asking her questions. She
> couldn't possibly go back to the gentleman's flat; she
> had no right to cry in strangers' houses. If she sat on
> some steps a policeman would speak to her.
> "Oh, wasn't there anywhere where she could hide
> and keep herself and stay as long as she liked, not dis-
> turbing anybody, and nobody worrying her? Wasn't
> there anywhere in the world where she could have her
> cry out—at last?
> "Ma Parker stood, looking up and down. The icy
> wind blew out her apron into a balloon. And now it be-
> gan to rain. There was nowhere."

The sad beauty of this story is due to the fact that when
the situation has reached the crisis of action, there can be no
action. Miss Mansfield knew her character and that is why
she was able to build so sympathetic a story about her. We are
interested not only in the heroes who can act, but in the un-
fortunates who can only suffer.

It is a difficult thing to write a good story like *The Life of
Ma Parker.* The best advice to a beginner would be: don't
attempt it. Stories of action are easier to write, and are as a
rule more popular. Select the characters who can do things;
describe and analyze them briefly; and then put them into a

crisis where they will have to act. This, on the whole, is the safest formula for you to follow until you have attained the skill of a professional writer.

When you come to the action of your story, you have reached the point where your story becomes a drama. In other words, you must use dialogue. Action can best be expressed by means of dialogue.

Let every word of your dialogue contribute to the action of the story. Don't waste ammunition. Let your speeches be short and to the point. Let each speaker be heard several times, a few words at a time. A give-and-take conversation is much more interesting than a debate. Avoid, in your dialogue, any long arguments. Dialogue should reveal character through action. There can be no action in long speeches.

Have plenty of dialogue in your stories. It is good for the eye as well as for the mind. The magazine reader generally seeks out the stories with a good deal of conversation in them. "In fiction," said Earl Derr Biggers, "I use dialogue all I can."

Make your dialogue true to your characters. A common fault with young writers is to make every character speak like the author. This is a fault of which even Oscar Wilde and Bernard Shaw have been guilty at times. In the drama this is not so fatal as in the short story. When you hear dialogue, you have no time to analyze it; but when you *see* it, you have the opportunity to weigh it critically and at your leisure. For this reason it is very important for the short-story writer to watch his dialogue.

In writing your dialogue, try to avoid dialect. It is difficult to handle, and looks strange to the eye. The average reader doesn't like it. If you *must* resort to dialect occasionally, try to *suggest* the strange speech instead of "laying it on thick." A dialect that is merely suggested is easier both for the writer and the reader.

The young writer often asks himself the question: "How shall I introduce the speeches of my characters?" Among the words that are most commonly used to introduce speeches are the following: said, remarked, exclaimed, asked, broke in, whispered, smiled, ventured, interrupted, sneered, retorted, murmured, muttered, hissed, growled. A good way to indicate a speech is to describe the action that accompanies it. For example:

> He flicked the ashes from his cigar. "You are quite right. I should have done the same myself."

Don't precede every speech with the words "he said" or "she said." To do so is a sign of amateurishness. The skillful writer will sometimes write page after page of dialogue without a single prefatory phrase. If you are unable to dispense entirely with introductions to your speeches, try to vary these introductions as much as possible. Don't use merely a subject and a verb. Add modifiers that will enable the reader to *see* as well as to *hear* the speaker. O. Henry was a master of dialogue. Observe carefully this passage from his *An Adjustment of Nature:*

> "There is a certain fate hanging over Milly," said Kraft, "and if it overtakes her she is lost to Cypher's and to us."
>
> "She will grow fat?" asked Judkins, fearsomely.
>
> "She will go to night school and become refined?" I ventured anxiously.
>
> "It is this," said Kraft, punctuating in a puddle of spilled coffee with a stiff forefinger. "Caesar had his Brutus—the cotton has its bollworm, the chorus girl has her Pittsburgher, the summer boarder has his poison ivy, the hero has his Carnegie medal, art has its Morgan, the rose has its——"
>
> "Speak," I interrupted, much perturbed. "You do not think that Milly will begin to lace?"
>
> "One day," concluded Kraft, solemnly, "there will come to Cypher's for a plate of beans a millionaire lumberman from Wisconsin, and he will marry Milly."
>
> "Never!" exclaimed Judkins and I, in horror.
>
> "A lumberman," repeated Kraft, hoarsely.
>
> "And a millionaire lumberman!" I sighed, despairingly.
>
> "From Wisconsin!" groaned Judkins.

The above dialogue sparkles not only because of what the speakers say, but also because of the manner in which they say it. You notice that they say, they ask, they venture, they interrupt, they conclude, they exclaim, they repeat, they sigh, and they groan. Observe, too, that they are not merely talking machines, but acting and feeling human creatures. They fear, they punctuate their speeches with their fingers, they are perturbed, they feel solemn, they are horror-stricken, they become hoarse, and they despair. In other words, when O. Henry presents his characters in dialogue, he not only makes them speak, but he shows their *motions* and their *emotions*. This is the sort of thing that makes characters alive.

PLOT

When you have selected your characters, build your plot around them. Show them in action and bring them through a crisis. This plot-building is a difficult matter. It takes ingenuity and time and patience. You must create an atmosphere around your characters, give them a locale, and weave around them a net of circumstances out of which they try to disentangle themselves as best they can.

Your plot should begin with an incident. The incident may be trivial, like the appearance of a stranger at an inn, or important, like a Mississippi flood. Out of this incident will grow all the subsequent action of the story. This action should slope upward from the incident to the climax. There must be an intercrossing of paths, a struggle, and a denouement.

The intercrossing of paths will result from the fact that the characters are at cross purposes. For example, two men may be in love with the same woman, or a detective may pursue a criminal, or a scoundrel may persecute an innocent man, or a spy may attempt an escape from prison. Sometimes the crossing of the paths may be between the will of man and the forces of nature, as in Hawthorne's *The Ambitious Guest*. In this story a young man seeks for shelter at the house of a New England family in the White Mountains. It is a sharp September night. A brisk fire is roaring up the chimney. The newcomer is invited into the family circle. He tells his hosts that he is on his way to the city. He has a dream to fulfill. He wants to become a great man. "I cannot die," he cries, "until I have achieved my destiny."

As they are talking, a crunching sound is heard. It comes

from the mountain that overhangs the cottage. The sound grows into a roar. A shriek bursts simultaneously from all their lips:

"The slide! The slide!"

The mountain comes down upon them, and the young man is buried together with his ambition and his dream.

Fate is not always triumphant in such a struggle. In *Belle-mamma,* by Eleanor Mercein, published in the April 24 (1937) issue of the *Saturday Evening Post,* a courageous old lady not only defies the Ohio flood, but marries her elderly admirer while the waters rage around the house in which she lives.

Frequently the struggle in a story consists in the involuntary crossing of interests between two people who love each other. This takes a rather amusing and at the same time pathetic turn in O. Henry's *The Gift of the Magi.* Della Young wants to buy her husband, Jim, a Christmas present. But she has only $1.87 in her possession. This is all she has been able to save up on her husband's $20 a week salary.

Jim, too, wants to buy a present for Della, but he hasn't the money.

Somehow they manage to find a way. Della buys a chain for Jim's watch, and Jim buys a pair of combs for Della's hair.

The climax comes when they discover that Della has sold her hair to buy the chain and Jim has sold his watch to buy the combs!

The simple story has a simple plot: one struggle, one complication, and a climax. The complex story has an involved plot: two or more struggles, two or more complications crossing each other and intertwining the motivations and the actions, with the climax at the end. O. Henry's *The Last of the Troubadours,* Stockton's *A Tale of Negative Gravity* and Kipling's *Wireless* are good examples of the complex story. Read them and study them, but don't imitate them at the beginning of your career as a short-story writer. First try to master the simple story. There is a good enough field for it at the present time.

Whether your plot is simple or complex, be sure to have an incident, a struggle, and a climax—that is, a beginning, a middle, and an end. When you have acquired some skill in the weaving of plots, you may start with a glance at the middle of the story, and then return with a flash-back to the beginning. This effect is cleverly produced in Stevenson's *Sire de Maletroit's Door*. It is the inverted type of action so common in the drama. Ibsen begins almost all his plays in the middle, or close to the end, and then carries the scene back in order to explain the earlier events which led up to the opening incident.

This method is used to good effect in O. Henry's *An Unfinished Story*. This story, considered by some critics to be O. Henry's best, begins with a dream: "I had a dream. . . . Gabriel had played his trump; and those of us who could not follow suit were arraigned for examination . . . A fly cop—an angel policeman—flew over to me and took me by the left wing. Near at hand was a group of very prosperous-looking spirits arraigned for judgment.

" 'Do you belong with that bunch?' the policeman asked.

" 'Who are they?' was my answer.

" 'Why,' said he, 'they are——' "

At this point of the story we expect the author to go on with his dream about the trial of the spirits in heaven. But he doesn't do so. Instead, he takes us abruptly down to earth and begins with a narrative of the events that led up to the dream:

"Dulcie worked in a department store . . . Of what she earned, Dulcie received six dollars per week . . ."

One day she made a date with Piggy. "Piggy needs but a word. When the girls named him, an undeserving stigma was cast upon the noble family of swine."

She broke the date. Her misery had not as yet dragged her down to *that* level. Poverty was still better than degradation.

But—there was another time, when Dulcie's spirits were a little lower and her desire to live was a little stronger. Piggy asked her again to dine with him; and then——

Here the author takes us back to the scene at the beginning of the story:

"As I said before, I dreamed that I was standing near a crowd of prosperous-looking angels, and a policeman took me by the wing and asked if I belonged with them.

" 'Who are they?' I asked.

" 'Why,' said he, 'they are the men who hired working-girls, and paid 'em five or six dollars a week to live on. Are you one of the bunch?'

" 'Not on your immortality,' said I. 'I'm only the fellow that set fire to an orphan asylum, and murdered a blind man for his pennies.' "

* * *

The flash-back technique is especially useful in the detective story. In the author's mind, the final chapter of a detective story is written first. The author must know the criminal at the very start, or else he can't write the story. The reader, on the other hand, must not know the criminal until the very end, or else the story is a failure. The detective story writer, therefore, must work his plot backwards. He must begin the story *after* the crime is committed, and then bring his reader back to a point *before* the crime is committed. G. K. Chesterton, Edgar Allan Poe, Arthur Conan Doyle, Mary Roberts Rinehart, and Agatha Christie are especially successful with this technique. In most of their stories the action takes place before the real story begins. Read Agatha Christie's *The Tuesday Night Club* as a good example of the short-story detective plot.

The plot of your short story should be well organized. Each event should follow as a logical result of the previous events. The amateur writer is likely to put together a plot that creaks. A good way to overcome this fault is to practice on the plots of famous old stories, just as the automobile mechanic practices on old motors. The Greek tragedians, you know, took old plots and turned them into new masterpieces. So did Shakespeare. Some of the best of modern short stories are adaptations of earlier plots. Shakespeare's *King Lear* has served as a subject for at least three competent modern works: Turgenev's *A Lear of the Steppes*, Mrs. Freeman's *A Village Lear*, and J. Gordin's *A Modern King Lear*. The *Electra* of the Greek poet, Euripides, gave Eugene O'Neill the plot material for his *Mourning Becomes Electra*. These are only a few of many similar cases. Practice on the old masters in order to acquire skill in plot-weaving. And then, when you have learned to transform another writer's plot into something that is entirely your own, begin to create your original plots.

As an aid in the creation of your own plots, consider the following situations, based upon the commonest of human emotions. You can learn to build your plots either upon one of these emotions or upon a combination of them:

1. Accidental crime	18. Jealousy
2. Adultery	19. Loss
3. Adventure	20. Love
4. Ambition	21. Madness
5. Capture	22. Mystery
6. Courage	23. Neglect
7. Curiosity	24. Persecution
8. Defeat	25. Rebellion
9. Deliberate crime	26. Refusal
10. Dishonor	27. Remorse
11. Entreaty	28. Rescue
12. Error	29. Revenge
13. Forgiveness	30. Rivalry
14. Friendship	31. Sacrifice of others
15. Greed	32. Self-sacrifice
16. Hatred	33. Strife
17. Injustice	

Create characters through whom you can depict some of the above situations or emotions, put them into an interesting environment, and set them at cross purposes. If you do this, you have the nucleus of a good story. What you need to complete the story is a good climax.

CLIMAX

The climax is the explosion of the story. In order that this explosion may be effective you must lead up to it by means of suspense. Keep your reader guessing. Tease him along through the course of the story. Don't bring on the climax too soon. The vaudeville comedian has learned this trick of suspense in telling his story to the audience. When he brings out a particularly good point, and the audience sits back to applaud, he rouses further curiosity and expectation with the words: "Wait, you ain't heard nothing yet!" Anthony Trollope gave an excellent recipe for a short story: "Make 'em laugh; make 'em weep; make 'em wait."

Nature has taught us this trick of suspense. First comes the dawn, then the occasional sound of a bird, and finally the outburst of song and the climax of the sunrise.

Do as Nature does. Prepare the way for the climax. Coax your reader along to the end. Keep him in suspense. Anton Chekhov was a master of suspense. In *Vengeance* he tells about a man who accidentally overhears a compromising conversation between his wife and another man. These two are planning an illicit correspondence. The wife is to write a letter which she is to insert in a marble vase at the Public Garden. The lover is to get it on his way from the office at six o'clock. The husband is furious when he overhears this. What is he to do to get even with them? And the reader, too, is kept guessing. What, indeed, will the husband do?

Then the husband hits upon a plan. Further suspense. The reader is anxious to go on and learn what is the nature of this plan.

The husband's plan, in brief, is as follows: The husband writes a forged letter, in an illiterate hand, threatening a certain rich merchant in the city with bodily harm unless this merchant puts two hundred dollars into the marble vase at the Public Garden before six o'clock.

The plan seems excellent. The merchant will of course report this letter to the police, a squad will be sent to the Public Garden, and when the lover comes to get his letter in the marble vase he will be arrested.

The suspense is now at its height. The reader is waiting anxiously for the moment when the lover will come to the Public Garden for his letter.

At the appointed time the author takes the reader, together with the husband, to the Public Garden. A policeman is seen lounging near the marble vase. "Aha!" says the reader. "Now the fun will begin!"

Promptly at six o'clock the lover appears. Whistling a popular tune, he approaches the vase. The reader is tense with excitement. Now what will happen? And then comes the climax. The lover puts his hand into the vase and takes a tiny package out of it. He unwraps the package and his mouth opens with astonishment. The package contains two hundred dollars!

The husband swears under his breath, while the lover, shrugging his shoulders, pockets the money and walks off.

* * *

You will find an excellent example of suspense piled upon suspense in Stevenson's *The Adventure of the Hansom Cab*. Lieutenant Brackenbury Rich was walking early one evening in the London streets. He was accosted by a cab-driver. "Where to, sir?" asked the driver. "Where you please," said Brackenbury.

Here comes suspense number one. The cab-driver takes Brackenbury, at a rapid pace, to a house in the suburbs. A reception is being held in the house.

"Here we are, sir," says the driver.

"Here!" cries Brackenbury. "Where?"

"You told me to take you where I pleased, sir," chuckles the driver, "and here we are."

The reader is at once intrigued. What is this place to which Brackenbury has been brought? And what is going to happen to him here?

We read on:

Brackenbury, as mystified as the reader himself, steps into the house. He is welcomed by a young man, slender and singularly handsome. A group of about sixteen guests surrounds a roulette table. There is not a woman present.

Suspense number two. Is this a gambling house? But no, a few words exchanged with the host convinces Brackenbury that the man is no professional gambler. Then who is he? And what is the meaning of this strange company?

Brackenbury is all eyes and ears. He observes that every few minutes the host speaks to one of the guests, escorts him to the door, and returns alone. Brackenbury overhears one of these conversations:

"I beg you a thousand pardons!" says the host. "But I fear you have made a mistake and honored the wrong house with the pleasure of your company. Under whose roof do you suppose yourself to be?"

"That of Mr. Morris," replies the guest.

"Mr. John Morris or Mr. James Morris?"

"I really don't know. The cab-man who brought me here told me to ask for Mr. Morris."

"I see," said the host. "It was all a mistake. There is another person of the same name farther down the street."

Suspense number three. Who is this host who thus strangely invites and dismisses his guests? And what is he up to?

The author hurries on with his story. Brackenbury steps out of the drawing room into the hall for a breath of fresh air. And here he makes a most surprising discovery. The house is being dismantled, and three large furniture vans stand before the door.

Suspense number four. Is all this a sham? Or is it the prelude to still further surprising adventures?

Brackenbury returns to the company. There are now only five guests left. "It is now time, gentlemen," says the host, "to explain my purpose . . . I have asked you to come here on a dangerous mission . . . If there is anyone who is afraid and wants to leave right now—I wish him good-night and Godspeed."

Three of the five remaining guests accept the invitation and depart.

Suspense number five. Now, at last, together with the two remaining guests, we shall learn something of the mystery.

The host explains his mission: "Three days ago a distinguished gentleman disappeared . . . He is engaged upon a work of private justice . . . He finds it necessary to rid the earth of an insidious and bloody villain . . . He has managed to get a letter into my hands . . . We must arrive this morning, promptly at 3, at Rochester House, Regent's Park . . . Beyond this information," concludes the host, "I am as wholly in the dark as either of yourselves."

Suspense number six. What now?

The three young men drink a glass of wine and set off on their strange adventure.

They arrive at Rochester House. It is now 10 minutes before three. The three adventurers are about to enter the house, when they hear two voices.

"Is the grave dug?" asks one.

"It is," replies the other.

The first speaker laughs. "In an hour from now."

Suspense number seven. What's going on in that house?

A postern door is opened in the garden wall, and the three men enter.

They are ushered into a small apartment, lighted by a smoky

lamp and the glow of a modest fire. At the chimney corner sits a young man. His attitude and expression are "of the most unmoved composure."

One of the two companions of "Mr. Morris" recognizes the young man at the fireplace. Prince Florizel of Bohemia!

Suspense number eight. Are we now at last going to get the full explanation? No, not yet. "You will excuse me, gentlemen," smiles Prince Florizel, "if I have to leave you in the dark. The moment now approaches."

The lamp is extinguished. A short period of tense waiting. Then a hand is laid on the door. The door is opened. In the dim gray light of the early dawn the figure of a man appears on the threshold and stands motionless. His upper teeth are bare and glistening. He carries a knife in his hand.

Suspense number nine. Who is he? And what is going to happen?

The newcomer crosses the threshold. There is a leap, a cry, a struggle. The prince overpowers the man.

And now comes the explanation. This man is the President of the Suicide Club. His criminal insanity has caused the death of several people. Prince Florizel has set out to capture and to kill this man. He now has him in his power.

Suspense number ten. The two go out into the garden to fight a duel. Who is going to come out the victor?

The three young men await the outcome in an agony of sweat. It is broad daylight when the sound of returning footsteps is heard. The Prince enters. . . .

And then the story ends upon a reflective note. Stevenson the story-teller bows himself out and Stevenson the philosopher comes upon the stage to deliver his epilogue:

"I have killed this man," muses the Prince . . . "I have attained my end . . . What then? The existence of a man is so small a thing to take, so mighty a thing to employ . . . Is there anything in life so disenchanting as attainment?"

* * *

The climax of the story is best achieved through the skillful handling of suspense. To come back to the homely figure of the sneeze, a quick explosion that follows immediately after the warning is unsatisfactory. The snuff-takers of past generations knew how to inhale just enough snuff to produce a series of ticklings that followed one after the other in a pleasurable crescendo of suspense until the climactic delight of the explosion in the end.

Produce this effect, and you will be a successful writer of short stories.

* * *

What type of stories are you going to write? At the present time there is a good market for the following types: the humorous story; the story of adventure; the domestic story; the business story; the mystery story. Try your hand at all these types, and learn from experience which of them best fits your individual talent.

How long are you going to make your stories? This, too, depends upon your individual talent and temperament. Some writers are at their best in short and brilliant leaps; others can display their skill to the best advantage in long and sustained flights. Observe your own gifts and limitations, and study the requirements of the magazines. There is a market for short stories of all lengths ranging from 1000 to 10,000 words. The most practical length is about 5000.

A final word on this subject: The success of a short story depends largely upon the end. The end should be one that the reader desires, or fears, or expects—or, still better, one that the reader does *not* expect. The surprise ending is still a great favorite among the readers of the most popular magazines.

B

Novels

Within the past few years the sale of the novel has increased tremendously. Some of our most recent novels, like *Anthony Adverse*, have passed the half-million mark; and one of them, *Gone with the Wind*, has already sold better than a million. What makes a best-seller? In other words, what is there in such books as *Anthony Adverse, Gone with the Wind, The Bridge of San Luis Rey, Drums Along the Mohawk, So Red the Rose, Of Human Bondage, Northwest Passage, Kristin Lavransdatter*, and *The Forty Days of Musa Dagh* that compels so many tens of thousands of people to spend their time and their money on them? Externally, no two of these books are alike. Is there some internal common denominator that makes these books popular? Without giving a positive answer to this question—for there is no ready-made formula for a best-seller—let us note those qualities which the above books, and indeed most of the best-sellers, possess in common.

1. A best-seller is honest. If you want to produce a popular book, be honest with yourself and with your public. Don't "spoof" your readers. Don't sneer at them or look down upon them. Sympathize with them. Touch upon that chord which binds you and your readers into a universal brotherhood of frequent suffering and occasional joy. Be human and humane. Show a sincere affection for your reader, a frank understanding and discussion of his problems, and he will come to you for entertainment and advice. The first requisite of a best-seller, therefore, is honesty.

2. A best-seller is interesting. It has a good plot. It is full of physical or mental or moral action. It takes the reader away from himself and carries him into a land of adventure. That is why you see so many historical novels on the best-seller lists. A historical novel is a magic carpet which takes the reader on a journey. It transports him to other times and other places. And yet it depicts problems which have a universal application— problems which have perplexed mankind at all times and in all places. A book, in order to be interesting, must tell a story that is human and universal.

3. A best-seller must have an ending which is morally happy. It may be physically sad, or even tragic, as in *The Bridge of San Luis Rey*. But it must be ethically sound and hopeful. The idea must be the same as that expressed in *The Bridge of San Luis Rey*. Though in accordance with our human hindsight the killing of seven people in the catastrophe of the bridge is a meaningless tragedy, it is in the foresight of Heaven a necessary bringing together of seven completed lives into an immortal harmony. A novel that is to become a best-seller must be a dream-fulfillment, either here or in the hereafter.

4. A novel that is a best-seller must be passionately devoted to an ideal. It may glorify the ideal of a family, or of a city, or of a state, or of a country, or of the entire world. It must

bind a group of characters together, either in a small or in a large way, with the golden thread of a common human bond. The search for unity is one of the eternal quests of mankind. Create a group of people united in a good cause, and you have the ingredients that make a best-seller.

5. A best-seller must be timely. It must be published at the moment when the public is psychologically ripe for the subject. This is a difficult thing to achieve. It takes months, and even years, to write a good novel. Your subject may be timely when you begin your book, but stale when you finish it. If that happens, you must have patience. Public taste moves in cycles. Once in every few years a wave of interest in a certain subject will sweep over the reading public. If two years ago there was a tremendous interest in psychological novels, and today the interest has died down, the public is merely catching its breath. In five years, or in ten years, this interest will be fanned once more into a white heat.

6. A best-seller must have a fetching title. E. Haldeman-Julius, publisher of the popular *Little Blue Books,* experimented widely with the titles of his books. And he achieved some striking results. Some of his books sold only 5000 copies under one title, and jumped to 20,000 and 25,000, and in a few cases even to 50,000 and 100,000 copies when he changed their titles.

7. A novel must be well-written in order to be a best-seller. This requisite, curiously enough, is not so important as the other seven requisites. Some of the most successful of the recent best-sellers are poorly written. *Gone with the Wind,* for example, has many stylistic shortcomings. But it contains all the other necessary ingredients to a high degree.

The above seven ingredients, if well mixed, *may* turn out a best-seller. But it is not at all certain that they will. It is easy enough to follow a recipe for the baking of an appetizing pudding. It is not quite so easy to follow a recipe for the writing of an appetizing novel. Yet it is a fact that most of the best-sellers, or near-best-sellers, or better-than-average sellers, have been written, consciously or subconsciously, in accordance with the above pattern.

If you want to write a salable novel—don't, at the start, aim at the best-seller—study the above seven principles. Or, still better, read the books that have enjoyed the best sales for the past twelve months. You will find these books listed in *Publishers' Weekly*. Read these books with a note-book at your side. Jot down, in each book, all the qualities which have made *you* interested in that book. Then compare those qualities which are common to *all* the books that have been the current best-sellers. In this way you will have worked out your own formula for the successful novel. It is hard work to do this. But no writer as yet has succeeded without hard work. The good Lord must have had the young novelist in mind when he said: "By the sweat of thy brow shalt thou earn thy daily bread."

Types of Novels

There are several types of successful novels:

1. The romantic novel. Everybody loves a lover and wants to read about him. Indeed, every novel, no matter what its subject, must have its love element. Without a romance, there can be no good plot. This romance may center around young or middle-aged or old people. Frequently a good plot may be based upon the union between a young woman and an old man, or vice versa. In such a case, however, you need a young outsider to act as a foil against the older member of the marriage. This will give you the necessary triangle. A triangle is always a good nucleus for the plot of a novel.

2. The humorous novel. This is a difficult type. First-class humorous writers are few and far between. Jerome K. Jerome in England and Mark Twain in America have left no successors of their calibre. The demand for this type of novel is great, and the writers who can supply this demand are few. If you can turn out a truly humorous novel, something reminiscent but not imitative of Jerome K. Jerome or Mark Twain or Anatole France or G. K. Chesterton or P. G. Wodehouse, you will find an eager public.

The humorous story is so difficult to write because a sense of humor is a peculiar thing. No two nations—indeed, no two individuals—have the same sense of humor. A story that seems funny to an American may sound lugubrious to an Englishman. An incident that sends Tom into paroxysms of laughter may send Dick and Harry to sleep. There are today only a few novelists who can write a humorous story with a wide appeal. Try your hand at it, if you wish. You never can tell. This sort of story may just exactly suit your talents. Write a humorous story, and then try it on ten different types of people: a maid, a professor, a chauffeur, a lawyer, a hod-carrier, a housewife, a bachelor, a high-school girl, a business-man, and an automobile mechanic. If your story has caused all these people either to laugh or to chuckle, then you may set yourself up as a professional humorist, and feel pretty certain that Fortune is on her way to your door.

3. The picaresque novel. In this novel your hero is a rogue. If you can make your rogue companionable, you have a good story; if you can make him lovable, you have an excellent story. The greatest of the picaresque novels is, of course, Le Sage's *Gil Blas*. Anatole France's *Queen Pedauque* is a first-rate modern specimen of this type. A good English picaresque novel is Compton Mackenzie's *Sinister Street*. Read these three books, and then see whether you have the inclination and the talent to write a book of this kind. There is always a big public interested in the beloved vagabonds of the human race.

4. The adventure story has always been in demand. From Alexandre Dumas to Rafael Sabatini and Hervey Allen, the competent writers of adventure stories have enjoyed deserved success. The adventure story is easier to write than the humor-ous or the picaresque story. And there is a bigger public for it. There are today a good many writers who make a comfortable living in this field. Harold Bell Wright, Zane Grey, Edison Marshall, James B. Connolly, and H. G. Wells (in his earlier stories) are only a few of them. In the past generation, there was a steady demand for the works of such writers as Robert Louis Stevenson, H. Rider Haggard, Jack London, James Oliver Curwood, Joseph Conrad, and Jules Verne. Indeed, the zest for adventure stories has remained undiminished ever since Homer took his reader on a vicarious journey over land and sea. It bids fair to persist for a long time to come.

There are two kinds of adventure stories: the realistic story and the imaginative story. *Anthony Adverse, The Three Musketeers,* and *Captain Blood* belong to the realistic or rather to the pseudo-realistic type. They are based upon his-toric data. *The Time Machine, A Voyage to the Moon* and

Buck Rogers belong to the imaginative type. They are built up entirely of the author's fantasy. There is a profitable and permanent field for both of the above types of adventure stories. Practice writing this type of story. It is decidedly worth while.

5. The historical novel. Ten years ago a well-known critic made the assertion that "the historical novel is all played out." Yet today the historical novel enjoys a vogue such as it has rarely enjoyed before. Indeed, within the past few years the historical novel has been the best-seller among all the best-sellers. *Gone with the Wind* bids fair to smash all sales records for fiction. And this is only one of a host of successful novels in the same field. The history of the United States offers a field of inexhaustible wealth to the writer of fiction. And this field is still virgin. It has merely been scratched thus far. See what James Boyd and Kenneth Roberts and Hervey Allen and Margaret Mitchell have done with it. If you can make our past history alive, you have an enviable career awaiting you.

6. The detective novel. There is always a big demand for this type. All of us enjoy the thrill of the chase and the capture. And all of us are fond of solving riddles. A good detective story has two requisites: a baffling plot and an interesting detective.

Your detective story must have a baffling plot. Give your reader plenty of suspense. Keep him guessing. Mislead him by means of false clues. Yet be honest with him. Give him a hint of the real clue. This is a delicate matter. Your hint must be fair and yet obscure. Study the stories of S. S. Van Dine and see how he manages his false and his true clues. For ingenuity of plot in general, study the classics of Conan Doyle and the more modern stories of Edgar Wallace, of E. Phillips Oppenheim, and of Mary Roberts Rinehart.

Your detective story must have an interesting detective. Try to create a character as intriguing as Agatha Christie's M. Poirot, or R. Austin Freeman's Dr. Thorndyke, or S. S. Van Dine's Philo Vance. Make your detective pleasing and colorful and unique, or else your readers will not be interested in him.

The detective story offers to the young writer perhaps the most encouraging field of all. If you decide to enter this field, don't get the impression that you are going to write down to a "low-brow" audience. Some of the most intelligent people alive today are detective-story enthusiasts. Stanley Baldwin, Clarence Darrow, Lloyd George, and Bernard Shaw, to mention only a few, have expressed their fondness for this type of story. Among our past presidents, there have been at least three detective story "fans": Theodore Roosevelt, Woodrow Wilson, and Herbert Hoover. When you enter this field, therefore, you are in good company.

7. The war novel. Novels dealing with the great wars of history have a good chance for success. But a novel of this kind must be written at a time when the passions resulting from the war have had a chance to cool off. This cooling-off process may sometimes take an entire generation or even longer. The French Revolution was most successfully depicted, several decades after the event, in Dickens' *A Tale of Two Cities*. Our own Civil War has just served as a background for the most popular book ever written about that period—*Gone with the Wind*. The World War will at some time undoubtedly give a novelist the theme for a literary masterpiece that will prove to be a best-seller. Whether or not the time is ripe for such a masterpiece, it is hard to say. I venture to believe, however, that this time will come within the life-span of the younger writers of today. So—here's your chance!

The Length of the Novel

There is no arbitrary limit to the length of a novel. Edith Wharton's *Ethan Frome* is about 50,000 words. Hervey Allen's *Anthony Adverse,* on the other hand, runs to 700,000 words. Artistically, the short novel is preferable. Anatole France believed that it was the only possible kind of good novel. Nobody, he maintained, can write a long novel that is aesthetically sound. I think it is axiomatic that any novel would be twice as good if it were half as long. The present-day taste, however, is for long novels. Sigrid Undset, Franz Werfel, Sholom Ash, Hervey Allen, and Margaret Mitchell are among the most popular writers today. And most of their novels are of the three-decker type. The public is used to bargains. It demands quantity as well as quality. The tendency in publishing is toward bigger books at lower prices. It is therefore impossible to advise the young writer as to how long to make his novels. A long story, you know, takes considerable time. And fashions may change while you are writing it. The ideal length for the novel in the first three decades of the twentieth century was 90,000 words. Books of this size still command a good sale.

Your novel should be long enough to differentiate it from the long short story. But it must be meaty from beginning to end. The commonest mistake of the literary recruit is to spin out a long story with a thin plot. A novel should have a "thick" plot. It should not, like a short story, depend upon one or two or three incidents. It should contain sub-plots as well as the main plot. A novel is the result of many tributaries of action flowing at the end into a single stream. The competent handling of all these contributory streams requires space. A novel with an adequate plot can hardly be developed in less than 90,000 words.

EXAMPLES OF NOVEL-PLOTS

The mechanic learns how to put machines together by taking a number of them apart. Let us try to do the same with the novel. Let us select a few of the world's classics and examine their clockwork.

The Toilers of the Sea
by
Victor Hugo

Here the author brings together a number of characters and throws about them a net of circumstances which entangles them into a plot of tragic beauty. Some of these characters are:

Deruchette, a charming young girl.

Lethierry, her uncle with whom Deruchette is living.

Gilliatt, a young man of doubtful birth but doubtless courage.

A young Episcopalian curate.

Rantaine, an adventurer and thief.

Clubin, an honest and capable ship captain.

Now let us see what Victor Hugo has been able to do with these characters:

Lethierry befriends Rantaine. The latter repays the favor by stealing 50,000 francs from Lethierry. This money, saved over a period of forty years, has been intended for Deruchette's dowry.

Gilliatt worships Deruchette from a distance. He is too humble, however, to tell her of his love.

One day Gilliatt rescues the young curate from the high tide. The curate offers him a sovereign, which Gilliatt refuses. He accepts a Bible instead.

Here you have a situation which promises an interesting entanglement. A beautiful girl whose dowry has been stolen; a young man of humble station who is desperately in love with the girl; and another young man, of higher station and learning. This is obviously a situation for the inevitable triangle. But let us go on and see how the fates of the other characters are intertangled with the fates of these three young people.

Clubin is a captain. He commands Lethierry's steamboat, the *Durande*. Lethierry has lost all his other ships, and all his hopes are centered in the *Durande* and its captain. He is an honest man, this captain, and well worthy of his master's trust.

On one of his trips, Captain Clubin runs across Rantaine, the scoundrel who has stolen Lethierry's money and who is about to escape from the country with a fortune of 75,000 francs. Clubin compels Rantaine, at the point of a pistol, to deliver the money to him. He then sets sail to bring the money back to Lethierry.

And now observe what the author does to complicate the plot and lengthen the story. The steamship *Durande* is wrecked. Clubin sends the passengers off in the long-boat, and calmly awaits death on the sinking ship.

Lethierry's last hope for Deruchette is gone. The *Durande* is a total wreck, except—note this clever device by which the story is continued—except for the engines which Lethierry himself has designed. If only he can recover the engines, he can build another ship around them.

Is there anyone who can find a way to save the engines? If there is any man who can do it, he shall have the hand of Deruchette.

There is one man in the crowd who undertakes this almost impossible task. It is Gilliatt.

He sets out for the wreck. It is situated underneath a precipice in the channel. In order to reach it, he must climb down by means of a knotted rope. It is a superhuman task fraught with the greatest danger. For many a day he toils and starves himself, for part of the food which he has brought along with him has been swept away by the sea. He lives on shell-fish and crabs—whenever he can get them.

Once, as he wades into the shallow water of a cave in pursuit of a crab, he is attacked by a devil-fish and barely escapes with his life.

At this point in the story the author begins to prepare us for the climax. He takes Gilliatt into the further recesses of the cave where he finds the skeleton of a man. By means of a belt with a name upon it, Gilliatt is able to identify the skeleton. It is that of the ship captain, Clubin. Tied firmly to the belt is an iron box. It contains 75,000 francs.

Gilliatt takes the money and returns to his toil.

He finally succeeds in rescuing the engines. He is ready for his reward—the hand of Deruchette.

In the evening he approaches the house in which she lives. A nightingale is singing. In his heart, too, there is a song.

Deruchette is in the garden. She is not alone. The young curate whose life Gilliatt has saved is with her. Deruchette and the curate embrace. Gilliatt turns away and leaves them to their love.

Deruchette and her lover are married. They set sail for England. Gilliatt stands on a rock at the water's edge and watches the ship. The tide is rising. It comes up to his knees, his shoulders, over his head. And thus ends the tragic life of the toiler of the sea.

* * *

The Scarlet Letter
by
Nathaniel Hawthorne

Here we have, among others, the following characters:

Hester Prynne, a woman with a great yearning for love and a great capacity for suffering.

The Reverend Mr. Dimmesdale, a young minister whose courage is not equal to his devotion.

Hester Prynne's husband, Dr. Roger Chillingworth, a man with a great intellect and a little soul.

Pearl, the child of Hester's sin.

With these four major characters for a start, Hawthorne has woven one of the immortal plots in the history of literature.

The action does not begin at the beginning. Hawthorne uses the flash-back method in this novel. The scene opens upon Hester Prynne's discharge from prison. She carries a three-months-old baby in her arms. On the breast of her gown, in scarlet cloth, appears the letter A.

Outwardly serene, but with agony in her heart, she walks to the pillory.

On the outskirts of the gaping crowd stands a small man. He has an intelligent brow and cruel eyes. He is Roger Chillingworth, Hester Prynne's husband. He has been abroad for a number of years and is now a stranger in this town.

A young minister, Arthur Dimmesdale, makes his way through the throng. He comes to Hester's side and urges her to name her fellow-sinner.

Here, in the first few pages of the book, we are introduced to the four leading characters. The author begins without delay to weave the strands of their fate. That night Hester's child falls ill, and Dr. Chillingworth is called in.

"I have greatly wronged thee," murmurs Hester.

"It was my fault as well as thine," replies her husband. "I am a man of thought, you a woman of beauty. What right had we to marry?"

Roger Chillingworth understands, but he does not forgive. His mind and his heart are not in harmony. He is determined to learn the name of her fellow-sinner and to punish him.

Hester takes up needlework for a living. The worthy people of the town at first insist upon taking her "sin-child" away from Hester. But Mr. Dimmesdale prevails upon them to let the child remain with her.

"You take, my friend, a strange interest in this poor woman," smiles Roger Chillingworth.

Mr. Dimmesdale's health is failing. Dr. Chillingworth becomes his physician. He moves into the same lodging with the minister. For he is determined to ferret out the secrets of Dimmesdale's heart.

Note how the author brings these two men together physically in order to interweave the threads of their mental and moral reactions. Chillingworth becomes the incarnated conscience of the guilty minister.

Dimmesdale regards Chillingworth with increasing horror. Time and again he tries to confess his sin from the pulpit, but his courage always fails him.

Once, in the dead of night, he mounts the pillory where Hester has stood exposed in her shame. He believes that everybody is asleep. Yet three people see him: Hester and Pearl, who are returning from the home of a dying woman—and Dr. Roger Chillingworth.

In mock pity the doctor takes him home. "You should not study so hard, good Master Dimmesdale!"

The strands of the plot have now been interwoven into a definite and tragic pattern. We are ready for the climax. And this is how the author brings about the climax:

Hester plans to escape from the baleful influence of Roger Chillingworth. She takes passage for England. Dimmesdale and Pearl are to go with her.

But they cannot evade Chillingworth as easily as all that. Hester learns that he, too, has booked passage on the same ship for England. This information comes—note the skill of the author—on a very important holiday: the day on which Mr. Dimmesdale has been chosen to preach the election sermon in honor of the newly appointed governor. Thus the height of Mr. Dimmesdale's fame and the bitter culmination of his tragedy come together on the same day. For it is no longer possible for Dimmesdale to conceal his sin with Hester. Better that than the future torture of Chillingworth's endless probing into the deepest recesses of his soul.

Accordingly, Dimmesdale preaches the election sermon to an adoring crowd; and then, in a dramatic gesture, he mounts the pillory together with Hester and little Pearl.

"People of New England," he cries. "At last, at last I stand where seven years since I should have stood. . . ."

And now comes the moment of tragic revelation:

"Lo," he continues in a ringing voice, "the scarlet letter which Hester wears. . . . I, too, have my scarlet letter!"

He tears away his ministerial robe from his breast. Seared upon his flesh stands out the scarlet letter A.

Then, as the populace stares at him in amazement and pity, his head sinks down upon Hester's bosom. He has paid for his sin with his life.

* * *

Adam Bede
by
George Eliot

For this story the author brings together a group of English countryfolk in the last year of the eighteenth century:

Dinah Morris, a vigorous and attractive and fearless young woman who turns "Methody" preacher.

Hetty Sorrel, a beautiful young creature with an intense love of life.

Adam Bede, a carpenter who worships Dinah but who loves Hetty.

Captain Arthur Donnithorne, heir to a rich estate, who has a way of whispering into Hetty's ear many pretty things that he doesn't mean.

With these four widely contrasted characters as a nucleus, the author is ready to begin her colorful story:

One August evening Adam is walking home through a grove of glorious beech trees. He stops to admire one of the trees when he stumbles upon a scene that makes his heart stop still. Arthur and Hetty are standing close together—hands clasped, faces flushed, voices tense in a passionate whisper.

At the sight of Adam, the girl hurries away. But Arthur comes forward.

"Well, Adam, so you've been admiring the beeches? . . . Grand old trees, aren't they? . . . Remember, you have just seen the trees, nothing else. . . . Let's say no more. . . . The whole thing will soon be forgotten."

"Oh, no, it'll not be soon forgot . . . You have robbed me of my happiness when I thought you my best friend . . . You're a scoundrel and a coward."

There is a scuffle, and Arthur is overpowered.

"Promise Hetty that you'll marry her. Or else, write to her that you'll never see her again. Do this, or by God, I'll kill you!"

Arthur promises to write.

When Hetty receives the letter, she gives way to despair. She has two alternatives: death, or marriage with Adam Bede. She decides to marry Adam at some time in the future.

In the meantime, Arthur has rejoined his regiment. After a brief campaign, he learns that his grandfather has died and that he has become the lord of the Donnithorne estate.

He comes home, eager to enter upon his inheritance and to marry some rich and respectable lady.

Immediately upon his arrival, he learns that Hetty Sorrel is in prison for the crime of child murder.

Springing upon a saddled horse, he dashes off to save her.

While he is on his way to the prison, a visitor comes to see Hetty in her cell. It is Dinah Morris, the young evangelist.

"I was so miserable, Dinah," cries Hetty. . . . "I dared not keep the baby. . . . I buried it in the wood. . . . It cried. . . . I heard it all night. . . . Dinah, do you think God will forgive me? . . ."

"Let us pray, Hetty. God is All Merciful."

Heaven hears their prayer. Arthur earns a reprieve for Hetty.

She is saved from death, but she is sentenced to transportation. Arthur returns to the army.

Thus the strands of two of the characters are disentangled, each to be spun out in a destiny apart from the other. But there are two strands that are still left. Dinah returns to her evangelical work, and Adam to his carpentry. For a time their paths do not cross. But one day his mother mentions the name of Dinah. And then he realizes that what he has regarded as his worship for her, might be more correctly defined as love.

He marries Dinah.

* * *

Tess of the D'Urbervilles
by
Thomas Hardy

Like all the other great novelists, Thomas Hardy selects a group of widely contrasted personalities for the spinning of his colorful plot:

John Durbeyfield, a shiftless peddler who learns that he is a descendant of the noble family of D'Urberville.

Joan, his handsome and foolish wife.

Tess, their pretty daughter who is anxious to restore the family fortunes.

Alec D'Urberville, dissolute son of a blind old woman (not related to the Durbeyfields).

Angel Clare, idealist son of an old clergyman.

This story, though its plot is in some respects similar to that of *Adam Bede,* is more loosely and more leisurely constructed. And that is where the novel has an advantage over the short story. A novel can meander like a long and winding river, taking the reader into all sorts of interesting fields and forests and meadows and nooks and crannies. A short story, on the other hand, must rush like a rapid mountain stream from the start to the crisis.

But let us return to *Tess of the D'Urbervilles.*

When John Durbeyfield learns that he, a vagabond, bears a noble name, he is ready to burst with pride. His wife, Joan, begins to dream of a brilliant match for their daughter, Tess. They therefore prevail upon her to get a job as poultry girl on the farm of the vulgar old lady D'Urberville.

Here Tess meets the old lady's son, Alec D'Urberville, a handsome and unprincipled young scoundrel. A brief romance, disillusionment, and a child. The child soon dies.

Tess returns home.

It is some time before she finds the courage to face the world again. Finally, however, she accepts a job as dairymaid on the Talbothy farm. Here she meets Angel Clare. Son of an old clergyman, Angel has, much to his father's regret, turned from the shepherding of souls to gentleman farming.

The two are drawn closely together. When Angel Clare declares his love, Tess hasn't the courage to reveal her past life. Her dream is too beautiful to be shattered.

The wedding day approaches. In a moment of honest despair she writes a long letter of confession. She thrusts it under the door. But her hand is guided by the mysterious hand of fate. The letter slips under the carpet. Just before the wedding she discovers it and tears it up.

They are married. As they depart from the church, they hear the crowing of a cock. An afternoon crow is an evil omen.

It should be noted at this point that there is a sixth leading character in this, as well as in all of Thomas Hardy's stories— Fate. In Hardy, it is always Fate, cruel, blind, and mysterious, that spins the plot.

Tess and Angel come to live in a picturesque old farmhouse. Here Angel confesses his one sin—a two days' dissipation with a scarlet woman. He asks for his young wife's forgiveness. This she readily grants, and then relates the story of her own sin. But Angel Clare is not so ready to forgive.

There is a separation, and Tess returns home. Her mother takes the matter lightly, but her father's drunken D'Urberville pride is deeply hurt at what he regards as her inexcusable conduct.

Tess finds summer work on the farms. A large part of her pay she spends on the support of her parents. But with the coming of winter she loses most of her work. An occasional drab and difficult and poorly paid job, and then long stretches of hunger and despair. At last she decides to make one desperate attempt to see Angel's parents. Perhaps they will give her news of him. Through the rain and snow she trudges for many miles—but she finds the vicarage empty.

She turns back. Again there are long days of hunger and hopeless degradation. Once, as she passes by a barn, she hears a boisterous evangelist. The voice is familiar. She looks inside and recognizes Alec D'Urberville.

Alec pleads with her to return to him. At first she refuses. But her father's death and her mother's poverty weaken her resolution. To earn bread for her mother, Tess goes back to Alec.

She yields her body to Alec. But her heart is still wandering in search of Angel Clare. And he, too, is now seeking for Tess. He is unhappy and ill. His old anger has died down, leaving nothing in its place but a deep longing for his bride.

He finds her in a fashionable boarding-house,—a degraded woman. The relentlessness of Fate has so tangled the threads of their lives that they cannot meet. Angel Clare starts on his way home.

On the outskirts of the town she overtakes him. "I have killed him. . . . He called you by a foul name. . . . I owed it to you. . . . It was the only way I could get you back."

Hand in hand they depart from the scene of her suffering. Fate has brought them together at last, but only for a moment of tragic irony. At the dawn of day she is arrested—note the contrast between the rising of the sun and the setting of her hope. She is tried and found guilty.

Eight strokes of the bell, and a black figure twists convulsively in the air.

Tess has paid her debt to Fate.

* * *

A Tale of Two Cities
by
Charles Dickens

This plot is based upon the striking resemblance between two characters. It is a common theme, both in fiction and in drama. It dates back over two thousand years. The Latin dramatist, Plautus, first used it in his play *The Twins*. Sixteen hundred years later, Shakespeare adopted the idea and the plot in his *Comedy of Errors*. Within the past three centuries, several successful stories have been based upon this resemblance theme.

In *A Tale of Two Cities,* Dickens brings together the following group of characters for the weaving of his intricate plot:

Charles Darnay, a young French nobleman.

Sydney Carton, a young English lawyer who looks like a twin brother of Darnay's.

Jarvis Lorry, a London banker.
Dr. Manette, a French physician.
Lucie, his daughter.
Defarge, the owner of a wine-shop in Paris.
Madame Defarge, his wife.

Having collected these seven characters, Dickens begins to intertwine the tale of their lives against a background of the French Revolution. At first the threads are loose. Dr. Manette, a prominent young physician in Paris, has suddenly disappeared. Nobody knows what has happened to him. His distracted wife puts her little daughter, Lucie, into the care of Mr. Jarvis Lorry, a member of the well-known London banking firm of Tellson & Co.

Two years later Dr. Manette's wife dies.

Sixteen more years pass since the disappearance of Dr. Manette. Mr. Lorry has just heard strange news about him. He makes his way to Lucie.

"Your father has been found. He is alive, but greatly changed."

Mr. Lorry takes Lucie to the house of an old servant of Manette's, the wine-shop keeper, Defarge. Here, in an attic, they find Dr. Manette. He is haggard and feeble-minded. He sits on a bench making shoes.

Another five years pass. The author then transports us to a London courtroom. A dapper young Frenchman, Charles Darnay, is on trial for his life. Near by sits a dishevelled young lawyer, Sydney Carton. There is an amazing resemblance between them, and Sydney Carton is aware of it. Sydney rescues Darnay, and the two become fast friends.

Darnay is a nobleman. Carton is a commoner. Darnay is a man of exemplary character. Carton is a dissipated wreck of a man. Note the trick of character-drawing by means of contrasting colors. This contrast in their character is utilized later on in the weaving of the plot.

Charles Darnay and Sydney Carton become acquainted with Lucie Manette. The loose threads of the story have now become interlaced into the beginning of a definite design. The two young men fall in love with Lucie. She, in turn, is gracious to Carton, but is passionately devoted to Darnay.

Carton knows that his suit is hopeless. Yet he tells Lucie of

his love. "Do not weep, dear Miss Manette. I know I am
unworthy of you. . . . Yet I want you to remember this—
that there is a man who would give his life to save the life of
someone you love." Thus the author prepares us for the climax
that is to come later in the story.

The action now takes on a quicker tempo. Dangerous days
are ahead. The rumblings of the French Revolution are
heard. We are in the year 1789. The people are marching
through the streets with a song on their lips and blood in their
hearts. One of their leaders is Madame Defarge. She heads a
frenzied mob against the Bastille. The Reign of Terror has
begun.

Three years pass in a deluge of blood. Charles Darnay comes
to Paris in order to help an old servant of the family. Darnay
is arrested and recognized as a member of the noble house of
Evremonde. Madame Defarge is loud in her denunciation of
this young nobleman. For it was the selfishness and the cruelty
of the French nobility that had brought misery upon her own
family.

Dr. Manette appeals to Defarge, but in vain. Darnay's fate is
sealed. "Death within twenty-four hours."

And now, the climax. Sydney Carton has come to Paris in
the hope of saving Charles Darnay. He has promised Lucie to
give his life, if need be, in order to save the life of someone
she loves. He bribes the jailers to admit him into Darnay's cell.
Darnay is carried out from the cell unconscious. Carton sits
down to await his death.

The strands of the plot have now been woven into the complete design. There is left only the final scene. Six death-carts
are rolling along the Paris streets. They are carrying "the day's
wine" to the guillotine. In the third sits Sydney Carton.

The tumbrils arrive at the guillotine. The grim executions
begin. The knitting women count the falling heads. Twenty-one.
Twenty-two. Twenty-three.

Sydney Carton has performed the most sublime of human
acts. He has laid down his life for another. "It is a far, far
better thing that I do, than I have ever done; it is a far, far
better rest that I go to than I have ever known."

*   *   *

Anna Karenina
by
Leo Tolstoi

This book offers a large canvas of many colorful characters. For our plot-sketching purposes, however, we can reduce these characters to seven:

Alexei Karenin, a high official in the Russian court at St. Petersburg. He is a capable, hard-working, honest, but entirely unlovable personality.

Anna Karenina, his laughter-loving wife. She is twenty years younger than her husband.

Serozha, their seven-year-old son.

Stepan Oblonsky, Anna Karenina's brother who lives in Moscow. He is an easy-going, affable, and somewhat irresponsible family man who is not averse to the charms of other women.

Kitty, Stepan's sister-in-law, light-hearted, pretty, and popular.

Count Vronsky, rich, handsome, suave, a man who loves a good horse, a good fight, and a pretty woman.

Konstantin Levin, a Moscow nobleman. He is a well-to-do and serious young man with a skeptical turn of mind. "He is unable to believe; he is equally unable to disbelieve."

These are the people whose intertangled fates form the plot of the story.

For eight years Anna is faithful to her husband and happy in the love of her little son, Serozha. The child adores his mother like a goddess.

All would have been well but for an unfortunate visit that Anna Karenina pays to her brother Stepan in Moscow. Here, in the gay and heartless society of the Russian nobility, she meets Count Vronsky. They fall an easy prey to a mutual attraction.

Anna is not the first of Vronsky's conquests. Indeed, at the very moment of his meeting with Anna he is involved in a love affair with Kitty. This charming young debutante has many admirers. But of them all, she prefers Vronsky—and looks upon another, Konstantin Levin, as a convenient man to fall back upon in case of necessity.

Anna and Vronsky are aware of the danger of their love. Anna is afraid. She longs for the adoration of her son and the protection of her husband. She cuts her visit to her brother short and takes a return ticket to St. Petersburg. On the train she finds Vronsky.

He is determined to follow her.

They meet often in the social circles of St. Petersburg. Society looks upon their affair with a snickering approbation. It is an interesting diversion for them—and a good subject for gossip.

As for Anna's husband, he calmly points out to her the folly of her course, and then prudently shuts his eyes. He will not run the risk of a divorce scandal, and he will not endanger his life in a duel.

But things are coming to a head. Note how the author invents the following incident in order to find new threads for the weaving of his plot: There is an accident at a horse race. Count Vronsky is seriously hurt. Anna makes a public display of her anxiety. And, when Karenin upbraids her, she confesses her love for Vronsky.

Anna implores her husband to set her free. But he is determined to have his revenge. He compels her to remain under his roof.

Tortured and humiliated and desperate, Anna continues her relations with Vronsky. She is torn between three emotions: her love for her little Serozha, her loyalty toward Kitty from whom she has taken Vronsky, and her passion for Vronsky. Kitty finally manages to forget Vronsky and marries Konstantin Levin. One of the difficulties of Anna's position is therefore removed. But the other two, her love for Serozha and her passion for Vronsky, are still present in all their bitter intensity.

And now arises a new complication. Anna gives birth to a daughter. Karenin is magnanimous toward Vronsky's child; but Vronsky, in his humiliation, attempts suicide.

Anna's position has become intolerable. She must make a choice between Serozha and Vronsky. She decides in Vronsky's favor.

But the story is not yet ended. The author has another sombre thread to weave into the plot. Anna and Vronsky go abroad. For a time they enjoy a measure of happiness in their illicit love. Then they return to Russia and once again implore Karenin to grant Anna a divorce. But Karenin refuses.

Anna grows meditative, then morose. And finally a flaming jealousy begins to consume her. She suspects Vronsky of unfaithfulness. Her only relief is in oblivion—the death-in-life that comes through morphine.

And then—the end. Suicide under the wheels of a train.

*   *   *

The six foregoing plots are merely skeleton outlines. Every good novel is a stream of many tributaries. Study the six novels in their entirety with a notebook in your hand. Watch the many situations, the many scenes, and the many characters. Observe the way in which every one of them contributes to the plot. Then, and not till then, will you have a working knowledge of how a novel is written.

§ 3

NON FICTION

A

Poems

Miracle of miracles! There is today a fairly good market for poetry! Stephen Vincent Benét, Samuel Hoffenstein, Ogden Nash, Dorothy Parker, Edna St. Vincent Millay, and—of course—Edgar A. Guest have found poetry a profitable field. There is a market for the satirical, the humorous, the sophisticated, the realistic, and the sentimental in poetry. And, like the historical novel, the historical poem may sometimes become a best seller. One of the most successful books within recent years was Benét's *John Brown's Body*.

If you have a talent for poetry, cultivate it. There may be a market for it. Study the technique of versification. Learn the important rules that govern rhythm and rhyme. Find out what it is in a poem that makes it sing itself into the reader's mind and heart.

RHYTHM

All life is rhythmical. The rising and the falling of the tides, the succession of day and night, the recurrence of the seasons, the movement of the stars and the planets, the breathing of the lungs, the beating of the heart—all obey the rhythmical laws of nature. The poet is only an imitator of nature. He is catering to a universal human instinct—an instinct that may be called the musical pattern of life.

The poet has caught this pattern in many ways:

1. In the Iambic Pentameter line. An *iambic* is a foot of two syllables with the accent on the second syllable. For example:

> because
> observe
> defeat

A *pentameter* is a line of five feet. An *iambic pentameter,* therefore, is a line containing five feet with the accent on the second syllable of each foot. Example:

> For fools rush in where angels fear to tread.

This is the rhythm of dignified poetry. Shakespeare's plays and Milton's *Paradise Lost* are written in iambic pentameter. A recent dramatic success, Maxwell Anderson's *The Masque of Kings,* is written largely in iambic pentameter. This meter is also used, with modern shades and variations, in much of Miss Millay's poetry. Note, for example, the following lines from her sonnet, *I Shall Go Back:*

> I shall go back again to the bleak shore
> And build a little shanty on the sand . . .

The tendency in modern iambic pentameter, as in all other types of modern verse, is to use simple expressions and homely words. The poets have brought down their wares from Parnassus to Main Street. This, I think, is one of the chief reasons for the popularity of much of our present-day verse. A colloquial style on the part of our poets has shown to the public that almost everybody can understand poetry and enjoy it. Even the stately iambic pentameter has caught the nervous lilt and motion of our hurried life today.

2. The Iambic Tetrameter. A *tetrameter* is a line of four feet. It moves more rapidly than the pentameter. It expresses ideas and emotions that are more common to our everyday

experience. It is more easily set to music. It is a lyrical rather than a dramatic rhythm. Example:

> I burned my life that I might find
> A passion wholly of the mind. . . .

These lines, from Louise Bogan's *The Alchemist,* are in tune with the swift and eager searchings of the modern mind.

3. The Iambic Trimeter. A *trimeter* is a line of three feet. It moves even more rapidly than the tetrameter. Indeed, it gives a jerky motion to the poet's thought. Note the effect of the following lines from Tennyson's *Maud:*

> O, let the solid ground
> Not fail beneath my feet
> Before my life has found
> What some have found so sweet!

There are many other kinds of rhythmic patterns. I shall mention only a few:

4. The Trochaic Tetrameter. A *trochee* is a foot of two syllables with the accent on the first syllable. There is more life and more excitement to a trochee than there is to an iambus. Note, for example, the difference between the iambic words

> now come, my friend

and the trochaic words

> come now, Henry.

The trochaic tetrameter is a swinging, marching music, as you will see from the following specimen:

> First a single marching column
> Swinging past the cheering thousands,
> Then another and another,
> Hearts exultant, eyes a-glitter,
> Rushed the army to the battle.

5. The Dactyllic Hexameter. A *dactyl* (from the Greek *daktylon,* finger) is a foot of three syllables, with the accent on the first syllable. Examples:

> competent
> actual
> sympathy

A *hexameter* is a line of six feet. A *dactyllic hexameter,* therefore, is a line of six feet with the accent on the first syllable of each foot. Example:

> This is the forest primeval, the murmuring pines and
> the hemlocks.

The dactyllic hexameter is the favorite rhythm in Greek and in Latin poetry. But it has not been successful in English. Longfellow tried it in his *Evangeline* with fairly good results. No other English or American poet, however, has been able to produce a poem of melodious hexameters. This rhythm has always been a challenge to British and to American poets. If you can introduce this new type of music into the English language, you will be hailed as a pioneer in poetry. But it is a difficult—some poets say an impossible—job.

6. The Anapestic Line. An *anapest* is a foot of three syllables with the accent on the last syllable. Examples:

> inferfere
> correspond
> rat-a-tat

This rhythm adapts itself easily to the English language. It is very popular with the poets both here and in England. It produces the effect of a drum-beat, swift, stirring, and passionate. It is a galloping verse. Read this, for instance:

> And the drums beat a tune,
> And the bugle resounds,
> And the horses come clattering down from the
> mounds.

These are only a few of the possible rhythms in poetry. The professional poet tries them all, varying the style to the mood, and the mood to the music of his thought. If you want to be a professional poet, study the effects produced by various rhythms in the poems of Edna St. Vincent Millay, of Ogden Nash (who has tried a number of new rhythmical tricks with surprising results), of Robert Frost, of Louis Untermeyer, of Joseph Auslander, and of Dorothy Parker. Of the earlier poets, be sure to familiarize yourself with the rhythmic effects of Tennyson, of Shelley, of Keats, and especially of Swinburne. And, although Free Verse is at present undergoing an eclipse, sit at the feet of Walt Whitman, of Amy Lowell, and of Carl Sandburg. The most successful poets today have learned much from these teachers. Even in your regular verse you will be able to introduce cadences and echoes derived from the irregular experiments of the Free Verse poets.

RHYME

Rhyme in poetry is like the tinkling of a bell which brings a pleasant memory to the mind. It is the echo of a delightful experience. This is why an imperfect rhyme displeases us. It is a false echo. It produces a jarring note in a harmony of sound.

There are two important laws that govern the use of rhyme: first, the last vowels of the rhyming words must have the same sound; second, the consonants before the last vowels must *not* have the same sound.

1. The last vowels of the rhyming words must have the same sound. Examples:

show and *slow*
kind and *mind*
mended and *descended*

This law is frequently violated, especially in the work of the amateur poet. Thus, we often see *love* rhymed with *move, strong* with *flung,* and *thought* with *note*. These false rhymes are very disagreeable to the sensitive ear. Though some critics find no fault with such rhymes, it is wise for the young writer to avoid them.

2. The consonants before the last vowels must *not* have the same sound. Examples:

*b*orn and *m*orn
*s*weet and *g*reet
*ch*ill and *f*ill

This law, too, is frequently violated. It is wrong to try to rhyme *light* with *delight, reception* with *deception,* or *ring* with *bring*. It is true that the greatest poets, like Shelley and Browning and Swinburne, occasionally fall into this error. It is your business, however, to copy the virtues and not the faults of the great poets.

Avoid any rhyme that may give pain to the delicately trained ear. Don't rhyme *lover* with *brother, robin* with *sobbing, sinful* with *dimple,* or *endeavor* with *feather*. Even Tennyson, the most perfect technician of them all, rhymes *river* with *mirror*. This, however, is one of his few rare slips. In a young poet writing today, such an error is inexcusable.

There are a few words in English which, in the opinion of the critics, cannot be rhymed. Yet the clever poet—read Ogden Nash, for example—can find a rhyme for almost any word. A college professor recently told his students that it was impossible to rhyme *window*. Whereupon one of the students recited the following bit of doggerel:

> "I have a splendid recipe
>   For making *thick* dough out of *thin* dough;
> I treat the dough with Fleischmann's yeast,
>   And then I place it on the window."

The story is told of James Russell Lowell that a friend of his once challenged him to find rhymes for the two most difficult words in the Bible: *Sennacherib* and *Jehosaphat*. Whereupon Lowell nonchalantly remarked:

> "Why, old Sennacherib
>   He could never crack a rib
> Of Jehoshaphat,
>   Because he was so fat."

To the clever rhymester nothing is impossible.

SOUND EFFECTS IN POETRY

The poet is often able to use words whose sound expresses their meaning. The English language is pretty rich in such words. To mention only a few: *thud, splash, roar, bang, whizz, moan, hubbub, shriek, crag*. Kipling, in one of his poems, tells about the *sludgy, squudgy creek*. As you read these words, you can actually feel the mud oozing up between your toes. In Tennyson's line, *the innumerable murmur of the bees,* you can hear the droning and the humming of the insects as they flit from flower to flower. Note the frothy sound of Browning's line, *the wroth sea's waves are edged with foam;* and the long gliding motion of the river in Vachel Lindsay's lines:

> Then I saw the Congo, creeping through the black,
> Cutting through the jungle with a golden track.

One of the most pleasing sound effects in poetry is produced by means of alliteration. But you must know how to handle this. The mere repetition of a vowel or a consonant may be monotonous and at times even decidedly unpleasant. Try this and see how it sounds:

Theophrastus Throttlebottom threw three threadbare thimbles through the thrusting throng.

If gracefully handled, however, alliteration will add beauty to your poetry. Note the following lines from Swinburne:

> When the hounds of spring are on winter's traces,
>   The mother of months, in meadow or plain,
> Fills the shadows and windy places
>   With lisp of leaves and ripple of rain.

The soothing effect is here produced by the skillful interlacing of three liquid consonants: *m,* in *mother, months,* and *meadow; l,* in *lisp* and *leaves;* and *r,* in *ripple* and *rain.*

Swinburne is the perfect artist of tone effect. Study him faithfully if you want to learn the art of writing colorful poetry. And remember this: through the practice of writing colorful poetry, you will also learn how to write colorful prose.

B

Plays

"The Play's the thing." The drama is one of the oldest, as well as one of the most popular, of literary forms. It was born about two thousand years before the birth of the novel, and about twenty-two hundred years before the rise of the modern short story. One of the most successful plays in the twentieth century A. D. was a comedy written in the fifth century B. C. I refer, of course, to Aristophanes' *Lysistrata,* which played to full houses in New York only a few years ago.

For a short time it looked as if the stage drama would be eclipsed by the screen play. Today, however, the drama has come back into its own. It is as popular as ever.

A literary form that is so old, so universal, and so vital is a form well worth cultivating. The young professional writer should give it a thorough trial. If he succeeds in this field, he has a pleasant and remunerative career before him.

It pays, emotionally as well as financially, to write an acceptable play. The dramatist is in some respects more fortunate than the novelist. If you write a good novel, you can never see the effect produced upon your readers. For they are scattered far and wide. You can have no personal contact with them. But if you write a good play, you can see and hear the results for yourself. You meet your audience face to face. There is nothing that so stimulates an author to better work as the concrete applause of an appreciative audience.

Try, then, to write for a visible audience. Learn the technique of a good drama.

A drama, to define it briefly, is a story in dialogue form, just as a story is a drama in narrative form. Dramas may be roughly divided into two main types: tragedy and comedy.

TRAGEDY

Great literature, wrote Anatole France, arouses in us the emotions of irony and pity. This is especially true of tragedy. When we see a great tragedy, we realize the littleness of man and we pity him for it. The Greek philosopher, Aristotle, said that tragedy is a moral cleanser. He uses the term *Katharsis* (from which our English word *cathartic* is derived) to define this purging effect produced upon us by great tragedy.

Most of us like to see good tragedy upon the stage. Shakespeare's *Hamlet* and *Julius Caesar* and *Macbeth* are popular to this very day. Among the outstanding dramatic successes within recent years we find a goodly proportion of tragedies: Ibsen's *Ghosts* and *Hedda Gabler,* Bernard Shaw's *Saint Joan,* Eugene O'Neill's *Emperor Jones* and *Mourning Becomes Electra,* Maxwell Anderson's *Masque of Kings,* and Elmer Rice's *Street Scene,* to mention only a few.

If you write a tragedy, be honest with yourself. If your

characters are the victims of fate, let your art be as inexorable as fate itself. Don't, in your capacity as an honest writer of tragedy, be more considerate than nature. Don't let your personal pity, or your desire to please your audience, sentimentalize a tragic situation into a happy ending. There has been a recent tendency, among certain playwrights, to truckle to what they consider the public desire for the happy ending. Such plays never ring true, and they are almost always unsuccessful.

Don't attempt a tragedy unless you yourself have suffered. Literature, as you know, is the picture of our moments of perturbation that we paint in our moments of tranquillity. We can best understand our own troubles. Only those who have experienced sorrow can write a good tragedy. If your life has been tranquil—and let us hope that it has been and will continue to be so—then it is best for you to leave tragedy alone.

If, however, you are one of those whose "bread has been dipped in tears," then tragedy is within your province. Select a character through whom you can depict and ennoble your own suffering. Let the character, in other words, possess a noble soul. At least, let there be a *striving* after something noble. A man who is a downright scoundrel is not a fit subject for tragedy. His sufferings may arouse irony, but they will arouse no pity. Even Faust, you will remember, had the divine spark in his sordid soul. "In whatever he did, he erred," his creator, Goethe, tells us. "And yet, in all his erring moments, he had the instinct of the one true way."

A petty character is no subject for tragedy. His misfortunes may harass and even destroy him. But they do not sear and ennoble his soul. Disaster in itself is not tragedy. To become a fit subject for tragedy, disaster must be experienced in the heat of a cleansing fire.

Must a tragedy on the stage always end in death? Not necessarily. A life protracted without love or hope may be worse than death. This is the tragedy of the three principal characters in *Ethan Frome*. A noble life uprooted from its moorings, let us say in a Communist or in a Fascist revolution, may be an excellent subject for tragedy. A childless woman who loves children, an artist who loses his eyesight, a violinist whose hand is amputated as the result of an accident, a man whose

ambition is thwarted by poverty or illness—all these may, in
the hands of the talented dramatist, rise to the stature of
tragic characters. There are in your vicinity, in every vicinity,
stunted and bitter lives that will give you material for tragedy
if only you have the eye and the heart to see them.

If you want to know how to write a good modern tragedy,
study the ancient tragedies of the Greeks. This is what Eugene
O'Neill did. He took the plays of Aeschylus, of Sophocles, and
of Euripides, and he gave the characters of those plays a
modern setting and modern names. He preserved their ancient
passions because those passions were universal. In his *Mourning Becomes Electra,* O'Neill did just exactly what Shakespeare
did in his historical plays. He breathed new life into an old
theme. Eugene O'Neill is a profound student of the ancient
dramatists. He has learned many a dramatic and psychological
trick from them. Study these old Greek masters. Read the
Agamemnon in the translation of Edward FitzGerald; the
Antigone in the translation of Gilbert Murray; and the *Prome-
theus* in the translation of Elizabeth Barrett Browning. Then
read the French tragedians, especially Racine's *Phaedra.* Like
O'Neill's *Mourning Becomes Electra,* it derives its inspiration
from the Greek.

From the French tragedies turn to *Faust.* Goethe was amazingly modern in his outlook on life. Yet he sat at the feet of
the ancient masters for his inspiration.

Finally, you must turn to our modern tragedians. You will
find that some of their best work is based upon the genius of
the Greek dramatists. Read Maugham's *The Sacred Flame,*
Masefield's *The Tragedy of Nan,* and St. John Ervine's *John
Ferguson.* From these plays you will get a definite idea as to
what constitutes a good modern tragedy.

COMEDY

I believe it was Schopenhauer who said that "every life is
a tragedy when seen as a whole, and a comedy when examined
only in part." A comedy, therefore, is a tragedy with the final
act omitted. It is a play with a happy ending. A comedy may
be full of painful situations, but it must end in a good laugh
over these situations.

A good comedy, like Oscar Wilde's *Lady Windermere's Fan*, or Bernard Shaw's *Arms and the Man,* or Robert Sherwood's *The Road to Rome,* owes its success to the fact that it can arouse "thoughtful laughter," a term invented by George Meredith.

This element of thoughtful laughter in comedy frequently brings it very close to tragedy. "My laughter is always bitter," wrote the great humorist, Voltaire. Many a comedy leaves the spectator with the feeling that he ought to laugh and weep at the same time. We have had in the United States within recent years several such comedies, including *The Show-Off, Dulcy, Expressing Willie, The Goose Hangs High,* and *Idiot's Delight.* Study these plays. There is a touch of sadness in their laughter. And the modern public seems to be fond of this intermingling of emotions.

In comedy, as well as in tragedy, the ancient Greeks have shown us the way. The wit and the universality of Aristophanes' *Lysistrata* have not lost their sparkle even at the present time. Aristophanes was the first pacifist in history. In this play he ridicules the belligerency of the Athenian warriors. The wives of the soldiers declare a "sit-down" strike. They refuse to do the housework unless peace is declared. And they have their way. The modern playwright will be wise to dip his pen in Aristophanes' well of inexhaustible laughter. No less successful a dramatist than Robert Sherwood has done this, and with excellent results.

In your study of the technique of comedy, you must next turn to the Latin dramatists. Read Plautus' *The Twins (Menaechmi)* and *The Mostellaria (The Haunted House).* These comedies have served as models for some of the most popular of European plays. Shakespeare's *Comedy of Errors* is practically a translation (touched, of course, into new life by Shakespeare's genius) of *The Twins.* Read also Terence's *Phormio* and *Andria.* Their humor and their technique are amazingly universal. The great Molière is a humble disciple of Terence. Even in our own day Terence has been brought to life again. Thornton Wilder's *The Woman of Andros* is based almost wholly upon Terence's *Andria.*

If you want to write a successful *new* play, study the masters of the successful *old* plays.

Coming closer to our own day, don't neglect the comedies of Shakespeare. Change the names and the locale of his characters, and you have people and places that are just as thoroughly alive in the twentieth century as they were in the seventeenth.

Study Molière. The revivals of his plays are almost always successful. His technique is still as fresh and as brilliant as ever. Study especially his *Le Bourgeois Gentilhomme* and his *Tartuffe*.

Study, again and again, Sheridan's *A School for Scandal* and Goldsmith's *She Stoops to Conquer*. These two plays contain all the necessary ingredients for a successful modern comedy.

Turn next to Oscar Wilde. From him you will learn the word that glitters and the epigram that crackles into contagious laughter. Note, for example, this bit of dialogue from his *An Ideal Husband*:

> Lady Basildon: I delight in talking politics. I talk them all day long. But I can't bear listening to them. I don't know how the unfortunate men in the House stand these long debates.
>
> Lord Goring: By never listening.
>
> Lady Basildon: Really?
>
> Lord Goring (*in his most serious manner*): Of course. You see, it is a very dangerous thing to listen. If one listens one may be convinced; and a man who allows himself to be convinced by an argument is a thoroughly unreasonable person.
>
> Lady Basildon: Ah! that accounts for so much in men that I have never understood, and so much in women that their husbands never appreciate in them!
>
> Mrs. Marchmont (*with a sigh*): Our husbands never appreciate anything in us. We have to go to others for that!

Study the plays of Bernard Shaw. The success of these plays depends largely, I think, upon a very clever formula: Mr. Shaw makes his characters talk like libertines and act like puritans. They tell you about the naughty things they would like to do, but they never do them. In this way Mr. Shaw gives his spectators a vicarious thrill, but he never offends their sense of propriety.

To come to our American dramatists of the present day, study the comedies of Philip Barry, of S. N. Behrmann, of George S. Kaufman, of George Kelly, and of Robert Sherwood. Familiarize yourself especially with *The Second Man*. In this play Mr. Behrmann uses the classic technique with the Shavian formula. It has met with great success.

* * *

Tragedy and comedy, as stated above, are the two main divisions of the drama. These two divisions may be further subdivided into various groups. It is unnecessary, and to the beginner confusing, to go minutely into these subdivisions. Let me, however, mention two of them: the first as a warning, and the second as a guide.

These two subdivisions are the *melodrama* and the *farce*.

A melodrama is an exaggerated drama. It is a subconscious caricature of life. The author is probably unaware of his distortion of the truth. At least, he hasn't the skill to prevent this distortion. A striking example of the bad melodrama is *Way Down East*. In a sophisticated audience this sort of play arouses laughter instead of tears. It has bathos instead of pathos. Avoid this type. The American public is becoming too sophisticated to enjoy it.

A farce, on the other hand, is an exaggerated comedy. Unlike the melodrama, it is a *conscious* caricature of life. The author knows that he is exaggerating his characters and his situations. He is deliberately exhibiting life through a distorted mirror.

Farce contains the element of laughter without the element of thought. Anatole France's *The Man Who Married a Dumb Wife* and Oscar Wilde's *The Importance of Being Earnest* are excellent examples of this type.

If you are a good caricaturist, try your hand at farce. There is today a good market for it.

THE TECHNIQUE OF THE DRAMA

In order to become a good dramatist, you must have three qualities: the dramatic instinct; a profound passion for reading and witnessing the best plays; and an infinite capacity for hard work.

You may have all the literary talent in the world; but if you haven't the dramatic instinct, you had better leave the stage alone. Try the short story or the novel instead. Thomas Hardy and Joseph Conrad failed as dramatists. In spite of their genius, they wrote their dramas under the mistaken assumption that they were writing novels. They recognized the similarities between these two types of literature, but they failed to notice the differences. It is true that a drama, like a novel, is based upon character, dialogue, plot, and climax. But there the similarity ends. Starting from the same point, the novel and the drama go off in different directions.

Let us glance at some of the more important distinctions between the novel and the drama:

A novel has descriptive and narrative passages. A drama depends almost entirely upon dialogue. Here is where the novelist makes his mistake when he tries to dramatize his story. He allows his characters to *tell* the story instead of compelling them to *act* it. Long narrative passages in drama are taboo.

The novelist writes his dialogue to be seen by the eye. The dramatist writes it to be heard by the ear. When you compose the dialogue of a drama, be sure that the words sound right and blend right when spoken aloud. Indeed, you should *speak* your words aloud after you have written them.

The novel may be of any length, from 50,000 to 500,000 words. The drama must be limited to 30,000 words. People who live in the suburbs come to the theater late and leave early. This puts an arbitrary acting period of two hours upon the modern play. A play that takes two hours to act is about 30,000 words in length.

The novel may have a hundred characters and scenes. The play can have only a few. The tendency among producers nowadays is to curtail expenses by limiting the number of characters and scenes. Other things being equal, a play with ten characters and only one or two settings has a better chance for production than a play with twenty characters and half a dozen settings. Incidentally, your play will be better with fewer characters and less scenery and shorter speeches. Brevity in the drama is the soul of wit. The Greek and the Roman dramas took about an hour to act. The best plays of Molière were shorter than most of our present dramas.

Yet you must avoid excessive brevity. Impressionistic plays, whose characters talk in symbols and half-expressed innuendos, are as a rule unsuccessful. Ernst Toller's *Man and the Masses,* though good philosophy, was poor drama. It was a failure on the stage.

* * *

If you want to be a successful playwright, spend all your spare time reading and seeing plays. Take them apart. Watch the springs of their action. Study how the author has put them together. You will find that the dramatist, like the novelist, frequently starts with his characters. He brings together several widely contrasted persons, and he lets them act out their own story. You will discover that the great dramatist follows his own instinct for the theater rather than any conventional laws of technique. The dramatist does not learn his technique from the teacher. The teacher learns it from the dramatist. Aristotle wrote a famous book on the technique of the drama. But —observe this—the greatest Greek dramatists came *before,* and not *after,* Aristotle.

The competent playwright learns rules in order to break them. Shakespeare read Aristotle's rules about the unity of time and place, and then he threw the rules into the waste-basket. Ibsen studied the old dramatic masterpieces, and then developed a dramatic art of his own. Shaw studied Ibsen, and then struck out for himself. The critics told Shaw that he would never be a playwright because he didn't follow the rules. But Shaw had the dramatic instinct. He studied the *stage,* rather than the *critics.* Do as Bernard Shaw did. Study the stage. Note the physical limitations of the drama as compared with those of the novel. Then develop your own technique in accordance with these physical limitations.

It is a good plan to outline the lives of your characters, as well as the plot of your play, before you write it. Some dramatists find it convenient to have before them a toy stage on which they manipulate the actions of their characters as they write their plays.

Know your characters and know the stage upon which they are to act. Study it from behind as well as from the front of the footlights. Don't ask your characters or your producers to do things which cannot be done upon the stage. Don't put impossible people into impossible scenes. Be true to life. This cannot be emphasized any too strongly. Truthfulness to life is as important to the playwright as an instinct for the stage. Is your character acting in accordance with human nature? In accordance with his own nature? Does his speech ring true? Don't be literary in your dialogue. Submerge your fine style. Let your character speak in his own style. For lifelike dialogue, read Sean O'Casey's *Juno and the Paycock*.

Give life to your characters. The spectator of your play, like the reader of your novel, wants to read about living and interesting characters. He wants to see your characters in action. He wants to see the action precipitated rapidly— much more rapidly than in a novel—to a thrilling climax. And he wants the characters and the action and the climax to be convincing.

"There are no arbitrarily right ways and wrong ways of composing a play," writes Granville Barker. The technique of the drama keeps changing in accordance with the changes in public taste. At one time the play of five acts may be all the rage. At another time, the public may prefer a play of four or of three or of two acts. At still another time, the fashion may demand a series of loosely connected scenes without any division into acts. These are minor distinctions, and teachers and critics have placed too much emphasis upon them. The essentials of good drama have remained the same at all times. Whatever your technique—and this you must work out for yourself—remember that you are writing for an audience. Your characters must please this audience. And they will best please it if they talk and act like human beings, and if they meet a common human crisis in an interesting human way. This, in brief, is the whole technique of the drama.

And how can you master it? Let Pinero give you the answer: "By severer mental tension, by more actual manual labor than (you would put into) any novel . . . By sleepless nights, days of gloom and discouragement, and other days again of feverish toil."

C

Scenarios

The technique of the stage play is constantly changing, because the stage is a rapidly evolving medium of art. This is even more true of the screen play. The scenario of 1927 is already a dead form of drama. Ten years from now it is likely that our present-day scenario will be equally dead. The motion picture is developing much more rapidly than the stage play.

The best advice to the young scenario writer, therefore, is this: Watch the screen and follow its rapid development.

The most important advance in the screen play has resulted from the introduction of sound and dialogue. The old silent drama appealed mainly to the eye. The new talking picture must appeal not only to the eye, but to the ear. It comes closer to the stage play. And yet it is essentially different from the stage play.

What are some of these differences between the stage play and the screen play?

1. The stage play is limited in space and in action. You can depict only a few scenes, and only a small number of people in each scene. You can't bring a battle or a shipwreck or a tornado upon the stage with any degree of realistic effect. But you can do so on the screen. On the stage, your characters must either remain in one place or travel very sparingly if the action necessitates a change of locale. You can rarely show your characters in the *process* of travelling. On the screen, however, you can take your characters on a rapid journey from heaven to earth and back again, and show them to the spectator while they are actually travelling. This tends to *widen* the action of your screen play, and to *speed it up*. In other words, you can devote more space and allow greater freedom of action to your screen play than to your stage play.

2. The stage play is unable to show simultaneous action in two widely separated parts of the world. The limitations of scenery and the difficulty of shifting the sets with any rapidity prevent this simultaneousness of action. The screen play, however, can at least approach this ideal if it cannot actually

attain it. Within a single minute, the producer can flash upon the screen a group of people in London, another group in Shanghai, and a third group in New York. He can thus show you what various widely separated characters are doing at the same time. This technique tends to make the screen play more *flexible* than the stage play.

3. The stage play is most effective when it has a small number of long scenes. The screen play, on the other hand, is at its best when it has a large number of short scenes. In the scenario, each scene has its rising action, with its dramatic climax and fade-out at the end. It requires a greater degree of plot-weaving ingenuity on the part of the author, but it produces a more exciting effect upon the spectator. A drama is like a slow fist-fight, where only a few telling punches are exchanged. A screen play is like a rapid prize-fight, where blow follows blow in dazzling succession, and the knock-out punch inflames the audience into an outburst of enthusiastic appreciation.

4. The stage play can have only a few characters. In the screen play there is almost no limit to the number of characters that may be used. The richer the moving-picture industry grows, the more liberal the producers become in this respect. Consider the increasing number of recent screen plays in which scores of characters are used,—some of them only in one or two brief scenes. Note, for example, such plays as *Captain Blood, Anthony Adverse, Mutiny on the Bounty, A Tale of Two Cities, Lost Horizon, Grand Hotel,* and *Dinner at Eight.*

5. The stage play must be confined within a relatively short time. Plays that range over too long a period fail to grip the audience. *Milestones* was such a play. *Cimarron* would not make a very good drama on the stage. But it made a very good motion picture. A screen play can cover an entire lifetime, or even more than one lifetime. This is made possible because the action and the dialogue and the camera technique have been so speeded up that the spectator always gets the illusion of rapid motion. The years rush by like days. In the screen play, time doesn't *march* on; time *flies* on.

6. The writer for the stage must keep his imagination down to the level of the producer's pocketbook. He must cramp his

talent because imaginative flights are expensive to portray. The writer for the screen, however, should strive to whip his imagination *up* to the level of the producer's pocketbook. The more spectacular the play, the better the producers and the public like it. There is hardly a flight of the imagination that the producer's capital and the camera man's skill cannot depict upon the screen. Don't be afraid of your imagination if you are trying to write for the screen. Let yourself go.

Compare any successful stage play with its screen version. You will see that the screen play is wider in scope, more rapid, more flexible, more episodic, and more imaginative than the stage play.

We have already noted that the dialogue in the drama must be crisper and speedier than the dialogue in the novel. In the screen play, your dialogue should be even more crisp and swift. In the drama, the author explains by means of dialogue the things that have happened off-stage. In the screen play, these things must be shown by means of action rather than explained by means of talk.

Remember that your "movie fan" is less sophisticated than your playgoer. Your screen play must appeal to the eye more than to the ear, and to the ear more than to the intellect. Clever talk is generally lost on a motion-picture audience. Oscar Wilde's plays would find a very poor reception on the screen.

Never let your dialogue hamper the plot. Sacrifice your brilliant conversation, if necessary, to the action. Let your dialogue be natural rather than "smart." The average person is neither an oracle of wisdom nor an orator. His everyday talk is brief, homely, and occasionally pithy. Picture your character as *he* acts and talks, not as *you* act and talk. Submerge your own superiority into the averageness of your character. Even if your character is brilliant, like Disraeli or Voltaire or Richelieu, don't smother him with too many epigrams. Give him just a few epigrams to show his cleverness, but supplement these with enough homely speeches to show his humanness.

Avoid smartness in your dialogue. And avoid poetic flights. The average person is not a poet. Even a lover doesn't speak "bouquets" to his beloved. As a matter of fact, love scenes in real life are characterized by a few words, spoken rather hesitantly and punctuated by eloquent pauses of silence. A glance of the eye, a half-stifled exclamation, a shy caress or a timely embrace are much more effective in a love scene than any number of spoken words.

How to Prepare a Scenario

The best form in which to prepare your scenario is the outline form. Write an *outline* of your story, telling briefly about your characters and your situations. This brief sketch of your story should consist of about 6000 words—17 typewritten pages. It is not necessary to write this in dramatic form.

Some authors prefer to write out their scenarios at length—either as a complete short story, or as a novel, or as a drama. This, for the young writer, is not advisable. It takes you too long to do it; and the chances are that some subordinate at the studio will merely prepare a synopsis of your script for the editor.

The short outline is the preferable type of scenario. If you *must* write a long manuscript, prepare it as a novel. You then have a chance to get two bites out of the same pie. You can first sell your manuscript to a book publisher, and you can then resell it, at a higher price, to a motion-picture producer.

As regards the subject-matter of your scenarios, there are two types of story that are almost always in demand: the topical story, and the period story.

The topical story deals with those events that are currently popular in the newspapers. Floods, earthquakes, insurrections, gang wars, criminal organizations, notorious murders and divorces—these are the subjects that will make successful photoplays while the events are still fresh in the public mind. Watch the papers, and watch the screen. If you can take a timely event and build an interesting story around it, you have a good chance for a sale.

The period story is always popular. Time and again the producers have announced that they want no more period or costume stories. But the public is always clamoring for more and more. It seems that for years to come there will be no end to the public interest in such plays as *Richelieu, The House* of *Rothschild, Disraeli, Louis Pasteur, Mary Queen of Scots,* and *King Henry VIII.*

A third type of screen story that bids fair to be popular for some time to come is the sentimental story. In the stage drama sentimentalism is fatal. In the novel it is almost equally taboo. But on the screen it continues to attract a large and unsophisticated public. For there are many who still love a good-old-fashioned cry over the good-old-fashioned "homely" virtues and vices. Call this type of play *tripe,* if you like. But there is a big public that demands it.

There is a fourth type of screen story that you are likely to sell if you do a good job on it. This is the best-seller novel type. Let me explain what I mean. If a novel happens to be a best seller, some producer will buy it for the screen. All the other producers will be in the market for something like it. You will do well, therefore, to keep abreast of the best sellers and to prepare scenarios dealing with similar themes. You will know for a certainty that within a few months the producers will be looking for such material as you have prepared. Be careful, however, not to plagiarize any of your material. Deal with a similar theme to that of the best seller, but don't appropriate that theme. Plagiarism is not only dishonest, but dangerous.

Whichever of the above types you select, be sure that your screen story has *human appeal.* This term has been overworked, perhaps. And yet, for want of a better term, it is still used as a measuring rod by which a film play is finally accepted or rejected. Most of the producers want stories with human appeal —that is, stories that strike an emotional response on the part of the public. A play that calls forth many laughs and a few tears is always likely to be a successful play.

D

News Writing

If you want to be a professional writer, try to get a job as a reporter. Whether or not you remain a journalist, your training will have taught you how to write. For you will have learned, as a reporter, to say much in a few words. You will have developed a style that is clear, simple, accurate, and compact. And, if you are a *good* reporter, you will have acquired two other virtues as a writer. Your style will be photographic and graphic.

A reporter's job is as difficult as it is fascinating. I am not here referring to the physical hardships of a newspaper career. I mean the mental task of presenting a complex world in a simple way. The late Arthur Brisbane had a genius for doing this sort of thing.

Your newspaper story must be almost telegraphic in its brevity. And yet it must tell a complete and interesting story. There is a tendency nowadays to dramatize the newspapers. The public is no longer interested in drab reports of the news. It demands color, motion, and life. The old-fashioned newspapers so dear to the spinsters of the last generation are dying out. One by one they have turned out to be financial failures.

The modern newspaper is like a screen play. It depicts the fascinating scenario of daily existence on this crazy planet we call the earth. Each scene must have its characters, its action, and its climax. Such magazines as *Time* and *News-Week* have paved the way to the new style in newspaper reporting. The more wide-awake of the dailies are rapidly adopting this style. The reporter nowadays is becoming a stylist. He doesn't merely transcribe life, he describes it. Brevity is still the motto in the newspaper editorial room. But it is brevity touched into life. The descriptive adjective, or still better, the descriptive verb —for a verb means action—is taking a prominent place in the modern newspaper story.

The life depicted in the daily papers is a pretty tragic affair. Accident, murder, suicide, robbery, graft, murder, divorce, slander, murder, robbery, divorce, suicide, graft, and so on and on and on. In order to make all this palatable, a sense of humor is necessary. If you want to be a reporter, you must be a natural humorist. Every good reporter has something of the cynic in him.

Cultivate a sense of humor if you want to be a good journalist. Humor is important not only in the news item, but in the feature story. The chief difference between the news item and the feature story is this: the news item is an impersonal report; the feature story is a personal photograph. The news story is concerned mainly with *what* happened; the feature story deals more intimately with the person to *whom* it happened.

Not every reporter can write a feature story. It requires a special skill. You must have the personal touch, the creative ability. Your character must be brought into life. In other words, if you are a good feature-story writer, you have the makings of a novelist or a dramatist.

GATHERING YOUR NEWS

In order to write your news item or your feature story, you must know how to get your material. There are three good ways to gather material: keep your eyes and your ears open; interview people; and read articles and books.

The skillful reporter will use all three methods. To be a good writer, you must be a good listener and a good reader. If your feature is to be timely, "hot off the griddle" so to speak, get your information by ear, at first hand, rather than by eye, through an article or a book. Some of the best reporters have confessed that they depend much more upon "watching and listening" than they do upon reading.

In order to get your material, you must go after it. Meet people. Talk to them. Let them talk to you. If you can afford it, travel. You'll meet new scenes and new people—and new ideas.

Try to get your material at first hand. A good reporter can't afford to play second fiddle. A woman reporter for one of the Boston papers travelled all the way to Monts, France, in order to secure an interview with "Wally" Simpson. She knew that Mrs. Simpson had persistently refused to be interviewed. But she was determined to get her information at first hand. She got it. Mrs. Simpson granted her an exclusive personal interview.

Not everybody can afford to travel, however. If you are one of those who can't, don't be discouraged. Some of the finest feature articles are written by men and women who stay at home. A good way to get material when you cannot go after it in person is to send out a questionnaire. You will find that most people are very coöperative in answering your questionnaire. A form letter of this kind, if carefully worded, will give you as much information as a series of personal interviews.

Keep a notebook. Jot down in it important names, dates, and items of general interest. Some journalists make it a practice to keep a biographical card system of all the important world personalities. Always carry around with you, in your pocket, some blank paper and a pencil. Jot down whatever information and ideas you pick up in the street, in the subway, in the office, in the library, in the lecture hall. I know a prominent feature writer who gets his most brilliant ideas while listening to a symphony orchestra. He always has his notebook and his pencil ready with him at the music hall.

Prepare a file of important anniversaries—dates of famous battles, centenaries, bicentenaries, and tercentenaries of famous people and events,—anything, in short, that has a historic or human interest. Prepare your material on these events a month or even two months in advance. Give your editor plenty of time to print the article.

Get into the habit of taking mental snapshots of interesting people and places and events. Some of the most popular columnists are doing just this. Walter Winchell and O. O. McIntyre are artists of the verbal snapshot. They catch people at psychological moments and transfer them to the printed page.

Wherever you go, try to make acquaintances and friends. The best journalist is the journalist who is most thoroughly human. Learn at first hand what is most likely to interest people, and then give it to your readers. Give it in a clear, simple, accurate, compact, and graphic style. I am deliberately repeating these words because they are so vital. The newspaper reader has plenty of material from which to make his selections. Unless your article possesses the qualities which will make him stop and read, your work will have been wasted. Never use vague and abstract words in your news article. Concrete, pictorial nouns and verbs that are full of action—these are the factors that make a good newspaper style.

The Five W's

Every good news story must be based upon the so-called five w's. It must tell *who, what, where, when* and *why*. In order to illustrate this point, let us look at the story of a burglary as related in a recent issue of the *Boston Herald*. The names are fictitious:

"Hampton Beach, N. H., June 29—A lone marauder broke into Edgemere, the country estate of William H. Sloane, president of the Walkeasy Shoe Company, early this morning and escaped with jewelry valued at $50,000 and a small sum in cash.

"From the efficient way in which the burglar operated—he entered and left the Sloane home without awakening either the family or the servants in the rambling three-story mansion—state police were convinced that it was a professional job.

. . . .

"Sloane discovered the theft at 4 A.M. when he awoke and went into the bathroom which adjoins the second-floor master's bedroom . . . for a drink of water. He found a section of the bathroom screen cut out and the wall-safe in a closet off the bathroom open and stripped of its contents. He aroused the household and summoned the police.

"Before the police arrived, a further check of the house showed that the marauder had entered the room of Mrs. Stanley Jones, Sloane's sister, who was an overnight guest, and had stolen jewelry from a handbag which she had left on a dressing table."

In the above report, there are three important characters: the thief, Mr. Sloane, and Mr. Sloane's sister. Observe how the story of each of these characters is based briefly upon the five essential w's: *who* performed the action or suffered from it; *what* the action was; *where* it took place; *when* it took place; and *why* the person was in that particular place at that particular time. If you bear in mind these five essentials, and omit all the non-essentials, your newspaper story will be brief, pithy, and interesting.

E

Magazine Articles

The magazine article is closely allied to the feature story. The style of your magazine article—unless you are writing for the "arty" magazines—should be exactly the same as the style of your feature story. The range of your subjects is somewhat wider, since the intellectual horizon of the magazine reader is somewhat more extended than that of the news feature reader. Your magazine essay should be personal and specific. Avoid generalizations. Fill your essay with anecdotes. If necessary, create characters upon which to hang these anecdotes. Remember that most readers are interested not so much in ideas as in people. The more people you put upon the page, the more human will be the tone of your article.

Read the best articles in the magazines and try to develop the features that have made these articles alive. Study especially the beginning of an article. It is important to capture the reader's interest. Just as in the sales talk, so too in the magazine article the beginning should be a surprise. Stir the reader out of his nonchalance. Throw a pebble into the smooth surface of his indifference. Make a challenging statement. Put him on the defensive. And then go on with the explanation of the challenge. You thus get him to take sides at the very outset. You start a personal debate with him. Everybody loves an interesting debate.

Write as you would talk. Imagine your reader to be in actual conversation with you. The conversational style in an article is the best style. Assume that you are talking to an intelligent high school senior. This is about the mental average of the general magazine reader.

Use the second person as much as possible. Your reader likes to feel that you had him personally in mind when you prepared your article. Give your reader the honest impression that you are writing for him because you are concerned with his welfare.

Use questions. Put your reader on his mettle. Ask him how he would meet a certain situation, and then go on to tell him how you, as a result of your experience and research, would advise him to meet it. You thus establish yourself both as a teacher and as a friend.

Explain every point as clearly as possible. Remember that your reader knows much less about the subject than you do. For you have made a special study of it. Examine the subject from every possible angle. Don't be afraid of repeating yourself, provided every repetition throws a new light on a hitherto obscure or semi-obscure idea.

Have your magazine clearly in mind when you write your article. A style that would suit the requirements of *Atlantic Monthly* would fall flat if submitted to *Liberty*.

Think of ideas rather than words. The right idea will generally find for itself the right word. If you have something to say, you will be able to say it. You will never succeed in selling an article that consists merely of a fine style. Pretty words without a thought are like rouge on a dead man's face.

Don't write down to your readers, and don't write up to them. Put yourself on a level with them. Interest yourself in their interests. If you can't do that, you had better leave writing alone. An article is written to be read. It will fall upon barren ground if it is either too abstruse or too puerile to make good reading.

And, finally, whether you are writing a news item or a feature story or a magazine article, try to be a simple and honest and accurate reporter of life.

Types of Popular Articles

In order to learn what types of articles the readers of the most popular magazines demand, study these magazines. Note the articles that are selected for condensation in such magazines as *Reader's Digest*. These are the articles with the strongest appeal for the greatest number. A survey of a single month's issues of the best-known magazines shows the following list of titles, to mention only a few:

> Consumer's Dollar
> Neutrality and Common Sense
> The Child Labor Amendment
> Subsidized Athletics
> War Clouds in Asia
> The Future of the Sit-Down Strike
> Accidents Can Be Stopped
> Better Babies
> Machinery and the Worker
> Interesting Personalities
> Women and Patriotism
> Dictatorships—Will They Survive?

It *Can* Happen Here
How Near Is War?
But *Is* the World Going Mad?
Building Your Personality
Through a Trailer Window
Will Mussolini's Daughter Rule Over Italy?
Why These Airplane Crashes?
Whither Are We Drifting?
Life of a Share-Cropper
After Appomattox
The Great Goldwyn
Help Yourself to a Career
Birth Control
Labor on the March
The Errors of Television
Must We Have Another Boom?
Who Will be Our Next President?
The Farmer-Labor Alliance
What Next in Our Economic Drama?
The College for Women
Will Woman Become the Dominant Sex?

The above titles, you will note, cover a wide variety of subjects. The magazines from which these titles have been selected are of the general type. They appeal to the average class of readers. Each article is a colored bit of glass taken out of the whirling kaleidoscope of modern life.

Every one of these articles has its distinct human appeal. And every one of them is topical; that is, it deals with a personality or a theme that is of current interest. The subjects may be divided into fourteen general groups: the cost of living; self-improvement; the problem of war and peace; the labor and the education of our children; the question of safety; the relationship between capital and labor; dictatorship and democracy; foreign affairs, particularly as they are likely to affect the American public; the latest fads; politics; feminism; sports; the doings of the great and the near-great in our own day; and the high-lights of history. The last group is especially noteworthy. Recently there has been a revival of interest in the Civil War owing to the popularity of *Gone with the Wind*. Articles about the historic shrines of that war are in pretty good demand. *After Appomattox* is merely one of several such articles. Everything, in short, is grist for the free-lance writer's mill provided it has a news angle. You must select only those subjects in which the public is interested today.

But whatever you select as your subject, write about people. The most fascinating theme in the world is the romance of human life. The best article is the biographical article, and the most successful writer is the writer who reveals personalities. If you write about baseball or birth-control, farming or philosophy, education or politics or revolution or sport, introduce likable and colorful personalities into your article.

To sum it all up in a single sentence, let your article be, not an essay, but a story.

* * *

Do you want to be a successful writer? If you have the talent, my advice to you is this: Cultivate, in preference to all other forms, the short story. It offers the biggest field. There are today scores of magazines that publish short stories. The demand for good fiction is always greater than the supply. This is not quite so true of any other field in literature. If you think you have a salable plot and intriguing characters, don't waste them on a drama or on a scenario. Put them into a story. Your drama and your scenario would have to find a place in an overcrowded field. Your story, however, will find little competition—that is, if it is a *real* story.

Then there is this further advantage in writing a short story. If it strikes fire, it may possibly be purchased for the screen later on. Original scenarios, especially those submitted by unknown authors, are rarely accepted *unless they have hitherto been published in story form*.

Specialize in the short story.

§ 4

PREPARING YOUR MANUSCRIPT

Your manuscript is your salesman. Its object is to sell you to the publisher. It should not only have a good story to tell, but it should look spick and span when it arrives in the publisher's office.

Remember that a publisher's reader is human, even as you

and I. He wants his work to be as pleasant as possible. Save his eyes and his nerves. Give him a neat and readable script. It will predispose him in your favor.

Type your manuscript plainly on white paper, eleven inches long by about eight inches wide. Let your paper be of a medium weight. Use only one side of the paper, and don't scratch it up with erasures and insertions. If you are not a good typist yourself, have the work done by someone who is. Don't send your manuscript around too many times. When it begins to look worn, make a fresh copy.

Write your name and address on the outside cover of your manuscript, and also on the title page. Take no chances of your name and address being lost in the shuffle. If you use a pseudonym, be sure to indicate on the manuscript both your pseudonym and your real name.

Don't ever submit a hand-written script. No matter how legible your writing may be, it will give the publisher the impression of amateurishness.

Double-space your manuscript, and use wide margins on all sides. This will make your work pleasant to look at and easy to read.

Fasten each chapter of your manuscript together with a firm clasp. If the manuscript is fairly thick, have it bound so that it will open like a book. Be sure in that case that the inside margin is very wide. Don't irritate the reader with copy that comes too close to the binding.

If your manuscript is unusually thick, have it bound in two parts. The publisher's reader may want to take it home for the evening or the week end. A bulky manuscript is hard to handle.

Number your pages carefully. If you find it necessary to insert one or more pages, let us say between pages 53 and 54, number the revised pages as follows: 53, 53a, 53b, 54. If, on the other hand, you have to destroy one or more pages, number the revised pages 52, 53-54, 55;—or 52, 53-55, 56.

Be sure to make a carbon copy of everything you write. Manuscripts don't often get lost in editorial offices or in transit, but they do sometimes. I have known of one tragic case where an author had to rewrite *an entire book* because he lost the original manuscript and had made no copy of it.

Never submit your carbon copy to an editor. It will not only irritate him, but it will make him suspicious. Rightly or wrongly, he will conclude that you have submitted your best copy to another publisher, and that you are using him merely as a convenient second choice. Besides, carbon copies are difficult to read. Very few editors will give whole-hearted attention to a carbon copy.

In estimating the length of your manuscript, don't count the actual number of words. Take the average number of words to a line, and then multiply this average number of words by the average number of lines to a page. This, multiplied by the number of pages, will give you the total number of words in the manuscript. Count short lines at the ends of paragraphs and in quoted speeches as full lines. The ordinary double-spaced typewritten page has about 30 lines and about 12 words to a line—360 words to a page.

Don't fold your manuscripts when you send them out, unless they consist of only a few pages. In that case, fold them only once. Folded manuscripts are hard to read and get worn at the folds after a few trips. Wrap your manuscripts carefully. Use corrugated paper, if possible. Packages get hard knocks in trains and in express trucks. Enclose return postage with your manuscript, or else you may never get it back. If your manuscript is big, send it by express prepaid, with instructions that in the event of rejection it be returned to you by express collect.

If your name is difficult to spell or to pronounce or to remember, it is a good idea to use a pen name. Otherwise there is no special reason why you should do so. In any event, don't use several names. Your success depends upon your making your name known to the reading public. Stick to one name, and keep presenting it to the publishers and to the public as long and as frequently as you possibly can. In literature, familiarity spells success.

§ 5

MARKETING YOUR MANUSCRIPT

Your literary success depends upon incessant work and tireless salesmanship. Keep writing and sending out your manuscripts all the time. A mail-order return of 3% is considered good. As a writer you are in the mail-order business. Don't be discouraged if you have to make a hundred mailings in order to get three sales. To make a hundred mailings you don't have to write a hundred manuscripts. If you write ten manuscripts and send each of them out to ten publishers, you should, according to the law of averages, sell three of the ten manuscripts. That is, if your manuscripts have real merit. The better established you become, the higher will be the percentage of your sales. It all comes down to a matter of quantity production and aggressive marketing. If you want to make a profession of writing, let not a single day pass without your sending out at least one manuscript to some publisher. Success in literature, as in everything else, is cumulative.

If you feel that you have creative power but no business ability, get a literary agent to handle your work. Most of the well-known authors today are represented by agents. If you decide to get an agent, be sure that he is reputable. As a general rule, the reputable agent does not advertise for manuscripts. He has all that he needs. He works on a commission basis, 10% as a rule. He makes no charge for reading your manuscript. He does not suggest a fee for criticizing or correcting or revising it. Either he likes your manuscript and decides to handle it, or else he does not like it and returns it to you. There are, of course, a few exceptions to this rule. Occasionally a reputable agent does charge a fee for reading and correcting manuscripts, especially in the case of unknown authors. But there are so many disreputable agents who are interested merely in exploiting the inexperienced author that it is wise for you to find out who your prospective agent is and what he has accomplished in the way of actual sales.

There are three advantages in securing an agent:

1. He knows the publishers, and he knows what they want. Editorial requirements are constantly changing. The agent is kept in touch with these changes. He therefore knows just exactly where and when to submit your manuscript—something which you yourself cannot possibly know.

2. He can generally obtain a better price for your manuscript than you yourself would be able to get. Even after he deducts his commission, the chances are that the net results to you will still be greater.

3. The agent can take care of all the potential supplementary rights to your manuscript. He knows how to dispose of the first and second serial rights, the dramatic and film rights, the translation and foreign market rights, and so forth.

Remember that there are more good markets than there are good manuscripts. The demand is greater than the supply. The successful agent is always on the lookout for material. He generally recognizes a salable manuscript when he sees it. If he decides to handle your work, the chances are that he can sell it. He has neither the time nor the money to waste on unsalable material.

Unless, therefore, you are a clever businessman in addition to being a good author, it is best for you to get a literary agent. Specialization is a wise thing. You stick to your writing. Let your agent attend to the marketing.

At the outset of your career, however, you may find it difficult to interest an agent. You will probably be obliged at first to attend to your own sales. This will be a good experience for you, as it will teach you to watch the changes in the market and to meet them.

Watch the popular books and magazines. See what the public wants. Try to analyze *why* the public wants it. Then write accordingly, and keep up an incessant bombardment of the editorial offices. Laugh at rejections. Keep after the same editor again and again and again. He may reject your first ten manuscripts. When he gets the eleventh, your name will already be familiar to him. He may not remember *why* it is familiar, but no matter. After wading through a number of manuscripts by unknown writers—there are so many of them in every editorial office!—he will come to your script. "Ah," he will say to himself, "here at last is a chap I've heard of. Let's have a good look at his work."

When you submit your work to an editor, write a brief letter. The briefer, the better. Editors are perhaps the busiest people in the world. Just state that you are herewith submitting such-and-such a manuscript—and that's all. Make your letter formal. Don't assume a personal tone in writing to an editor who does not know you. Occasionally a daring note may get you a hearing. But this is a rare exception. The consensus of opinion among established authors is that letters to the editor do not produce sales. As Charles Caldwell Dobie puts it, "Obviously a good letter cannot possibly sell a poor story."

Why are certain manuscripts rejected? In answer to a questionnaire which I sent out to a number of editors, I received several illuminating reasons for the rejection of manuscripts. These reasons may be classified as follows:

1. A polished style, but a poor plot.
2. A good plot, but a poor style.
3. A sluggish beginning.
4. Too much narrative, and too little action.
5. The wrong type of story for that particular magazine.
6. A slovenly manuscript.
7. No punch at the end.
8. Lack of conviction. The characters sound counterfeit. They don't ring true.
9. Inadequate knowledge of the subject.
10. The manuscript is either too long or too short for the magazine considering it.

Be sure, in submitting your manuscript, that you have done everything in your power to prevent its coming back for any of the above reasons.

* * *

If you write an article, you have two possible markets for it: newspaper or magazine publication; and subsequent publication together with other articles in book form.

For a drama, you have three possible markets: the stage, the screen, and book publication.

For a short story, you have four possible markets: magazine publication, subsequent publication together with other stories in book form, the sale of the dramatic rights, and the sale of the film rights.

For a novel, you have seven possible markets: the sale of the first serial rights—that is, the serial publication of the novel in a magazine *before* its publication in book form; the sale of the second serial rights, or the serial publication of the novel in magazines and in newspapers *after* its publication in book form; book publication; the sale of the dramatic rights; the sale of the screen rights; publication in a reprint edition; and the sale of the translation rights. A successful novel may bring its author tens of thousands, and in some cases hundreds of thousands of dollars.

A short story may bring you anywhere from $25.00 to $5000.00, depending upon your popularity, the excellence of the story, and the affluence of the magazine that buys it. This price is paid for the magazine publication rights only. It does not, as a rule, include any of the other rights. The average price paid to well-known authors for a short story is $500.00. The stories that command the highest prices are not, as you might believe, the *plot* stories, but the *character* stories. A plot may occasionally creak, the atmosphere may fail to grip, and the settings may be unreal; yet if the story has one convincing and sympathetic character, the chances are that the editor will take it.

You must remember that the editor wants only those stories that have *the greatest appeal for the greatest number*. A magazine like the *Saturday Evening Post* is read by all sorts of people, from the bootblack to the professor. Strike a common denominator of human interest between them, and you have a story that will intrigue that vague public known as the readers of the *Saturday Evening Post*. The same holds true of practically all the other so-called "big" magazines. It is a fallacy to think that the average reader of the popular magazines is a low-brow. There are thousands of people who read both the *Atlantic Monthly* and *Liberty*. When you write a story, try to have in mind a million possible readers. For that is what the editor of the popular magazine will have to do when he considers your story for possible publication.

The short story—when you have made your mark—is profitable. But even more so is the novel. And it should be, for it takes about twenty times as long to write a novel as it does to write a short story. Now when I talk of the profits of a novel, please don't misunderstand me. Many a first and even a second and a third novel fails to net the author more than $500.00. Some novelists make even less than $250.00 on their first novel. But once the novelist really has arrived, he can command almost any price for the various rights in his book. For the first serial rights alone there are some novelists who receive $50,000.00. One of the more popular authors has recently been paid $75,000.00 for the first serial rights to her latest novel. The reason for this high price is that the novelist in question has learned the trick of suspense. Each installment ends upon a note which arouses the curiosity of the reader to a white heat. The serial publication of this author's novels in a magazine, therefore, both sustains and increases the circulation of that magazine.

But the above instances are rare. There are perhaps not more than half a dozen novelists who receive anywhere near $50,000.00 for the first serial rights. The average price for a successful serial is about $15,000.00 to $20,000.00.

When your novel has passed the first serial stage, it is then published in book form. The American public is gradually becoming book-minded. There is today a better market than ever for good fiction. Your novel, if it catches the public fancy, is likely to bring you a tidy sum. Your royalty will probably be computed on a sliding scale somewhat as follows: 10% on the first 2500 copies; 12½% on the next 2500 copies; and 15% on all subsequent sales. A few of the more successful authors sometimes receive a 20% royalty. In actual cash, your receipts on a novel that retails at $2.50 will be as follows:

> On the first 2500 copies, 25 cents per copy.
> On the next 2500 copies, 31¼ cents per copy.
> On all copies after 5000 have been sold, 37½ cents per copy.
> If the publisher sells 10,000 copies of your novel, you get about $3281.00.
> If he sells 25,000 copies, you get about $8906.00.
> If he sells 50,000 copies, you get about $18,281.00.
> If he sells 100,000 copies, you get about $37,031.00.

There has been a tendency, within recent years, to publish longer novels and to sell them at $3.00. One of these novels, *Gone with the Wind,* has sold more than a million copies. The author's royalties have probably reached the attractive figure of $500,000.00.

The average good novel, however, can hope to have no such sale as this. Even the successful author must expect to get far less for his book rights than he gets for his first serial rights. A royalty of $5000.00 is all that the established author should count on. The author of a first novel should be content with $1000.00 or even less.

With regard to the second serial rights, don't expect much from that source. The newspapers that reprint a novel in their columns pay very little for that service. The same holds true for the translation rights. Some of the foreign publishers pay as little as $25.00 for the sole right to republish a book in their country.

If your novel has been a success, it will be published in a reprint edition, to sell for about 75 cents. Your original publisher gets about 10 cents a copy for the reprint rights, and of this sum he gives five cents to you. If your book has had a pretty good sale in the regular edition, it should have an even better sale in the reprint edition. But its appeal must be popular.

There remain the dramatic and the film rights. Very few novels nowadays are dramatized. It is almost axiomatic that a dramatized novel rarely makes a hit. There are striking exceptions, of course. *Jane Eyre, Ethan Frome,* and *Dodsworth* turned out to be good box-office attractions. These exceptions, however, only prove the rule.

While very few good novels are bought for the stage, a great number of them are bought for the screen. The scenario editors are always on the lookout for good novels and for good short stories also—and the producers are ready to pay attractive prices for likely material. If your novel has screen possibilities, you or your agent will not have to bother about seeking out the scenario editors. The scenario editors will seek *you* out.

For a *good* novel you may expect to get $5000.00 or $10,000.00 from the motion-picture producer. For a *good* and *popular* novel, you may get $20,000.00 or $25,000.00. For a *popular best seller,* you may get as much as $50,000.00 or even $100,000.00.

Frequently a producer will take an option on your novel. He will pay you $500.00 or $1000.00 with the proviso that he may, if he wishes, buy the film rights on your book within 90 days. Such options are sometimes exercised within the specified period. More often, however, they are allowed to lapse without out the consummation of a sale. There is one writer in New York who is making a fairly good living on options. He sells several options on his stories every year. But he has never yet sold a story.

These, then, are your chances with a novel. If it strikes the fancy of the public, you can sell the first and the second serial rights, the book rights, which usually include the reprint rights, the translation rights, the screen rights, and possibly the stage rights. But—it takes a long time to write a novel; and there is always the possibility that after you have devoted all your time and energy to the work you may not succeed in disposing of it through any of the seven channels. Therefore my advice to the young writer again is this: Instead of writing one novel, write twenty short stories. Even though twenty successful short stories may in the long run net you less than one successful novel, you must think of *quantity* as well as of *quality* production. If you write twenty short stories instead of one novel, you increase your sales chances twenty to one.

* * *

When you have succeeded in selling your manuscript, you get a contract. This question of contracts, especially in the case of book manuscripts, is very important. You must learn to be on your guard against the contract that exploits the unwary beginner. There is in this country a group of unscrupulous printers who call themselves publishers. They advertise for manuscripts, either in the writers' magazines or through the mail. Many of these so-called "authors' publishers," or "vanity publishers," never read the manuscripts that are submitted to them. Instead, they send out to all the authors of these manuscripts a form letter to the effect that "our readers have found your manuscript highly interesting, and they have recommended its publication, provided——." This proviso is that you are to advance to the publisher a certain sum of money, in return for which he will give you, instead of the customary 10%, a much bigger royalty—about 30% or even 40%. What he fails to tell you is this: that the sum which you are asked to advance is about twice the cost of the printing and the binding of the manuscript, and that from his past experience he knows, or ought to know, that your book will not sell for the simple reason that he will not advertise it. These authors' publishers are looking for printing jobs and not for book sales.

If you want to publish a book of poetry, you may find it

necessary to pay for its publication. For there are very few publishers who will risk any money on poetry. But if you do decide to finance the publication of your poetry, try to get a "legitimate" publisher instead of a printer who parades as a publisher. On all manuscripts other than poetry it is best not to pay a fee to the publisher—unless, of course, you are willing to spend money for the pleasure of seeing your name in print.

In general, it is wise for the young author to set himself up as a professional, and not as an amateur writer. The professor doesn't pay for the pleasure of lecturing, and the doctor doesn't pay for the privilege of treating his patients. If you want to be regarded as a real author, you must insist upon a legitimate fee for your work,—an outright sum for your article or scenario or short story, and a royalty for your drama or novel.

In the case of the novel, try to insist upon a royalty. Don't sell the copyright for an outright sum. Once the publisher exclusively owns the copyright, he gets all the proceeds from the sale of the serial, the dramatic, the reprint, the screen, and the translation rights. The best arrangement for the novelist is publication on a royalty basis. The established novelist gets an advance against royalties,—that is, a sum of money which is paid in advance and which is later deducted from the royalties. The inexperienced novelist, however, should be content with a royalty without any advance.

If your book is published on a royalty basis, the publisher takes all the financial risk. You will have gambled your time, but no money. You get a royalty from the very first copy sold, whereas the publisher must sell two thousand copies or even more before he can realize any profit.

Don't expect more than 10% on the first 2500 copies. The first edition is the most expensive to produce. On subsequent editions the publisher can save the cost of typesetting and the plates. A copy of the first edition of a 500 page book may cost the publisher about 70 cents or even more. A copy of the later editions, however, will cost him only about 50 cents. He can therefore afford to allow you a larger royalty on all copies after the first edition has been disposed of.

Don't labor, as some authors do, under the erroneous impression that the publisher makes more money than you do out of your book. He actually makes less per copy sold. Consider the following items of expense that go into the producing and distributing of a book:

Typesetting	Office overhead
Plates	Salesmen's commissions
Paper	Booksellers' discounts
Press work	Advertising
Binding	Author's royalty

In general, unless a book sells beyond the first edition, the publisher may just break even on it. Bear this in mind when you receive his contract. Consider his point of view as well as your own. The author and the publisher of a book enter into a partnership. This partnership is most successful when each party is thoughtful about the problems of the other party.

Ask your publisher to specify in the contract a definite period within which your book is to be published. It is not fair for a publisher to tie up your manuscript indefinitely. Most publishers will agree with you on that point.

On the other hand, if you want your publisher to be fair with you, you must be fair with him. He will probably ask you for the first refusal on your next two or three books. That is, he will want you to submit these books to him before you submit them to any other publisher. Don't refuse this request. Your good will is likely to pay you dividends. If the publisher knows that he can have your other books, he will put more enthusiasm and energy into his efforts to put you over.

* * *

A word about copyrights. You may copyright a sermon, a speech, or a play in manuscript form. But a book must be printed before it can be copyrighted. Your book manuscript, however, is protected by the common law of the country.

* * *

Let us now assume that your manuscript has been accepted by a publisher. It goes to the printer, who sets it up and arranges the type into "galleys" about a hundred lines long. The galley proofs are sent to you for correction. Try to avoid making too many corrections. In other words, do all your correcting before your manuscript goes to the publisher. If your corrections in the galley proofs are too numerous, the publisher may find it necessary to deduct from your royalties the actual cost of resetting some of your corrected passages. The general practice among publishers is to charge the author for "all alterations in type or in plates required by the author, in excess of 10% of the original cost of the composition." This does not, of course, apply to the corrections necessitated by the printer's errors.

Make all your corrections in the margin, and be sure to point out in the printed copy the exact spot where each correction is to be inserted.

When you have returned the galley proofs, the printer resets the corrected passages and breaks the galleys up into pages. You then get a set of page proofs. On these page proofs, make only those corrections that are absolutely essential. For you must visualize the printer's problem. If your corrections dislocate a single word, this word may mean the dislocation of several pages. A printed word, you know, can be inserted only by removing other words from their proper place. If you *must* insert or omit a word in your page proofs, try to balance it by the omission or the insertion of another word containing an equal number of letters. This may necessitate the resetting of one line, or perhaps a few lines, but it will not compel the printer to rearrange several pages.

When you have returned the page proofs, your task, in so far as this particular book is concerned, is finished. Your publisher will attend to the rest. Sit down and do your next book.

Write, and write, and write! There is no other way to authorship. "Writing," said Flaubert, "is a dog's life. But it's the only life worth living."

* * *

A professional literary career is a long and oftentimes discouraging but decidedly fascinating uphill fight. Even the most successful authors have had their early struggles and disappointments. A number of them have generously written to me describing some of the difficulties they encountered in getting their literary start. The following extracts from their letters should serve as an inspiration to those young writers who are ready to give up:

CHARLES CALDWELL DOBIE

"My first serious work was a novel which I submitted to a literary broker. At the end of a year my story was returned with merely a list of the people who had refused it . . . I wrote ten years before achieving publication . . . *But everyone who works hard finally has the satisfaction of reaching the position where the struggle is not so heartrending.* Writers who complain that they are unappreciated have only themselves to thank."

* * *

RUPERT HUGHES

"I had hundreds of rejection slips before I was 25. Editors are as cordial as can be expected. *It is important to know what they want.*"

* * *

"HOLWORTHY HALL"
(HAROLD E. PORTER)

"I wrote 30 or 40 short stories before accomplishing a sale . . . When I finally got going, I had no trouble in keeping sold a year ahead."

* * *

SUSAN GLASPELL

"I have always had a certain number of unsuccessful stories, stories which failed with the magazines either because, in material or standpoint, they were outside the sort of thing the usual magazine wants, or else simply because I myself failed to treat them in the way to make them successful stories . . .

"I have found editors hospitable and friendly . . . I do not think it is true that they will not give the new writer a chance. Far from it. I think they want new writers."

* * *

FANNIE HURST

"My early history in placing manuscripts is rather a drab one!

"At about fourteen years of age I began my stubborn bombardment of the editorial fort.

"For four years the procession of my rejections came marching back often without even the questionable solace of a printed slip.

"During four years of college I submitted thirty-six manuscripts to one national weekly alone. They were all returned . . .

"Up to the time of selling my first story, I had never met an editor, a publisher, a journalist or an author.

"Probably one hundred short stories were rejected by almost every fiction magazine in America before I met with my first acceptance."

* * *

From the above letters, as well as from many others that I have received, it is possible to formulate three important rules for literary success:

1. Work hard.
2. Be patient.
3. Don't quit.

* * *

And so we come to the end. Have you decided to be an author? Very well, then, get ready to take off in the speediest of all the known vehicles,—the airship of your imagination. Up and away on your dangerous but fascinating flight to literary success. Good luck to you now—and to your manuscripts, many happy landings!

INDEX